Early Praise for *iOS 10 SDK Development*

iOS 10 SDK Development offers programmers an approachable, no-nonsense introduction to iOS development with Swift, leveraging the simplicity of Xcode's Playground support to have readers tinkering with real code in the first pages of the book. Careful elaboration of Swift's many unique features, and how Apple's iOS frameworks work with it, will leave readers with a solid foundation for pursuing whatever iOS development ambitions they have in mind.

➤ **Daniel Jalkut**
Founder, Red Sweater Software

I like this book. I like its approach to building something real in Swift. The result is an app that feels good and is useful. Along the way, you learn the basics of iOS development from an experienced pro. Highly recommended.

➤ **Eric J. Knapp**
Program director, Mobile Applications Development, Madison College

Once again, Chris Adamson delivers the must-have book for learning iOS development. Whether you're new to Swift or iOS—or both—you'll be able to hit the ground running by the time you finish.

➤ **Jeff Kelley**
iOS developer at Detroit Labs and author of *Developing for Apple Watch, Second Edition*

This book neatly covers building apps with iOS 10 from the ground up, starting with the basic tools and the nuances of the Swift language, and then progressing through interface design. You'll see how to build interfaces that auto-resize cleanly to multiple screen sizes. There's more to building an app than just assembling the pieces and getting it to compile. With *iOS 10 SDK Development*, you'll also learn invaluable testing practices, and the right approach to using the tools at your disposal to fix things when they go wrong. The chapters on closures are particularly well placed for people new to Swift. I'd recommend this book to anyone.

➤ **Kevin J. Garriott**
Director, Mobile Technology, Rockfish

Not many books cover both programming interfaces and deeper software engineering topics. It's refreshing to see both covered, expertly, in one book. Chris and Janie are masters at making technical content approachable. It's like having two of your best friends teaching you iOS.

➤ **Mark Dalrymple**
Author of *Advanced Mac OS X Programming: The Big Nerd Ranch Guide* and co-founder of CocoaHeads, the international Mac and iOS programming community

Whether you're new to iOS programming or just need some help getting up to speed on iOS and Swift, this is the perfect book for you. Chris and Janie take you on a well-thought-out and fun journey into iOS SDK development.

➤ **Dave Klein**
Founder of CocoaConf and author of *Grails: A Quick-Start Guide*

iOS 10 SDK Development

Creating iPhone and iPad Apps with Swift

Chris Adamson
with Janie Clayton

The Pragmatic Bookshelf

Raleigh, North Carolina

Our Pragmatic books, screencasts, and audio books can help you and your team create better software and have more fun. Visit us at *https://pragprog.com*.

The team that produced this book includes:

Publisher: Andy Hunt
VP of Operations: Janet Furlow
Executive Editor: Susannah Davidson Pfalzer
Development Editor: Rebecca Gulick
Indexing: Potomac Indexing, LLC
Copy Editor: Nicole Abramowitz
Layout: Gilson Graphics

For sales, volume licensing, and support, please contact *support@pragprog.com*.

For international rights, please contact *rights@pragprog.com*.

Printed in the United States of America.
ISBN-13: 978-1-68050-210-7
Printed on acid-free paper.
Book version: P1.0—March 2017

Contents

Acknowledgements

Ten versions of iOS (neé iPhone OS), and we've now managed to get Prags books out for half of them: 3, 6, 8, 9, and 10—more than half, if you recall there was no App Store or public SDK for version 1. Now that these releases have become an annual thing, we might finally be getting the hang of this.

My thanks for the latest edition start as always with Pragmatic Programmers, who have an efficient, comfortable workflow that gets out of authors' way and lets us write. (Rule number one for any competitors who might happen to be reading this: if you make authors use MS Word, add another two months to the schedule.) With Dave Thomas's retirement in 2016, Andy Hunt is doing a fine job of running the ship, and it's always a pleasure to work with the staff there, including Susannah Davidson Pfalzer and Janet Furlow. Most of all, it's important to have an editor whom I click with. Rebecca Gulick keeps me from going too deep into the woods of pounding out replicable instructions and makes sure I deliver the "big picture" themes and ideas of every chapter. Finally, I want to give a shout out to Prags's other iOS authors, including Jeff Kelley, Christina Moulton, Marcus Zarra, and Erica Sadun. And to Janie Clayton, who had other obligations and couldn't be a big part of this edition, but is always available on Twitter for constructive feedback or at least pictures of cooking and pugs.

I've had a day job doing Swift for a couple years now, and the important thing about it isn't just the language, but also working in an environment where the craft and quality of the code is of such high importance. So thanks to all my colleagues at MathElf (http://mathelf.com) for all the rigor in peer reviews, and Dan Kokotov in particular for pushing me hard to move past twenty years of accumulated bad habits.

In this edition, we've based our major example around writing a podcast client app. Part of the reason we did this is because there are so many good podcasts by and for iOS developers; hopefully, you'll check some of them out. Thanks to the CocoaConf Podcast (Dave Klein, Daniel Steinberg, and Cesare Rocchi) and Core Intuition (Daniel Jalkut and Manton Reece) for letting us feature them in our sample code and screenshots.

A big part of Prags's books is the feedback cycle, and this title benefits greatly from the input of our tech reviewers: Zach Jaquish, Jeff Kelley (him again!), Kevin Kim, and Scott Stevenson. I'm also grateful to everyone who posted to the book's forum or submitted errata during the book's beta, including (but hardly limited to) Mark Horrocks, David Lindelöf, Noah Patterson, Sean M. Paus, and Robert Sherwood.

Personally, it's been a difficult couple of years. Thanks to everyone I leaned on through iMessage or Twitter DM.

Obligatory end-of-book music check: this time it was Manic Street Preachers, BABYMETAL, Of Monsters and Men, The Flaming Lips, David Bowie, and Electric Light Orchestra. Current musical stats at http://www.last.fm/user/invalidname.

Preface

iOS *10*. Ten. Like the Roman numeral *X*. Perhaps more importantly, it's a sign that we're quickly approaching the tenth anniversary of the iPhone. Back in 2007, the operating system was called "iPhone OS," and we wouldn't even get a public SDK until a year later.

In that time, we've gone from an OS that ran on one model of one device to a variety of devices—iPhones, iPads, and iPod touches—and sizes. And it might be fair to also count the Apple Watch and Apple TV, whose OSes are offshoots of iOS, borrowing many of its frameworks and design patterns. Even the Touch Bar on the 2016 MacBook Pro can trace its roots back to iOS.

And along with the SDK, we got the revolutionary App Store. Much as Apple is criticized for its control over apps published through the store, it's far more open than what came before. One nugget of wisdom from the bad old days of Java-based J2ME phones was that "carriers can't stand you making a buck off their platform if they don't get to keep 99 cents." In historical context, Apple's 30% cut is arguably modest.

And it's because of that openness that we've seen an explosion of apps over the years, with over a million apps written for the platform. It's only recently that Apple has stopped boasting about the number of apps on the store, and it's even gone the other direction: stressing app quality over quantity, Apple has started pulling apps that haven't been updated to modern standards.

And this is where you come in. With deadweight being cast aside, there is a much better opportunity for good, *new* apps to have a chance. Whether you want to show us something we've never seen, do an existing thing better, or fix an old app, now is probably a great time to do it.

About This Edition

This is the fifth time Pragmatic Programmers has offered an introductory book for iOS developers. The previous entries were *iPhone SDK Development* in 2009 (covering iPhone OS 3), *iOS SDK Development* in 2012 (for iOS 6), *iOS 8 SDK Development* in 2014 (for iOS 8), and *iOS 9 SDK Development* in 2015 (for iOS 9).

As you might notice, we've gone from a sporadic update model to an annual one. This was motivated by Apple's introduction of the Swift programming language alongside iOS 8. Swift is exciting and fun, and we love coding in it, but there is a cost to living on the bleeding edge. Apple has aggressively evolved the language over the last three years, to the point where our iOS 8 book code wouldn't build in iOS 9, and the iOS 9 code is incompatible with iOS 10.

Since we can't realistically rewrite the entire book every year—at least not if we want to get it out soon enough to be useful—we've chosen our battles. For the iOS 8 book, we mostly focused on the iOS frameworks, and treated Swift as a means to an end. For iOS 9, Swift had settled down and we could dedicate the first three chapters of the book to really getting into the language itself, before playing with the frameworks.

For this edition, with few major changes in the iOS frameworks themselves, we took the opportunity to rework the core of the book. Like a lot of programming books, we built this around example code we hope will be fun to work with. For the last few editions, we built up a Twitter app as our example. It was fun, but it had some drawbacks—readers had to have a Twitter account to run the example, the Twitter API wasn't entirely analogous to client-server programming in general, and sometimes the example forced our hand in how we handled some topics.

So for this edition, we have a new sample project to work through: a podcast client app. This will give us a chance to touch on fun stuff like the media APIs—after all, Steve Jobs originally introduced the iPhone as "the best iPod we've ever made"—while using more generic networking APIs like URLSession and XMLParser. We think this will be more directly applicable to the apps you write after finishing the book.

Throughout the book, we have updated all the code to the new Swift 3, which significantly cleans up and simplifies much of the language. In particular, the C-like function calls we used to use for things like concurrency are largely a thing of the past—this year, the concurrency chapter (Chapter 7,

Handling Asynchronicity with Closures, on page 113) was a joy to write, because Dispatch.main.async(...) is a lot easier to remember and write than dispatch_async(dispatch_get_main_queue(), ...).

So Here's the Plan

Our goal for this book is to create a plausibly realistic and useful app, to the point where we can take it through the process of publication on the App Store in the final chapter. To accomplish this, we will spend a few chapters playing around with the Swift language, and then create the app project and slowly build out its functionality. This approach is similar to real-world development, so much so that we'll take time partway through to reorganize our work for maintainability and code reuse. We'll also spend time on important non-code topics, like testing and debugging, which are crucial and sometimes overlooked parts of the development process.

With that in mind, here's where our journey will take us:

- Chapter 1, *Playing with Xcode 8*, on page 1
- Chapter 2, *Starting with Swift*, on page 11
- Chapter 3, *Swift with Style*, on page 31
- Chapter 4, *Building User Interfaces*, on page 51
- Chapter 5, *Connecting the UI to Code*, on page 73
- Chapter 6, *Testing the App*, on page 89
- Chapter 7, *Handling Asynchronicity with Closures*, on page 113
- Chapter 8, *Loading and Parsing Network Data*, on page 129
- Chapter 9, *Presenting Data with Tables*, on page 151
- Chapter 10, *Navigating Through Scenes*, on page 171
- Chapter 11, *Fixing the App When It Breaks*, on page 187
- Chapter 12, *Publishing and Maintaining the App*, on page 201
- Chapter 13, *Taking the Next Step*, on page 221

Expectations and Technical Requirements

The technical requirements for iOS development are pretty simple: the latest version of Xcode, and a macOS computer that can run it. As of January 2017, that means Xcode 8 or later, and a Mac running 10.11 (El Capitan) or 10.12 (Sierra).

All code in this book uses the Swift programming language. Swift is a performant, practical language that Apple clearly intends to be the future of all development for its platforms. When it was open sourced in late 2015, the About Swift page declared:

The goal of the Swift project is to create the best available language for uses ranging from systems programming, to mobile and desktop apps, scaling up to cloud services. Most importantly, Swift is designed to make writing and maintaining correct programs easier for the developer.

On the same page, it says that Swift "is intended as a replacement for C-based languages (C, C++, and Objective-C)." That's not an unreasonable goal! Swift is a neat language that cleans out a lot of cruft from C and Objective-C, while also drawing inspiration from functional programming languages like Haskell.

We're sure you'll be able to pick it up quickly, provided you're a proficient programmer in at least one object-oriented language. That can be one of the many curly-brace descendants of C (C++, C#, or Java), or an OO scripting language like Ruby or Python. While we touch on Swift's appropriateness for functional programming, the iOS frameworks are largely OO in nature, so most of the functionality provided by Apple comes in the form of classes and objects.

Online Resources

This book isn't just about static words on a page or screen. It comes with a web page, https://www.pragprog.com/titles/adios4, where you can learn more and access useful resources:

- Download the complete source code for all the code examples in the book as ready-to-build Xcode projects.

- Participate in a discussion forum with other readers, fellow developers, and the authors.

- Help improve the book by reporting errata, such as content suggestions and typos.

If you're reading the ebook, you can also access the source file for any code listing by clicking the gray-green rectangle before the listing.

As we build our sample projects in this book, we will often write simple code, only to rewrite it with more ambitious code later as our knowledge increases.

All the different versions would be hard to put in one source file. So in the downloadable book code, we often have multiple copies of each project, each representing a different stage of its development. The different stages use numbered folders, like PragmaticPodcasts-1-1, PragmaticPodcasts-2-1, and so on, with the first number representing the chapter number and the second being a revision within that chapter. These folder names also appear in the captions for each code example in the text. You can either code along for the entire book from scratch, or copy over one of these "stages" and pick up from there.

And Here We Go

So, now that we've covered our goals and expectations, it's time to begin. We'll dive right into writing some code, and then step back to understand just what we're doing and how it works. Let's get started.

CHAPTER 1

Playing with Xcode 8

In this chapter, you'll get a taste of what iOS development is like. You'll set up the tools for creating iOS apps, flex your fingers by playing around with some code, and learn how to find your way in the development environment.

You'll start by simply playing around, and by the time you're done, you'll be ready to ship an app.

There is one must-have tool for iOS development: *Xcode*. This integrated development environment (IDE) will be where we do nearly all our work of developing, testing, and unleashing iOS apps. Xcode lets us build our apps, run them, debug them, and submit them to the App Store. There's very little in this book that *won't* involve working in Xcode.

Tooling Up with Xcode

So let's get Xcode on our Macs. Yes, we did say "Mac." Xcode is a native application that is only available for macOS (which until recently was called "Mac OS X"). Typically, it is available for the current version of macOS and (sometimes) one version back. For this book, we will be working with Xcode 8, which as of this writing can run on Sierra (macOS 10.12) or El Capitan (Mac OS X 10.11).

We get Xcode from the Mac App Store, which is always available from the Apple menu in any application. Search for Xcode in the store, and click the Get button. Don't worry, it's free, but you will need to have an Apple ID to get apps from the store. Actually, you'll need an Apple ID for a bunch of other tasks later, so create an Apple ID now if you don't have one, either in the Mac App Store app or at https://appleid.apple.com.

Xcode is an *integrated development environment* (IDE), meaning it combines many of the tools we need to create apps:

- A *text editor*, in which we write code

- *Interface Builder*, for creating user interfaces visually, rather than in code

- A *build system*, to convert our source code and user interface files into runnable apps

- A *Simulator*, allowing us to run our apps in a window on the Mac, which is sometimes more convenient than running on an actual device

- *Debugging tools*, which help us find and fix errors in our code

- *Profiling tools*, for finding performance bottlenecks at runtime

- *Testing tools*, to verify the correctness of our code and ensure that fixed bugs don't return

- A *documentation viewer*, containing the full developer documentation for the iOS, macOS, tvOS, and watchOS SDKs

- *Organizational tools*, for preparing and archiving the apps we submit to the App Store

That's a lot of stuff to fit in one app! It might be overwhelming, but our first run of Xcode will offer a pretty gentle introduction. Launch Xcode from the Applications folder (you may want to put it in your Dock, too), and click OK if it asks to install additional components, which are the command-line executables that will build our projects for us. When we get to the first window, Xcode keeps things simple:

We start with three simple options: "Get started with a playground," "Create a new Xcode project," and "Check out an existing project." On the right, there's a blank space that says No Recent Projects as we start working in Xcode; this will fill in with a list of our Xcode creations.

For now, let's start off with a little directed play.

Messing Around in a Playground

We'll start getting a feel for programming for iOS in what Xcode calls a *playground*, so click the "Get started with a playground" button. This brings up a new window, with a sheet showing two options for the playground: a name (defaulting to MyPlayground) and a platform. Make sure the platform is set to iOS, accept the default name, and click Next. Now we have to choose a destination folder to store the playground file. Anything will do here—Desktop, Documents, whatever—so pick something and click Create.

This brings up a window like the figure on page 4, with a toolbar and status pane at the top, a source editor on the left, an empty pane on the right, and a play/stop button at the bottom. For a moment, the status indicator will say Running MyPlayground..., and then the text "Hello, playground" will appear in the right pane, directly across from the source code line var str = "Hello, playground" (if you can't see it, the right pane may be too narrow; resize it by dragging the divider to the left).

What's happening here is that the playground is an interactive environment for writing and running small snippets of code. Anything we type in will be

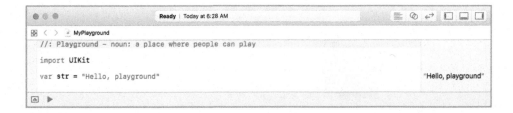

immediately executed—as long as it's valid code—and the results shown on the right side. By default, there is a single line of code that creates a string ("Hello, playground") and assigns it to the variable str. The result of this assignment is also the return value, which is why it shows up in the results pane.

Well, two can play at that game, right? On a new line at the bottom, let's write something really simple:

```
var two = 1 + 1
```

After a moment, the number 2 appears in the results pane.

Great, now we can do some math. Let's add another line to use that result:

```
two = two * two
```

As we expect, the number 4 appears in the results pane.

That's all well and good, but it's not much better than we could achieve with a calculator, or even by punching mathematical expressions into the Spotlight search bar. Let's think of something a little more ambitious.

Getting Serious on the Playground

I know, let's write a streaming web radio application!

Don't panic; this isn't as scary as you think. We can get this running with shockingly little code. But let's do so in a new playground. Close the current playground window, and use File > New > Playground to create a new playground. Call it WebRadioPlayground. Keep the line that says import UIKit, but delete the var str = "Hello, playground" line, and replace it with the following:

playing/WebRadioPlayground.playground/Contents.swift
```
Line 1  import AVFoundation
    2   let url = URL(string:
    3       "http://www.npr.org/streams/aac/live1_aac.pls")
    4   let player = AVPlayer(url: url!)
    5   player.play()
```

Nothing will happen just yet, but hang in there...

Xcode Console Garbage

As you start writing the code, you may see an error message like:

```
2016-11-20 17:28:47.041 WebRadioPlayground[19048:8310129] Failed
to obtain sandbox extension for ...
```
This is harmless and can be ignored.

The code we've written is in a language called *Swift*, introduced by Apple in 2014 for iOS and macOS development (and, later, watchOS and tvOS). It's a flexible language that's well suited to various styles of programming, as we'll see throughout the book. Swift is also the *only* language we can use inside a playground. You can also use C, C++, or Objective-C to write apps, but we'll only use Swift in this book.

Line 1 tells the Swift compiler that we want to use *AV Foundation*, a programming framework that lets us bring audio and video features to our apps. On lines 2–3, we create a URL for the station we want to play. Technically, this is an object of type URL, and not just a string. Instead, we create the URL by passing a string to its *initializer*, which creates and sets up the object.

Line 4 creates an AVPlayer, which is an object that can play various kinds of audio and video media. We create it with the url on the previous line, and the ! character is our assertion that the url is valid and not nil. This is actually a dangerous practice—we're not really in a position to know whether the URL is valid—and is something we will want to fix up a little later. Finally, on line 5, we tell the player to start playing.

Be Your Own DJ

You don't have to use our default URL; we just thought using a National Public Radio feed was a good bet for a URL that wouldn't get us sued and wouldn't disappear anytime soon. But we could be wrong; a URL we used in an earlier revision of this chapter disappeared in May, 2016, after more than a decade of non-stop streaming. So it's good to know how to choose and use a different URL for yourself.

To use a different stream, find a station you like in iTunes' Internet Radio section (but not the Radio section, which is only for Apple Music subscribers), and while it's playing, use Get Info (⌘I) to show its URL. Copy and paste this string in the playground, replacing our URL (make sure it's still in quotes). The AVPlayer class can handle the sort of HTTP-based audio streams seen in iTunes' Internet Radio section, so thousands of choices are available.

The results pane will show the URL string next to the line that creates the URL, and the lines involving the player will show AVPlayer and a big (64-bit) hexadecimal number (the player object's address in memory, which does us no good here). But nothing's actually playing, right?

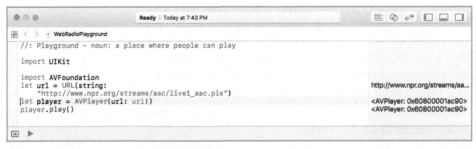

We need to do one special thing for this example. Swift is a language with built-in memory management that frees unused objects for us. Once we say player.play(), all the code in the playground has been executed, and Xcode assumes it's OK to clean everything up. Unfortunately, this results in the immediate destruction of the player object that we want to play our audio!

When we have a case where we want the contents of the playground to hang around after the initial execution finishes, we need to send a special command to Xcode to do so. Add the following to the end of the playground code:

playing/WebRadioPlayground.playground/Contents.swift

```
Line 1  import PlaygroundSupport
     2  PlaygroundPage.current.needsIndefiniteExecution = true
```

The import statement on line 1 tells the playground to load the functions and methods that let us interact with the playground execution itself, and setting the PlaygroundPage.current.needsIndefiniteExecution variable to true on line 2 gets the current page of the playground and tells it to keep executing indefinitely, instead of exiting (which would destroy the player variable).

Notice that as soon as you enter this last line and stop typing for a few seconds, you'll start hearing the web radio station playing (provided you have an Internet connection). Cool! Web radio with six lines of code!

Typing again causes the audio to stop, until you let up on the keyboard. Basically, when the playground thinks you're done editing, it tries to build and run the code, and in this case, that means music starts playing again.

So that's our first little bit of code that does something cool. Now let's look at how we got it to work at all.

Digging into Documentation

How did we know that an AVPlayer class exists, and that it can play an audio stream? Well, for now, your authors are happy to steer you in the right direction, but eventually you'll want to find features and functionality on your own, so let's see how that's done.

The documentation for the iOS SDK is available within Xcode itself, in a handy documentation viewer. Use the menu item Window > Documentation and API Reference (⇧⌘0) to show it.

When opened for the first time, the documentation viewer shows a two-pane window that lists three languages in the left pane—Swift, Objective-C, and JavaScript—and has an empty right pane. At the top, there's a toolbar with forward and back buttons, two other buttons, and a search field.

The two buttons hide and show two panes on the left side. The leftmost one, disabled by default, shows or hides the list of languages. This is actually the top-level *Navigator* for all documentation. Each language has a disclosure indicator (the triangle spinner) that lets us drill down for more information. Expand the Swift topic to see what it has to offer.

Under Swift, we find section headers like App Frameworks, App Services, and Developer Tools, and under each of these are topics that have disclosure triangles of their own. If we scroll down to Media and Web, we find an entry for AV Foundation, which you'll recall was something we used for creating our web radio player. Expand this topic and we find subheadings for classes, protocols, references, and more.

Under Classes, find AVPlayer and select it. This brings up the documentation for the class we used to play our web radio stream. We can scroll through this page or expand its disclosure triangle to see its topics in the Navigator: Creating a Player, Managing Playback, and more, as seen in the figure on page 8.

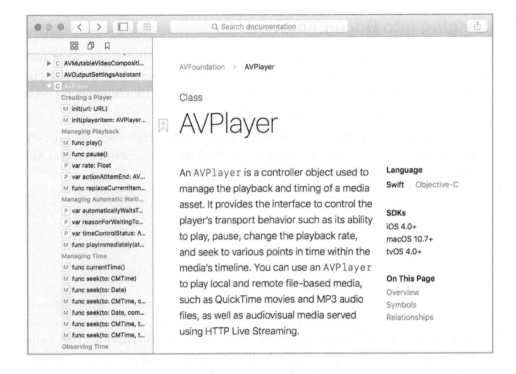

If we look under Creating a Player, we find init(url:). Click it to navigate to a page for this initializer. The page shows the syntax for creating an AVPlayer from a URL, describes the parameters and return value, and has a discussion section with further notes on its usage. All the documentation pages will use this general structure.

So now we know that to create an AVPlayer to play our audio, we just need to create a URL object and call AVPlayer(url: myURL). And if we look in the Navigator on the left, under Managing Playback we'll find the play() method that started playing our stream.

Searching Documentation

Now if we were working backward, we'd say to ourselves, "OK, to get an AVPlayer, we need to have a URL, so how do we do that?" In the documentation for init(url:), mousing over the URL reveals it to be a clickable hyperlink, so we could just follow that to get to its documentation. But let's learn how to do a search, too. Click in the search bar at the top, and type URL. The results of the search will immediately appear in a sheet beneath the search bar, as shown in the screenshot on page 9.

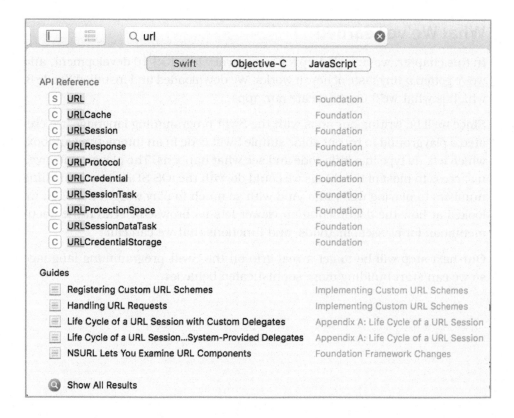

There are a bunch of different kinds of hits. The URL structure we want is at the top of the figure, denoted by a "S" icon to indicate it's a struct. There are other results, like classes that start with URL, and some guides on how to work with URLs in different APIs. If we clicked Show All Results, we would also see things like functions and methods that take URLs as their parameters. But let's select that first result and go to the URL structure's page. This documentation page is organized by topic, just like the last one, and under Initializers, we can find the one that takes a string.

So, by browsing, searching, and working backward, we can find the two classes we needed to create our streaming audio playground. We'll have more to say about the language itself in the next few chapters, but whenever we need functionality that we believe the SDK provides, we now know we can just bring up the documentation viewer and look for it.

What We've Learned

In this chapter, we've tooled up for our journey into iOS 10 development, and we've gotten a tiny taste of how it works. We downloaded and installed Xcode 8, which is what we'll use to create our apps.

Since we'll be writing our apps with the Swift programming language, we created a playground to try out some simple Swift code in an interactive sandbox, which lets us type in a little code and see what happens. The playground gives us access to most of the things we could do with the iOS SDK, from crunching numbers to playing web radio. And with so much to play with in the SDK, we looked at how the documentation viewer lets us browse or search the documentation for classes, methods, and functions that we can call.

Our next step will be to get a real grip on the Swift programming language so we can start building more sophisticated behavior.

CHAPTER 2

Starting with Swift

Playgrounds let us play around with iOS development, but it's not really obvious what we can do with them yet. When we browse the documentation, we can see there are thousands of classes and tens of thousands of methods and functions we can call. But how do we do that? It kind of feels like we opened up the box for a model kit and we now have a thousand plastic pieces to put together but no instructions and no glue.

In this chapter, we're going to start learning the Swift programming language, which will let us create our applications by giving us a way to call into the iOS SDK, and a way to compose our app's internal logic. We'll spend the entire chapter in playground mode, which will allow us to try things out, see what does and doesn't work, and quickly learn from our mistakes.

The Swift Programming Language

Swift is a programming language developed internally at Apple and released in 2014 for public use in developing iOS and OS X apps. Apple has made major changes and improvements on an annual basis, releasing Swift 2 in 2015 and Swift 3 in 2016. Swift 3 is the version of the language supported by Xcode 8, and the version we'll be using throughout this book. Apple is also open sourcing the language, and while it's a work in progress, this may eventually lead to opportunities for Swift developers beyond the Apple ecosystem.

Swift is defined by several essential traits. Swift is:

- *Compiled*, meaning that our source code is converted into executable machine code at build time, rather than being interpreted at runtime, as with scripting languages like JavaScript and Ruby.

- *Strongly typed*, meaning that objects we work with are clearly identified as strings, integers, floats, and so on. These types are *static*, meaning they can't change once they're assigned. Swift also provides *type inference*, so we don't have to explicitly indicate a type when the compiler can unambiguously figure it out.

- *Automatically reference counted*, meaning that objects allocated from memory keep track of how many incoming references they have, and their memory is freed up once there are zero references to them (since they're useless at this point, as no other objects now know about them). This is subtly different from the *garbage collection* system popular in many languages. The difference is that a garbage collector periodically goes out looking for unreferenced objects; Swift's *Automatic Reference Counting* (ARC) keeps constant track of references and frees objects immediately when they have zero references.

- *Name-spaced*, like many modern languages, but, importantly, not like Swift's predecessor, Objective-C. Name-spacing allows us to avoid collisions when multiple parts of our code (our app, frameworks we import, etc.) use the same name for different things. We can safely use a generic name like MyThing, because it's understood to be part of a *module* with a unique name like com.mycompany.myapp, so it won't be confused with com.othercompany.otherapp's MyThing (although we should still come up with better names than MyThing!)

Perhaps most importantly, Swift is a deeply *pragmatic* language, with a unique mission: providing a more modern and expressive way to code than Objective-C offered, while retaining compatibility with over 20 years of existing Apple frameworks and system code. The iOS SDK is written mostly in Objective-C, but parts of it are in C or even C++, and many different idioms are used in the various frameworks and libraries. Swift has to make it easy and natural to call all of it. As we'll see, Swift makes some accommodations to the past, because a more linguistically clean alternative that would require rewriting the iOS frameworks would be a non-starter.

In this book, we are covering Swift 3.0, which is supported by Xcode 8. Earlier versions of the language were supported by Xcodes 6 and 7. You can't write Swift 3 with earlier versions of Xcode, and future versions of Xcode will likely support yet newer versions of the language. Fortunately, the compiled code is forward- and backward-compatible, so Swift 2 code written in Xcode 7 will run on the new iOS 10, and Swift 3 code written in Xcode 8 will run on the older iOS 9 (provided that the app as a whole is marked as being backward-compatible with iOS 9). For simplicity, we are focusing only on current versions in this book: Swift 3, Xcode 8, and iOS 10.

Using Variables and Constants

Let's start writing some code and get a feel for how Swift works. Start a new playground (File > New > Playground), and call it NumbersPlayground. Delete the first line that creates the string (var str = "Hello, playground"), but leave the import UIKit. The import statement pulls in iOS frameworks we almost always want to use, so we will always leave that as the first line of our playgrounds.

Computers were originally built for math, so let's start with some simple numbers. Type the following:

startingswift/NumbersPlayground.playground/Contents.swift
```
let foo = 1
```

The right pane shows a 1. This is nice and simple: we've created foo and assigned it the value 1, which is what's shown in the results pane.

So far, so good. Now let's do some math. Like many languages, Swift has a += operator to add and assign, so let's try that.

startingswift/NumbersPlayground.playground/Contents.swift
```
foo += 1
```

Problem! It doesn't give us a 2! Instead, a red circle pops up in the left gutter next to our new line of code. Click the circle icon, and a red bar appears, saying:

```
Left side of mutating operator isn't mutable: 'foo' is a 'let' constant
```

That's bad! On the other hand, the circle icon means "instant fix," so that's good! When we clicked the icon, it also showed a pop-up box that looks like the following:

```
var foo = 1
foo += 1
```
Left side of mutating operator isn't mutable: 'foo' is a 'let' constant
Fix-it   Change 'let' to 'var' to make it mutable

The first line of the pop-up restates the error, and any subsequent lines give us instant-fix options. The error is that let creates a *constant*, a value that can't change. Once we set foo to 1, we can never change it again. If we do want foo to change, it needs to be a *variable*. That's what the second line is offering. In fact, it has even provisionally turned the let into a var to show us the effect of its proposed fix, as shown in the preceding figure.

This is what we want, so click the second line to accept the change to var. Now we can perform all the math on foo that we like.

Constants vs. variables might seem like a semantic difference: some languages like C make variables the default and constants uncommon, while JavaScript doesn't have constants at all. In Swift, using constants is preferred when you know that a value should not or cannot change. This allows the compiler to make certain performance optimizations for constants. We always have to choose between marking things as constants or variables, and this is on purpose; as we'll see again and again, many of Swift's design choices are built on the idea of the developer being explicit about his or her intentions.

Counting with Numeric Types

Let's play with some more math. We'll create another variable:

```
var bar = 0
```

That looks good, and since it's a variable, we can change its value:

```
bar = 0.5
```

Oh, no! We get another error, and this time without an instant fix. Worse yet, the description is unhelpful: "Cannot assign a value of type 'Double' to a value of type 'Int'."

So what's the deal? Can Swift seriously not convert between floating-point numbers and integers? Actually, Swift can, but our variable bar cannot. The problem is that we never specified what the type of bar is, so the Swift compiler made its best guess. And it guessed wrong. In fact, the instant fix proposes to replace 0.5 with Int(0.5); that will make an integer by rounding down 0.5 to the nearest Int, which is 0—not what we want! Instead, replace the bar = 0.5 line with the following:

```
type(of: bar)
```

The type(of:) function allows us to see what type a value has. In the right pane, we see that the type evaluates to Int.Type. That makes sense: since the original value was 0, Swift took a guess and assumed we wanted an integer, not a floating-point type. This inferring of types is called, appropriately, *type inference*.

We could tell Swift to use a floating-point type by using 0.0 as the initial value; try that and you'll see the inferred type becomes Double.Type. But if we want a given type, we should just declare it that way. Change the declaration like this:

```
var bar : Double = 0
```

Now Swift doesn't need to infer anything: we've explicitly declared that we want bar to be a Double, meaning a double-precision floating-point type.

There's also a lower-precision floating-point type, Float, and a Boolean type, Bool. In some languages, such as C, you can cast between integers, floats, doubles, and Bools, and the worst that will happen is that the compiler will warn you about loss of precision. Swift forbids this altogether, even if you wouldn't be losing anything. Try this:

```
startingswift/NumbersPlayground.playground/Contents.swift
let myInt = 1
let myDouble : Double = myInt
```

This leads to an error saying "Cannot convert value of type 'Int' to specified type 'Double'." We can't just cast between types like in many other languages; to create myDouble, we need to tell Swift to create a *new* Double:

```
startingswift/NumbersPlayground.playground/Contents.swift
let myInt = 1
let myDouble = Double(myInt)
```

The second line here uses Double's *initializer* to create a new Double, using the value passed in as a parameter.

Swift's numeric types work with many of the usual arithmetic operators popular in other languages: +, -, *, and /. The remainder operator, %, is available for the Int type, while Float and Double types need to use a related method, truncatingRemainder().

On the other hand, thanks to strong typing, Bools aren't just numeric values, and thus *none* of these mathematic operators works with Boolean values. And that's a good thing, because what would "false divided by true" mean, anyway? Instead, we use the usual Boolean operators ! (NOT), && (logical AND), and || (logical OR).

Storing Text in Strings

Strings—blocks of textual data—are another essential data type supported in nearly all programming languages, and Swift's are really great. Let's start a new playground to try them out: create the playground with File > New > Playground, and call it StringsPlayground.

Right off the bat, the playground template creates a string for us with var str = "Hello, playground", which evaluates as Hello, playground in the results pane.

Since str is defined with the var keyword, it's a variable, so let's change it up a bit. Type the following:

```
startingswift/StringsPlayground.playground/Contents.swift
str = str + "!!"
```

This evaluates as Hello, playground!!, and proves that we can combine strings with the + operator.

Swift strings are fully Unicode compliant, meaning they can contain any Unicode character, including all the various written languages and symbols supported by iOS. Let's add some of those characters now. Xcode offers quick access to Unicode characters with the menu item Edit > Emoji & Symbols (^⌘space). The popover, shown in the following figure, allows quick selection of groups of emojis and other characters like technical symbols and pictographs. Scroll to the top to find a search field to look up characters by name, and a button to switch to the full-size character input window.

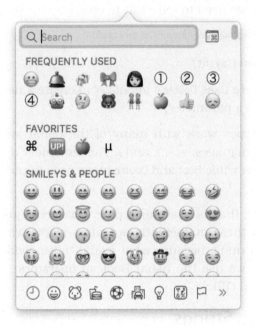

Let's see if we can add an emoji character to our string. Write the following code, and when you need to insert the emoji inside the quotes, bring up the symbols window, find an emoji character, and double-click it to insert it into the source code:

```
str += "🏃"
```

As you'll see in the results pane, this appends the emoji to the end of the string. And it turns out Swift's support for Unicode isn't just for strings; Unicode is fully supported throughout Swift source code as well. That means we can do something really silly, like this:

```
var 🏃 = str
```

This creates a variable whose name is actually the running person emoji, and the assignment operator (=) sets its value to the current value of str, so we see the same value as before in the results pane.

Aside from the + operator, we can also build up strings through a substitution technique. Whenever the sequence \() is found in a string in source code, the contents of the parentheses are evaluated and substituted into the string. The contents could be variables, mathematical expressions, or other strings, as in the following screenshot:

```
let book = "📖"                                              "📖"
let phone = "📱"                                             "📱"
let sentence = "This is a \(book) about \(phone) apps."     "This is a 📖 about 📱 apps."
```

Now what about the contents of a string? In some languages, such as C, a string is just an array of characters. That's largely true of Swift, subject to some technical details. Swift strings are really smart about Unicode, and sometimes multiple characters can be combined into one. Consider what happens when we combine Unicode's "combining accent character" (Unicode code point 301) with the letter "e," just as if we had typed ⌥e and then e:

startingswift/StringsPlayground.playground/Contents.swift
```
let accentedE = "e" + "\u{301}"
```

This evaluates to the single character "é." Two characters go in, and one comes out.

When we do want to pull out the contents of a string, we can use its characters property to let us treat the string contents as an array—one of the collection types we'll be talking about in the next section. This lets us count the number of user-readable characters, and for kicks, we'll substitute that number into a larger string:

startingswift/StringsPlayground.playground/Contents.swift
```
"Sentence has \(sentence.characters.count) characters"
```

This evaluates to "Sentence has 25 characters" in the right pane.

The contents of the characters array are of a type called Character, which represents a single human-readable character. Using our Unicode string from before, we can find the location in the string of the "book" emoji by representing it as a Character, and then using the array's indexOf() to find it in the characters array.

```
let bookChar : Character = "📖"
"book is at index \(sentence.characters.index(of: bookChar)) in sentence"
```

Once we write this, we see the result "book is at index Optional(Swift.String.Character-View.Index(_base: Swift.String.UnicodeScalarView.Index(_position: 10), _countUTF16: 2)) in sentence". The 10 is right, but all that Optional() stuff is weird, right? We're going to discover what's up with that a little later.

Packaging Data in Collections

With numeric types and strings, one thing we'll frequently want to do is to put them into *collections*. Nearly all languages have multiple ways of putting items into groups so we can then organize and perform operations on the entire group. Swift provides three main types of collections: arrays, sets, and dictionaries.

To start playing with these, start a new playground called CollectionsPlayground, and delete the line that creates the "Hello, playground!" string.

Arrays

For many of us, the most frequently used collection is the *array*. Arrays contain multiple items and maintain the ordering of those items. They also allow for the same item to appear multiple times in the array.

We'll start with an array of strings that lists our favorite iPhone models. Declare an array as follows, and immediately check its dynamicType:

```
startingswift/CollectionsPlayground.playground/Contents.swift
var models = ["iPhone SE", "iPhone 6s", "iPhone 7"]
type(of:models)
```

We can create an array by just putting its contents, comma-separated, inside square brackets. We can see from the results pane that this evaluates to these three strings, and the type(of:) is inferred to be Array<String>, meaning an Array of Strings.

Now let's add an item at the front of the array:

```
startingswift/CollectionsPlayground.playground/Contents.swift
models.insert("iPhone 7 Plus", at: 0)
```

Our array now has four strings. Keep in mind, however, that we can add *only* Strings because that's the type of the array. If we wanted to be able to add other types, like any of the numeric types, we would have had to originally declare that models accepts any Swift type, which we would write as var models : Array<Any>. There's also a simpler syntax for array type declarations: [Any].

As our array grows, it likely won't fit on one line of the results pane. Fortunately, there's a way to see the whole thing. Mouse over the last line in the results pane, and two icons will appear on the far right: Quick Look and Show Result.

["iPhone 7 Plus", "iPhone SE", "iPhone 6s", "iPhone... ⊙ ▦

Click the rightmost button, Show Result, to see the results shown directly below the line of code that produced them.

```
models.insert("iPhone 7 Plus", at: 0)                    ["iPhone 7 Plus", "iPhone SE", "iPhone 6s", "iPhone 7"] ▦

    0 "iPhone 7 Plus"
    1 "iPhone SE"
    2 "iPhone 6s"
    3 "iPhone 7"
```

The Quick Look button tries to do a similar presentation in a popover window rather than presenting the results in our source pane. In this case, the array members are too wide to fit in the popover, and have to be scrolled vertically as well, so it's not that useful this time.

Let's dig into our array. To access a member of an array by its index, we can use the square-brace syntax familiar from C, Java, and many other languages:

startingswift/CollectionsPlayground.playground/Contents.swift
```
let firstItem = models[0]
```

The evaluation pane shows that firstItem has been set to the value "iPhone 7 Plus", which we inserted a few lines back.

Since we can insert, we can, of course, remove items as well, either with removeAtIndex() or removeLast(). To see the shortened array in the results pane, we type models by itself on the next line.

startingswift/CollectionsPlayground.playground/Contents.swift
```
models.removeLast()
models
```

Keep in mind that all of these mutating operations are possible only because models was originally declared with the var keyword. If we'd used let, Swift would infer we wanted the array to be constant and would have created an immutable array.

Swift arrays have a few other neat tricks that make it easy to combine and split arrays, provided their types are compatible. Try this:

startingswift/CollectionsPlayground.playground/Contents.swift
```
Line 1  let iPhones = ["iPhone SE", "iPhone 6s", "iPhone 7", "iPhone 7 Plus"]
     2  let iPads = ["iPad Air 2", "iPad Pro", "iPad mini"]
     3  models = iPhones
     4  models.append(contentsOf: iPads)
     5  models.insert(contentsOf: ["iPod touch"], at: 4)
```

In this section of code, lines 1 and 2 create immutable arrays called iPhones and iPads, respectively. Line 3 assigns our models array to now be the contents of iPhones. Then, on line 4, we use the appendContentsOf() function to append the contents of the iPads array to the models array. If we don't want to add items at the end, we can use the insertContentsOf() function to insert an array at a given index. On line 5, we insert a one-element array of iPod touch models at index 4, putting it between the iPhones and iPads. As we can see in the evaluation pane, our array now has eight items.

Sets

Arrays are a bread-and-butter collection, but for certain tasks, *sets* make more sense. A set has no sense of order and does not allow duplicate items. Sets are useful for when you want to simply know whether or not a given item is part of a collection, and you don't care if it's "before" or "after" other members of the collection.

Let's kick off an empty set and start adding stuff to it.

startingswift/CollectionsPlayground.playground/Contents.swift

```
Line 1  var set = Set<String>()
     2  set.insert("iPhone 7")
     3  set.insert("iPhone 7")
     4  set
```

Line 1 shows the recipe for creating an empty collection of any type. We have to declare the type (because there are no objects to infer it from), so we use the type Set<String>, and empty parentheses to call the initializer for that type.

On line 2 we add the string "iPhone 7", and on line 3 we do it again. Then we just evaluate set on line 4 to see what's in it.

Look at the results on the last line: the set still only has one member. That's because a given item can appear only once in a Set; we don't care how many of something are in the set, just whether that thing is in or out. This is also reflected in the return value of each insert(): we get back a Bool indicating whether or not the insert succeeded, and an object that is either the newly inserted object, or an equivalent object already in the set that caused the new insert to be rejected.

Where sets really shine is their operators for determining membership between members of multiple sets. Let's create two sets to play with:

startingswift/CollectionsPlayground.playground/Contents.swift

```
var iPhoneSet : Set = ["iPhone 7"]
var iPadSet : Set = ["iPad Air 2", "iPad mini", "iPad Pro"]
```

Notice that as a convenience, we can create a Set from an Array. In this example, ["iPhone 7"] is one array, and ["iPad Air 2", "iPad mini", "iPad Pro"] is another. We have to declare the Set type (because otherwise the square-brace syntax would imply an Array), but at least the type of the Set's contents (Strings) can be inferred.

If we were interested in what members are in both sets, that's a one-line call:

startingswift/CollectionsPlayground.playground/Contents.swift
```
iPhoneSet.intersection(iPadSet)
```

The results pane shows us an empty set—Set([])—because no items are members of both sets. Let's change that. The iPhone 7 Plus feels nearly as big as an iPad mini, so let's add it to both sets and try another call to intersect().

startingswift/CollectionsPlayground.playground/Contents.swift
```
iPadSet.insert("iPhone 7 Plus")
iPhoneSet.insert("iPhone 7 Plus")
iPhoneSet.intersection(iPadSet)
```

Now the results pane shows us the one item in both sets, "iPhone 7 Plus".

If you studied set theory in high school, you'll recall that an *intersection* is the items that are in both sets, and that the *union* is all the members of both sets. Swift gives that to us, too:

startingswift/CollectionsPlayground.playground/Contents.swift
```
iPhoneSet.union(iPadSet)
```

This gives us everything from both sets (you might have to use the Quick Look or Show Results buttons to see them all). Notice that "iPhone 7 Plus" appears only once, despite being present in both sets. After all, the return type is a Set, and any object can appear only once in a set.

Dictionaries

Swift's third major collection type is *dictionaries*. A dictionary is a collection that maps *keys* to *values*, which gives you a way to quickly look up a given value in the future, provided you have the corresponding key.

Let's create a dictionary that lets us look up iOS device sizes by model name:

startingswift/CollectionsPlayground.playground/Contents.swift
```
let sizeInMm = [
    "iPhone 7": 138.1,
    "iPhone 7 Plus" : 158.1,
    "iPad Air 2" : 240.0,
    "iPad Pro" : 305.7]
type(of:sizeInMm)
```

As we can see in the results pane, this creates a dictionary with four key-value pairs, and the type of this collection is inferred to be Dictionary<String, Double>, meaning the keys are Strings and the values are Doubles.

To access a value, we put the key in square braces, like this:

```
sizeInMm["iPhone 7"]
sizeInMm["iPad mini"]
```

The results pane shows that we got back 138.1 for the "iPhone 7" key and nil for the "iPad mini" key, which makes sense because sizeInMm doesn't have that key.

Dictionaries are good for fast lookups of single items, although it's also possible to walk through the whole collection. To do that, though, we're going to need ways to have our code loop through the collection. So let's move on to that.

Looping and Branching: Control Flow

Control flow refers to how we specify the order of how our Swift instructions are executed, or in a bigger picture, what parts of our code are to be run and under what conditions. In Swift, as in other languages, this is mostly implemented as conditionals and loops. Conditionals are statements that do or don't execute code based on whether certain conditions are true or false at the time they're evaluated. Loops build on conditionals by running some part of the code zero or more times based on the conditions we provide.

Swift's tools for control flow are probably very familiar to most developers, since many languages have if, for, while, and so forth. We'll try them out now, so start a new playground called ControlFlowPlayground.

for Loops

Control flow also goes hand in hand with collections, which is why we're reaching it now: once you have a collection of items, it's natural to want to go through the collection and run some code on each item. We'll start with going through an array with for.

startingswift/ControlFlowPlayground.playground/Contents.swift
```
Line 1  let models = ["iPhone 7", "iPhone 7 Plus", "iPad Air 2",
     2      "iPad mini", "iPad Pro"]
     3  for model in models {
     4      print ("model: \(model)")
     5  }
```

On lines 1–2, we create the models array, consisting of five strings. Line 3 is the *for-in* loop syntax, which says we want to go through every member of the models collection, and each time through, the item we're working with will be represented with the local variable model.

The results pane doesn't show us anything about what happened each time through the loop. To see that we're actually doing something each time, we use the print() function on line 4 to write a message to the debug log. The output from print() isn't shown by default; bring it up with View > Debug Area > Activate Console (⇧⌘C), or the middle button on the pane-switcher on the toolbar:

Once the console pane is revealed, you should see the output of this loop:

```
model: iPhone 7
model: iPhone 7 Plus
model: iPad Air 2
model: iPad mini
model: iPad Pro
```

If it's useful to have the index of members of the collection, we can do a loop that counts the members of the collection numerically, like this:

startingswift/ControlFlowPlayground.playground/Contents.swift
```
for i in 0 ..< models.count {
    print ("model at index \(i): \(models[i])")
}
```

This style of for loop creates a variable for the index (i, in this case) and counts through a range of values. We create this with the *range operator*: ..<, which counts from the starting value (0) to one less than the ending value (models.count, the length of the array). If we wanted to include the ending value, we would use the range operator ... instead.

What if it would be convenient to have both the index and a local variable inside the loop? Sure, we could do let model = models[i] as the first line inside the loop, and then use that. However, Swift gives a much more elegant alternative, albeit one we'll have to wait to discover in the next chapter.

if-else Statements

We often want to execute some statements only if certain conditions are true, and while the if statement is unfashionable in some coding circles, it's familiar to nearly every programmer. Swift's are simple enough, with one or two unique wrinkles. Let's try an if statement that pulls a value out of a dictionary:

Get Your C-Style for Loops Out of Here

Swift giveth, but Swift also taketh away. In Swift 3, the language eliminates the old style of for loop popularized by C and its many descendants:

```
for (initialization_expression; loop_condition; increment_expression) {...}
```

The three elements of this construct are an initialization of some sort, a test for when to exit the loop, and an expression to perform each time through the loop. For example, for (i=0; i < 10; i++) is understood as meaning "loop through with values of i from 0 to 10 (non-inclusive)."

The combination of Swift's for-in syntax and the range operator does the same thing, and is arguably easier to read, so the old for syntax is now gone. In fact, that also led Swift 3 to eliminate the C-like ++ operator to increment numeric values by one; it was mostly used for this old style of for loop, and has order-of-operation subtleties that have caused bugs for *decades*.

startingswift/ControlFlowPlayground.playground/Contents.swift
```
Line 1  let sizeInMm = [
    -       "iPhone 7": 138.1,
    -       "iPhone 7 Plus" : 158.1,
    -       "iPad Air 2" : 240.0,
    5       "iPad Pro" : 305.7]
    -
    -   let model = "iPhone 7"
    -   if sizeInMm[model] != nil {
    -       print ("size of \(model) is \(sizeInMm[model])")
   10   } else {
    -       print ("couldn't find \(model)")
    -   }
```

After creating the sizeInMm dictionary, we define the model key we are interested in, and then try to get its matching value from the dictionary. If the value is not nil, we execute the print() on line 9, and otherwise the print() on 11. Change the value of model to different values to see each block of the if-else log its message to the console.

The one truly interesting thing to say here is that the curly braces in Swift if-else statements are *required*, even if only a single line is to be executed in either case. This is different from the single-line behavior of C and Java, and eliminates easy-to-miss bugs caused by the inconsistent syntax of making the curly braces optional.

Swift also offers a guard statement that is sort of like the opposite of if: it doesn't have a curly-brace clause for the true case, just an else for when the condition is not true. We typically use these for early exits when we don't want to run many lines of code if the condition isn't met, and we don't want to have to nest important code deeply in if-else indentation.

Typically, guard statements perform early returns to bail out of code we don't want to run, and we can't do that kind of early return in a playground, so we'll have to wait until we're writing a real app to get our guard on.

switch Statements

The last kind of control flow technique we need to be aware of is switch. The switch keyword lets us test a variable against several possible values, and execute different code in each case. Let's write a simple example:

`startingswift/ControlFlowPlayground.playground/Contents.swift`

```
switch model {
case "iPhone 7 Plus":
    print ("That's what I want")
case "iPhone 8":
    print ("Maybe next year?")
default:
    print ("Not my thing")
}
```

This switch will log "That's what I want" if model is "iPhone 7 Plus", or "Maybe next year" if it's "iPhone 8", or "Not my thing" in all other cases.

If you're familiar with C's switch, you'll be pleasantly surprised by one feature here: Swift's switch works on Strings (or any type that can be evaluated with ==, actually), and not just on numeric types. Another improvement from other languages is that a matched case *doesn't* fall through to the ones after it; in C, you would have to put a break at the end of the first case, or the code would execute the second case and the default as well.

One thing to be aware of is that switch statements must be *exhaustive*, meaning they must cover every possible value of the item being tested. Often, we use default as a catchall for this.

The switch statement gets heavily used in Swift because it's the perfect way to deal with enumerations, which you'll learn about in the next chapter.

Maybe It's There, Maybe It Isn't: Optionals

A few times so far, we've seen our result values log messages include the term "optional," a behavior we haven't explained yet. But it's time to deal with it, because optionals are one of Swift's defining features. Create a new playground called OptionalsPlayground and delete the "Hello, playground" line, as usual.

We'll start by adding the sizeInMm dictionary from a few sections back, since that's something that started giving us this "optional" stuff.

startingswift/OptionalsPlayground.playground/Contents.swift
```
let sizeInMm = [
    "iPhone 7": 138.1,
    "iPhone 7 Plus" : 158.1,
    "iPad Air 2" : 240.0,
    "iPad Pro" : 305.7]
```

Looking at this, we can see that sizeInMm["iPhone 7"] should evaluate to 138.1, which is a Double, meaning a double-precision floating-point number.

Well, that's great, but what if we evaluate sizeInMm["iPhone 8"], a key not in the dictionary? If our return value is a Double, what's the right value for its size? 0? -1? Some huge positive or negative value that we just interpret as a "no-value"?

Swift has a better answer for this: *optionals*. An optional is a type that represents two different things: whether there's a value at all and, if so, what the value actually is.

It turns out that dictionaries always return optionals for their values, as we can see by inspecting the type(of:) of the value we get back:

startingswift/OptionalsPlayground.playground/Contents.swift
```
let size7 = sizeInMm["iPhone 7"]
type(of:size7)
```

In the results pane, this shows size7 as 138.1 and the type(of:) as Optional<Double>.Type.

Now let's try the same thing with a nonexistent value, like the size of the fictional iPhone 8:

startingswift/OptionalsPlayground.playground/Contents.swift
```
let size8 = sizeInMm["iPhone 8"]
type(of:size8)
```

This shows us a size of nil and the dynamicType of Optional<Double>.Type. It's the same type as before—a Double optional—only this time there isn't a value.

Unwrapping Optionals

As you might imagine, we're frequently going to be concerned with whether an optional value is nil, and when it's not, we often want to get to the value itself. We do this through a process called *unwrapping*. To "unwrap" a Double optional like the values in our dictionary means to take an Optional<Double> and turn it into just a normal Double.

One way to unwrap is to use the *force-unwrap operator*, which is the ! character. Try it out on size7:

startingswift/OptionalsPlayground.playground/Contents.swift
```
type(of:size7!)
```

This force-unwraps size7 to be a non-optional type, and then gets its type(of:). The results pane shows the type as Double. Huzzah! We got our Double out from inside the optional!

Not so fast. Try the same thing with size8:

startingswift/OptionalsPlayground.playground/Contents.swift
```
type(of: size8!)
```

Ack! The results pane says "Error," and there's a red band with a bunch of scary text about EXC_BAD_INSTRUCTION.

```
type(of: size8!)
    error: Execution was interrupted, reason: EXC_BAD_INSTRUCTION (code=EXC_I386_INVOP, subcode=0x0).
```

This is pretty bad: our code has *crashed* inside the playground. And the reason for that is something we need to remember: *unwrapping nil values crashes our code!* size8 is nil; we said to unwrap it with the ! operator—bang, we're dead. Let's delete that line so it doesn't give us any more trouble!

Now we need to figure out what we're going to do to not crash anymore. One option would be to always test optionals against nil, and only unwrap if they're non-nil. That works, but it gets ugly. Nest a few if foo != nil blocks, and soon you've got what Swift developers call the "pyramid of doom" from all that indentation.

Unwrapping Optionals with if let

Fortunately, there's a way out of this mess. We can combine let and if to create an expression that says "if you can assign this to a non-optional value, then give it the following name." Here's what that looks like:

startingswift/OptionalsPlayground.playground/Contents.swift
```
if let size = size7 {
    type(of:size)
}

if let size = size8 {
    type(of:size)
}
```

Once we finish typing this, notice that the first if let block shows Double.Type for the type in the results pane, meaning that size is a normal Double inside the block and not an optional. But the second block of code doesn't show anything, because its if let fails (because size8 is nil, so the contents inside the curly braces are not executed and size is not assigned).

The if let keyword gets used a lot, so it has a few tricks that will help us write more concise code. The first is that we can combine several if lets on a single line, comma-separated:

```
if let size7 = size7, let size8 = size8 {
    type(of:size7)
    type(of:size8)
}
```

There are two things to notice here. First, each assignment in an if let creates a variable name that's only visible inside the scope of the curly braces. Often, it makes sense to just use the same name that a variable has outside the if let. So, in this case, if let size7 = size7 is *not* a meaningless tautology; instead, it looks at the right side (the optional size7) and says "if that's not nil, create an unwrapped variable *also* called size7 inside the curly-brace scope." At first it may look weird, but it's a convention that comes easily to Swift programmers and is better than having to come up with different variable names for use only inside the if let block.

Second, there's nothing in the results pane, because not all of the if let assignments succeeded. Since size8 is nil, we can't unwrap it, and the second let fails.

One other trick we use a lot is testing a value that we've just unwrapped, as part of the if let. For example, what if we want to run some code on an optional Double only if it's non-nil *and* its value is greater than some constant? We could use an if let followed by a if size7 > 100.0, but nesting ifs is going to give us that "pyramid of doom" we spoke of before. Instead, we can do this:

```
if let size7 = size7, size7 > 100.0 {
    size7
}
```

The logical expression after the comma on an if let allows us to perform logic with the unwrapped size7 Double while still on the if let line. This makes it clear that *everything* on the if let line has to pass for us to get into the curly-brace block.

It may seem like a lot of work to deal with optionals, but the concept ends up being powerful: we can use a single variable to both hold a value and to say "nothing to see here" if there isn't a value. In some languages, we'd either have to use two variables for that, or a magical flag value that we just agree to treat as a "no value" value. And programming history has shown that approach can cause a lot of unexpected problems.

What We've Learned

Optionals are a tricky subject to get your head around, so it's probably a good time to take a break and take stock of what we've learned so far.

This chapter has been all about working with the essential data types in Swift. We started with the numeric types—integers, floating-point numbers, and Booleans—and strings. We saw how to combine strings with the basic concatenation operator (+) and pattern substitution, and how to access their contents. Also, we went a little nuts with the Unicode support in Swift strings, but it'll pay off if we ever want to support multiple languages, or lots of emoji.

We also played around with the different types of collections—arrays, sets, and dictionaries—and what each is particularly good for. Then we looked at Swift's control flow operators, so we could use loops to go through the contents of collections.

Finally, since dictionaries may or may not give us a value for a given key, we started working with Swift optionals, to see how they represent the presence or absence of a value, and how to get to the value.

These are the building blocks we'll use to build full-blown iOS apps. In the next chapter, you'll see how to combine them into more sophisticated data structures, how to create functions to work with them, and how to do so with style and aplomb.

CHAPTER 3

Swift with Style

In the previous chapter, we explored the basics of Swift: the type system, control flow, optionals, and so on. And, assuming Swift isn't your first programming language, you've probably guessed the next step is combining these simple pieces together into more complex, more capable, and more interesting constructs. While that is what we're going to do, it's not as straightforward as you might think.

Swift is a remarkably flexible language, one that takes its inspiration from a number of different sources. It's true to both the object-oriented nature of Objective-C and to new ideas about design, elegance, and maintainability in functional programming languages. You can write Swift like Objective-C, like C, like Java, or even like Haskell, and it will still work.

Since there's no one right way to write Swift, we will be making choices about how we want to organize our code. In this chapter, we're going to look at what Swift offers us for building bigger data structures, and how our choices will affect the evolution of our apps as we write and rewrite them. If the one hammer in your toolbox when you started this book was the good ol' class, let's discover what we can do by taking lightweight types like structures and enumerations and extending them with custom functionality.

Creating Classes

Many programmers—professionals and students, hobbyists and cowboy coders—have grown up in the mind-set of *object-oriented programming*. As Janie once said on the NSBrief podcast, "I didn't think I was learning object-oriented programming. I thought I was learning programming...like that was the only way to do it."

And it's not like anyone's wrong to learn OO! It's the dominant paradigm for a good reason: it has proven over the decades to be a good way to write applications. Whole languages are built around the concepts of OO: it's nigh-impossible to break out of the OO paradigm in Java, and Objective-C has OO in its very name, after all!

So let's see how Swift supports object-oriented programming. The heart and soul of OO is to create *classes*, collections of common behavior from which we will create individual instances called *objects*. We'll begin by creating a new playground called ClassesPlayground, and deleting the "Hello, playground" line as usual.

In the last chapter's collections examples, we used arrays, sets, and dictionaries to represent various models of iOS devices. But it's not easy or elegant to collect much more than a name that way, and there are lots of things we want in an iOS device model. So we will create a class to represent iOS devices.

We'll start by tracking a device's model name and its physical dimensions: width and height. Type the following into the playground:

```
stylishswift/ClassesPlayground.playground/Contents.swift
class IOSDevice {
        var name : String
        var screenHeight : Double
        var screenWidth : Double
}
```

In Swift, we declare a class with the class keyword, followed by the class name. If we were subclassing some other class, we would have a colon and the name of the superclass, like class MyClass : MySuperclass, but we don't need that for this simple class.

Next, we have *properties*, the variables or constants associated with an object instance. In this case, we are creating three variables: name, screenHeight, and screenWidth.

There's just one problem: this code produces an error. We need to start thinking about how our properties work.

Properties

The error flag tells us "Class IOSDevice has no initializers," and the red-circle instant-fix icon offers three problems and solutions. The problem for each is that there is no initial value for these properties. Before accepting the instant fix, let's consider what the problem is.

The properties we have defined are not optionals, so, by definition, they must have values. The tricky implication of that is that they must *always* have values. The value can change, but it can't be absent: that's what optionals are for.

We have a couple of options. We could accept the instant-fix suggestions and assign default values for each. That would give us declarations like

```
var name : String = ""
var screenHeight : Double = 0.0
var screenWidth : Double = 0.0
```

That's one solution, as long as we're OK with the default values. But here they don't quite make sense because we probably never want an iOS device with an empty string for a name.

Plan B: we can make everything optionals. To do this, we append the optional type ? to the properties.

```
var name : String?
var screenHeight : Double?
var screenWidth : Double?
```

Again, no more error, so that's good. Problem now is that any code that wants to access these properties has to do the if let dance from the last chapter to safely unwrap the optionals. And again, do we ever want the device name to be nil? That seems kind of useless.

Fortunately, we have another alternative: Swift's rule is that all properties must be initialized *by the end of every initializer*. So we can write an *initializer* to take initial values for these properties, and since that will be the only way to create an IOSDevice, we can know that these values will always be populated.

So rewrite the class like this:

stylishswift/ClassesPlayground.playground/Contents.swift
```
class IOSDevice {
    var name : String
    var screenHeight : Double
    var screenWidth : Double

    init (name: String, screenHeight: Double, screenWidth: Double) {
        self.name = name
        self.screenHeight = screenHeight
        self.screenWidth = screenWidth
    }
}
```

The initializer runs from lines 6 to 10. The first line is the important one, as it starts with init and then takes a name and type for each of the parameters to be provided to the initializer code. In the initializer itself, we just use the self keyword to assign the properties to these arguments.

Easy Come, Easy Go

 All types also have a *deinitializer*, which is called when the object is destroyed. This means that if your object needs to clean things up before it disappears, you can just override deinit().

To create an instance of IOSDevice, we call the initializer by the name of the class, and provide these arguments by name. Create the constant iPhone7 after the class's closing brace, as follows (note that a line break has been added to suit the book's formatting; it's OK to write this all on one line).

stylishswift/ClassesPlayground.playground/Contents.swift
```
let iPhone7 = IOSDevice(name: "iPhone 7",
                 screenHeight: 138.1, screenWidth: 67.0)
```

Congratulations! You've instantiated your first custom object, as the "IOSDevice" in the results pane indicates. Notice that the names of the arguments to the initializer are used as labels in actually calling the initializer. This helps us keep track of which argument is which, something that can be a problem in other languages when you call things that have lots of arguments.

Computed Properties

The three properties we've added to our class are *stored properties*, meaning that Swift creates the in-memory storage for the String and the two Doubles. We access these properties on an instance with dot syntax, like iPhone7.name.

Swift also has another kind of property, the *computed property*, which is a property that doesn't need storage because it can be produced by other means.

Right now we have a screenWidth and a screenHeight. Obviously, it would be easy to get the screen's area by just multiplying those two together. Instead of making the caller do that math, we can have IOSDevice expose it as a computed property. Back inside the class's curly braces—just after the other variables and before the init() is the customary place for it—add the following:

stylishswift/ClassesPlayground.playground/Contents.swift
```
var screenArea : Double {
    get {
        return screenWidth * screenHeight
    }
}
```

Back at the bottom of the file, after creating the iPhone7 constant, fetch the computed property by calling it with the same dot syntax as with a stored property:

```
iPhone7.screenArea
```

The results pane shows the computed area, 9,252.7 (or possibly 9252.699...).

With only a get block, the screenArea is a read-only computed property. We could also provide a set, but that doesn't really make sense in this case.

It's also possible for stored properties to run arbitrary code; instead of computing values, we can give stored properties willSet and didSet blocks to run immediately before or after setting the property's value. We'll use this approach later on in the book.

Methods

Speaking of running arbitrary code, one other thing we expect classes to do is to let us, you know, *do stuff*. In object-oriented languages, classes have *methods* that instruct the class to perform some function. Of course, Swift makes this straightforward.

Let's take our web radio player from the first chapter and add that to our IOSDevice. After all, real iOS devices are used for playing music all the time, right? We'll start by adding the import statement to bring in the audio-video APIs, and the special code we used to let the playground keep playing. Add the following at the top of the file, below the existing import UIKit line:

```
stylishswift/ClassesPlayground.playground/Contents.swift
import AVFoundation
import PlaygroundSupport
PlaygroundPage.current.needsIndefiniteExecution = true
```

We need our IOSDevice to have an AVPlayer we can start and stop, so add that as a property after the existing name, screenHeight, and screenWidth:

```
stylishswift/ClassesPlayground.playground/Contents.swift
private var audioPlayer : AVPlayer?
```

Notice that this property is an optional type, AVPlayer?, since it will be nil until it is needed.

Now, let's add a method to the class. We do this with the func keyword, followed by the method name, a list of arguments, and a return type. Add this playAudio() method somewhere inside the class's curly braces, ideally after the init's closing brace, since we usually write our initializers first and our methods next.

```
stylishswift/ClassesPlayground.playground/Contents.swift
func playAudioFrom(url: URL) -> Void {
    audioPlayer = AVPlayer(url: url)
    audioPlayer!.play()
}
```

Like the init, the parentheses contain the parameters to the method and their types. In Swift, we label each parameter, which is why we have url: preceding the URL type. If playAudioFrom() also took a rate argument, we would call it like playAudioFrom(url: someURL, rate: 1.0). Compared to some languages, the labeled parameters may seem chatty or verbose, but in practice they make the code more readable by exposing what each value is there for.

Inner and Outer Parameter Names

 In fact, a parameter can have two names—an "outer" name that callers see, and an "inner" name used as a variable inside the method. So it would be somewhat more elegant to declare this method as:

```
func playAudio(fromURL url: URL)
```

and then call it like this:

```
playAudio(fromURL: foo)
```

We'll use outer names when they make our code more elegant, either for callers or inside the methods' implementations.

After the parameters, the return type is indicated by the -> arrow. In this case, the method returns nothing, so we return Void. (In fact, when we return Void we can omit the arrow and the return type.) The rest of the method is the two lines of code we used in the first chapter to create the AVPlayer and start playing.

Now let's call it and start playing music. Put the following at the bottom of the file, after where we create the iPhone7 instance.

```
stylishswift/ClassesPlayground.playground/Contents.swift
if let url = URL(string: "http://www.npr.org/streams/aac/live1_aac.pls") {
    iPhone7.playAudioFrom(url: url)
}
```

The first line attempts to create a URL out of the provided string. We use an if let because, if our string is garbage, what we get back from the initializer could be nil. This is because the URL type provides a *failable initializer*, one that reserves the right to return nil instead of a new object. It's denoted this way in the documentation with the keyword init?, where the ? clues us in to the fact that optionals are in play.

Wrapping this in an if let means that we will only enter the curly-braced region if the initialization succeeds and assigns the value to the local variable url. This is the proper practice for failable initializers and gets around the bad practice we used in the first chapter when we just force-unwrapped the URL? optional with the ! operator.

And once we're safely inside the if let, we call the playAudioFrom() method that we just wrote, and the music starts playing. If we wanted to write a proper stopAudio() method, that would look like this:

```
stylishswift/ClassesPlayground.playground/Contents.swift
func stopAudio() -> Void {
    if let audioPlayer = audioPlayer {
        audioPlayer.pause()
    }
    audioPlayer = nil
}
```

Again, we use an if let to safely unwrap the audioPlayer optional, and only if that succeeds do we pause() it. Then we can set audioPlayer back to nil.

Turn That Music Down

Remember that any change to the playground text will cause the contents to be rebuilt and rerun, which means that any change we make from here out will restart the audio. It's funny the first few times, but it gets annoying.

If you want to turn it off, just comment out the call to playAudioWith-URL(). Swift uses the same comment syntax as all C-derived languages (Objective-C, C#, Java, etc.). That means you can either put // on the start of a line to turn it into a comment, or surround a whole range of lines with a starting /* and a closing */.

Protocols

Swift classes are *single-inheritance*, in that a given class can have only a single superclass. We can't declare that IOSDevice is a subclass of two different classes and inherit the behaviors of both. (In practice, that kind of thing gets messy!) Actually, IOSDevice isn't currently declared as the subclass of anything, so it's just a generic top-level class.

In many languages, we can get common behavior across multiple classes by providing a list of methods that all of them are expected to implement. In Java and C#, for example, the interface keyword performs this function. In Swift, we have *protocols*, and types that provide implementations for methods defined in a protocol are said to "conform to" the protocol. In Swift, protocols aren't limited to methods: they can also specify that a given property is to be made available.

Let's try it out to do something useful. At the bottom of the file where we create the iPhone7, and then again on the line that plays the music, the evaluation pane on the right just says IOSDevice. That's because those lines evaluate to just the iPhone7 object, but the playground doesn't know what it can tell us about the object other than its class. We can do better than that.

Swift defines a protocol called CustomStringConvertible that lets any type declare how it is to be represented as a String. Playgrounds use this for the evaluation pane, as does print() when using the \() substitution syntax, like in print ("I just bought this: \(iPhone7)"). To implement CustomStringConvertible, we just need to provide a property called description, whose type is a String.

To implement the protocol, we first have to change our class definition. In Swift, the class keyword is followed by a colon, the superclass that our class subclasses (if any), and then a comma-separated list of protocols we implement. So rewrite the class definition like this:

stylishswift/ClassesPlayground.playground/Contents.swift
```
class IOSDevice : CustomStringConvertible {
```

As soon as we do this, we will start seeing an error message. That's OK, because the error is that we don't yet conform to the protocol, since we haven't provided a suitable description. Let's do so now, as a computed property. Put this right before or after our other computed property, the screenArea:

stylishswift/ClassesPlayground.playground/Contents.swift
```
var description: String {
    return "\(name), \(screenHeight) x \(screenWidth)"
}
```

This method just uses string substitution to show the device name and its dimensions. As soon as we finish writing this, the evaluation pane starts using this description instead of the bare class name:

```
let iPhone7 = IOSDevice(name: "iPhone 7", screenHeight: 138.1,       iPhone 7, 138.1 x 67.0
                        screenWidth: 67.0)
```

There are many other protocols we'll be implementing throughout the book. Some, like CustomStringConvertible, come from the Swift language itself, but most are from UIKit and the other iOS frameworks we'll be working with.

Returning Tuples

So far, we've taken a thorough tour of what Swift offers for object-oriented development. In a lot of languages, that would be enough. But in Swift, it's only half the story.

Swift is great for object-oriented programming, but it also allows for more of a *functional programming* style. In functional programming, there's an emphasis on passing data around, instead of maintaining state in classes and mutating it all the time.

One significant trait of functional programming is that it's better to pass *values* to and from functions, rather than *references*. If we have an object of some class, and two parts of our code can modify its data at the same time, it can lead to confusing bugs. In functions, we generally want to pass the data itself, not a containing object. In other words, we prefer *pass-by-value* to *pass-by-reference*.

One thing that makes this difficult is the fact that functions can take many parameters, but they can typically only return one thing. Sometimes, it's natural to want to return multiple values from a function, and in some languages the options to do so are either to define a new type solely to hold those multiple values, or to use some kind of collection.

In Swift, we have *tuples*, which are just simple lists of values. One way to think of it is that just as a function or method can take a list of values wrapped in a pair of parentheses, a tuple lets us *return* a list of values wrapped in a pair of parentheses.

Let's give our existing IOSDevice class a computed property that returns a tuple of the screenHeight and screenWidth. Up with the other computed properties, type the following code:

stylishswift/ClassesPlayground.playground/Contents.swift
```
var screenHeightAndWidth : (height: Double, width: Double) {
    get {
        return (screenHeight, screenWidth)
    }
}
```

This is a lot like our other computed properties, but the type of the variable is in parentheses, which makes it a tuple. Inside the tuple definition, we identify each member by a name (which is not required) and a type. So, this tuple has two members, named height and width. Then we just use parentheses in our return line to package these values into a tuple.

To use the tuple, just access it like any other variable. Outside the class, after creating the iPhone7 variable, pull out the values like this:

stylishswift/ClassesPlayground.playground/Contents.swift
```
iPhone7.screenHeightAndWidth
iPhone7.screenHeightAndWidth.height
iPhone7.screenHeightAndWidth.0
```

For the first line, the evaluation pane shows all the values of the tuple, as (.0 138.1, .1 67). We can then access a value inside the tuple either by the name, like height, or its index in the tuple, like .0. Both of these evaluate to 138.1.

One place that tuples really shine is in counting over collections. In the last chapter, we said that iterating over a collection meant going either by index or by object. Tuples let us have our cake and eat it too. That's because Swift defines an enumerated() function that returns members of a collection as tuples of each member and its index. This lets us do a for-in loop where we have access to both the member and the index inside the loop.

To try it out, we'll need a few new IOSDevice instances and a collection. Add the following at the bottom of the playground:

stylishswift/ClassesPlayground.playground/Contents.swift
```
let iPhone7Plus = IOSDevice(name: "iPhone 7 Plus",
                            screenHeight: 158.1, screenWidth: 77.8)
let iPhoneSE = IOSDevice (name: "iPhone SE",
                          screenHeight: 123.8, screenWidth: 58.6)
let iPhones = [iPhoneSE, iPhone7, iPhone7Plus]
```

This creates an array of three IOSDevice objects. If you like, check them out in the results pane with the Quick Look or Show Result button on the line that creates the iPhones array. Now we'll use enumerated() to count over them with a tuple:

stylishswift/ClassesPlayground.playground/Contents.swift
```
for (index, phone) in iPhones.enumerated() {
    print ("\(index): \(phone)")
}
```

Inside the for loop, we now have access to the index and the phone object each time, so we can easily log them out with print(). In the console (View > Debug Area > Show Debug Area, or ⇧⌘Y), we can see the output that shows each:

```
0: iPhone SE, 123.8 x 58.6
1: iPhone 7, 138.1 x 67.0
2: iPhone 7 Plus, 158.1 x 77.8
```

Building Lightweight Structures

If we want to get away from object-oriented programming and try something different, we have to free ourselves of classes. In the next few sections, we'll do just that, and see that we're not losing anything in the transition.

To make a clean start, close this playground and create a new playground called StructsPlayground.

Let's think about the IOSDevice that we created as a class: it had some simple properties for the device name and dimensions, and some methods that operated on those properties. If it mostly serves as a container for data, if we don't care about inheritance, and if the data is small and not difficult to copy around in memory, then it's the kind of thing that functional programmers would tell us doesn't need to be a class.

So what's the alternative? In Swift, we have *structures*, which are lighter containers for properties. Let's remake IOSDevice as a struct to see how they work. Delete the default "Hello playground" line and define the IODevice structure as follows:

stylishswift/StructsPlayground.playground/Contents.swift
```
struct IOSDevice {
    var name : String
    var screenHeight : Double
    var screenWidth : Double
}
```

This is a lot like the beginning of our old class: it's just the property names and their types. One thing has changed, though: we can define these properties as non-optional types, and we don't get an error message about how "IOSDevice has no initializers." That's because the struct gets an initializer for free: just pass in all the values, labeled by their property names in the structure. That means we can create an iPhone7 like this:

stylishswift/StructsPlayground.playground/Contents.swift
```
let iPhone7 = IOSDevice(name: "iPhone 7", screenHeight: 138.1,
                        screenWidth: 67.0)
```

This shows an IOSDevice in the results pane, which means we've successfully created an instance of the IOSDevice structure. That was easy!

"But," the critic says, "you can't really *do* anything with it, can you?" Well, sure.

If this were C, our next step would probably be to write some global functions that work with this struct, either taking it as a parameter or returning it as a result. And the difference would be that the functions would receive copies of all the members of the structure, not just a reference to an object in memory (that some other part of the code might also be using, unbeknownst to us).

But still, Swift can do a lot better than just making us write a bunch of global functions.

Extensions

Swift gives us the ability to attach code to arbitrary types: structures, classes, enumerations, and even numeric types. The bits of code are called *extensions*, and they're delightfully powerful. Let's use them to beef up our IOSDevice.

To extend a type, we just write extension and the type we are extending, and then in curly braces we put code for methods or computed properties. This goes *outside* the struct's curly braces. So we can give the IOSDevice structure the screenArea computed property that the class had like this:

```
stylishswift/StructsPlayground.playground/Contents.swift
extension IOSDevice {
    var screenArea : Double {
        get {
            return screenWidth * screenHeight
        }
    }
}
```

Now just call that with iPhone7.screenArea on a new line, and we'll see 9,252.7 (or perhaps 9252.699...) in the results pane.

The fact that we write the code as an extension outside the type's definition implies something very powerful: *we can provide extensions for anything*. We're not limited to extending the abilities of our own classes and structures; we can extend classes in UIKit, basic types in Swift, basically any named type. As a rather absurd example, we can add methods to Swift's Int type:

```
stylishswift/StructsPlayground.playground/Contents.swift
extension Int {
    func addOne() -> Int {
        return self + 1
    }
}
```

And then we would call this with 41.addOne() to get 42.

> **Joe asks:**
> # Why Is the Keyword func When It's Not Really a Function?
>
> The keyword func is so named because Swift does indeed have honest-to-goodness functions: executable segments of code that take parameters and can return a value, but that aren't attached to an instance of anything. We've been using these already: the print() function is a global function that we've used to log messages to the Xcode console pane.
>
> Defining a function is just like creating a method, just outside the scope of a class. Putting it inside the class makes it a method. Really, Swift methods are like a special case of functions: being inside a class, they pick up the stuff inside the class and are able to access its properties and other methods.
>
> In fact, both functions and methods are a special case of the even more general-purpose concept of "closures," but we'll hold off talking about them until Chapter 7, *Handling Asynchronicity with Closures*, on page 113.

Extensions and Protocols

We don't have to put all our code to extend a given type into one extension block; it's OK to use several. This is helpful when we split up our code more purposefully. For example, let's get back our nice description string to log the name and dimensions of an IOSDevice. When we were writing a class, we implemented the CustomStringConvertible protocol. With a struct, we just provide another extension that conforms to the protocol.

stylishswift/StructsPlayground.playground/Contents.swift
```
extension IOSDevice : CustomStringConvertible {
    var description: String {
        return "\(name), \(screenHeight) x \(screenWidth)"
    }
}
```

Notice that for a read-only computed property, we can omit the get {...} and just provide the code to compute the property in curly braces right after the variable declaration.

Once you write this extension, the IOSDevice gets a nicer representation in the results pane, just like before.

In fact, extensions can be used to extend protocols themselves: an extension can declare new functions, methods, and properties to implement, and can even provide default implementations. Used in this way, it's called a *protocol extension*, and gives us another way to provide object-oriented traits like abstraction and extensibility to simpler types, without classes.

Listing Possibilities with Enumerations

Structures are familiar to old C programmers, and they were available in Objective-C but were so limited that they were often ignored in favor of classes. Swift extensions tilt the balance back toward structs, as the language does with another old C type: *enumerations*. The enum is a type that enumerates all its possible values. It's nice for times when you want to know there are a small number of valid values for something, like the suits of playing cards, positions in a team sport, and so forth.

Start a new playground called EnumsPlayground, and delete the "Hello playground" line. We're going to use this playground to rethink our IOSDevice.

So far, whether class or struct, we've assumed our IOSDevice is a touchscreen device like an iPhone, iPad, or iPod touch. But that's not necessarily so, is it? The Apple TV is technically an iOS device, and we currently have no way to account for its lack of a screen, short of turning screenHeight and screenWidth into optionals (which will be a hassle for callers), or using 0.0 flag values, which would just be ugly. Surely, we can do better.

Swift's enumerations give us an elegant solution to this problem. We can define a ScreenType enumeration to indicate what kind of screen the device has. Currently that would be "Retina" or "none," and we can extend it if, say, the iPhone 9 employs a pop-up hologram or something.

Define our ScreenType enumeration like this:

stylishswift/EnumsPlayground.playground/Contents.swift
```
enum ScreenType {
    case none
    case retina (screenHeight: Double, screenWidth: Double)
}
```

The different values for the enumeration are marked off as separate cases, kind of like a switch statement. What's really interesting here is the retina case. The two Doubles in parentheses are called *associated values*, and only exist when a given ScreenType is retina. The none case has no associated values, and some other case might have completely different associated values; maybe a hypothetical case crystalBall would have a radius: Double for its associated value.

Now let's create a new struct that can use this enum to represent its display, or lack thereof:

```swift
struct IOSDevice {
    var name : String
    var screenType : ScreenType
}
```

That's easy enough; the enum acts like a new type, just like a String or Int. Now let's create some instances of this:

```swift
Line 1  let iPhone7 = IOSDevice(name: "iPhone 7",
     2                         screenType: ScreenType.retina(
     3                           screenHeight: 138.1, screenWidth: 67.0))
     4  let appleTV4thGen = IOSDevice(name: "Apple TV (4th Gen)",
     5                         screenType: ScreenType.none)
```

Notice that just like with the struct, we automatically pick up the syntax for populating the associated values of the ScreenType.retina case; we just label and provide a value for each one, comma-separated, in parentheses (see line 3).

Concise Swift

Swift likes concision, and many things that are redundant can be omitted. For example, the screenType variable in these initializers can only be of type ScreenType, so it's legal to omit the type and just write the value with the leading dot character. So we could create the appleTV4thGen like this:

```swift
let appleTV4thGen = IOSDevice(name: "Apple TV (4th Gen)",
                      screenType: .none)
```

As opportunities for omitting syntax occur throughout the book, we'll generally spell it out the long way first, mention what can be left out, and use the concise version from then on.

Using Associated Values in Enumerations

As before, the results pane evaluates the two instances of our new structure as just IOSDevice, because we no longer have a CustomStringConvertible implementation to provide a pretty string for them. We can provide one with an extension, and in the process we'll see how to use the associated values we provided for the screenHeight and screenWidth.

When we work with enumerations, we almost always need to use a switch statement to pick apart the possible cases. switch and enum go together perfectly, since they make it clear that we are walking through each possible value of the enum with case statements. In fact, Swift requires that the switch be exhaustive, meaning that it handles every possible case of the enum. There are only two in ScreenType, so it's easy here; with lots of cases, we could use default at the end of the switch to deal with otherwise-unhandled cases.

So to implement the description method, we need to return a string. It will include the name of the device and, only if it has a .retina screen type, the dimensions of the screen. Here's how we can do that with a switch:

stylishswift/EnumsPlayground.playground/Contents.swift

```
Line 1  extension IOSDevice : CustomStringConvertible {
    -       var description : String {
    -           var screenDescription: String
    -           switch screenType {
    5           case .none:
    -               screenDescription = "No screen"
    -           case .retina (let screenHeight, let screenWidth):
    -               screenDescription = "Retina screen " +
    -                   "\(screenHeight) x \(screenWidth)"
   10           }
    -           return "\(name): \(screenDescription)"
    -       }
    - }
```

We begin on line 1 with an extension that says we are going to make IOSDevice conform to CustomStringConvertible. This means defining a description computed variable of type String.

Our description should provide a different string based on whether or not we have a screen. We declare the screenDescription on line 3. Notice that this is not an optional, yet we haven't provided a value for it; Swift lets us get away with this if it can tell that we are providing a value in all cases before the value is read. We start the switch on line 4, and the .none case that starts on line 5 is easy: we can just set screenDescription to "No Screen".

The interesting part is on line 7, which starts the .retina case. We use the let keyword in parentheses to receive the associated values as local variables. If we didn't care about one or more of these values, we could use the underscore character _ instead of let and the local variable name to say "I don't need this value." But in this case, we want both the screenHeight and screenWidth as local variables, so we can build a screenDescription that shows the dimensions.

Once this is written, the playground will immediately rebuild and rerun our playground, and the IOSDevice, now that it conforms to CustomStringConvertible, will pretty-print nice descriptions for our two devices in the evaluation pane:

```
let iPhone7 = IOSDevice(name: "iPhone 7",                        iPhone 7: Retina screen 138.1 x 67.0
                 screenType: ScreenType.retina(
                        screenHeight: 138.1, screenWidth: 67.0))
let appleTV4thGen = IOSDevice(name: "Apple TV (4th Gen)",        Apple TV (4th Gen): No screen
                 screenType: ScreenType.none)
```

Swift's So Functional!

So, between structs, enums, protocols, and especially extensions, we can replicate most of the power of object-oriented programming, without needing to use classes and the usual practices of maintaining and mutating state. Swift isn't the most pure functional programming language by a long shot, but functional programming (FP) fans have found much to like in it.

Keep in mind that many of the iOS frameworks are very object-oriented in nature—they were written for use with Objective-C, after all—so much of the code we write will be of an OO style by necessity. Having said that, when we see an option to do things with a lighter touch, we'll try to do so.

Optionals Are Enumerations!

Here's a nifty little implementation detail that sometimes turns out to be useful: optionals are actually enumerations! An optional type is an enum with two cases, called .none and .some. The .none case is where the optional is nil, whereas .some has an associated value: the unwrapped value of the optional.

Some developers use this as a means of performing logic on the optional, particularly if we want to do something in the nil case. Rather than doing an if let and then testing the value against some other logic, we can put the logic in a switch like this:

```
stylishswift/EnumsPlayground.playground/Contents.swift
let optionalString : String? = "iPhone7"
switch optionalString {
case .none:
    print ("nil!")
case .some(let value):
    print ("some! \(value)")
}
```

Handling Errors the Swift Way

One thing we haven't considered is what to do when things go wrong. So far, our only defensive tactic has been the cautious use of if let to avoid crashing when we unwrap optionals that turn out to be nil. But there's more to robust coding practices than that.

Swift 2 introduced a new error-handling paradigm that is supported by many of the iOS frameworks. It will be familiar to readers who've seen try-catch–style semantics in other languages, but its differences are important to understand: these aren't your father's java.lang.Exceptions.

In Swift, methods (including initializers) can indicate that they signal errors by including the throws keyword. To call code that may throw, we need to do two things:

1. Wrap all related code in a do-catch block, where the catch will pull out and handle any thrown object.

2. Explicitly put the keyword try immediately before each method or initializer that can throw. Of course, the compiler could figure it out for us; putting the onus on the coder is meant as a means of annotating the code by explicitly calling attention to parts of the code that can produce errors.

Let's try an example. The iOS frameworks have a number of APIs that throw errors in Swift. In many cases, these were implemented in Objective-C with an "in-out" system where a caller would provide a pointer to an NSError object. The caller would send in nil for this pointer, and check its value after the method returned. If it was now a non-nil pointer to an NSError, it meant that an error had occurred. Any such "in-out" APIs are converted automatically to the throws idiom in Swift, so don't let the documentation scare you if you see those Objective-C asterisks (**NSError always freaked us out).

As an example, there's a class called Data that wraps an in-memory data buffer of any size. It can be populated with the contents of any URL with the init(contentsOf:options:) initializer, *but*...it's marked with throws, which means if we use it, we have to deal with a possible error. And that makes sense, of course: what should it do if your URL is nonsense or if there's a network error? Throwing an error describing the problem at least gives us a chance of recovering or telling the user what happened.

Start a new playground called ErrorHandlingPlayground, and delete the "Hello, playground" line. It's been a long chapter, so we'll make this short:

stylishswift/ErrorHandlingPlayground.playground/Contents.swift
```
Line 1  if let myURL = URL(string: "foo") {
     2      do {
     3          let myData = try Data (contentsOf: myURL, options: [])
     4          let myString = String(data: myData, encoding: .utf8)
     5      } catch let nserror as NSError {
     6          print ("NSError: \(nserror)")
     7      } catch {
     8          print ("No idea what happened there: \(error)")
     9      }
    10  }
```

Line 3 tries to create the Data from the provided myURL. This initializer throws, so the initializer itself needs to have the try keyword right before it; when a method or function throws, the try will be at the beginning of the line.

If we successfully download the Data, we use it on line 4, where it's used to create a String from the data, and a hint about what text encoding the data uses (UTF-8 is often a good bet). This line needs to be inside the do-catch only because it needs to have the myData in scope.

So, when this works, we'll see the Data and String represented over in the result area: the data will be clusters of hexadecimal digits, and the string will be the raw HTML.

Now let's get ourselves into the error handling. We'll do that by mangling the URL string. A simple way to do this is to change the URL scheme from http to some nonsense like foo. Do this, and the evaluation pane will go blank. Instead, down in the debug console, we'll see an error message:

```
NSError: Error Domain=NSCocoaErrorDomain Code=256 "The file "foo" couldn't
be opened." UserInfo={NSURL=foo}
```

This is coming from the block on line 5 that catches thrown NSErrors, the errors from the older Cocoa frameworks that underlie much of iOS. The later catch on line 7 catches anything, although nothing in our code is declared as throwing something other than NSError, so it will never be reached and is shown only for demonstration.

So, in a nutshell, that's Swift error-handling: if something declares that it throws, wrap the call in a do-catch, decorate all calls that can throw with try, and then catch whatever was thrown, using the let as construct to pick apart the type that was thrown.

Oh, and let's please be sure to do more to recover than just logging an error to the Xcode console. In real life, we would want to tell the user what happened, or maybe automatically retry, or *something*.

What We've Learned

You came into this chapter knowing about strings, numeric types, control flow, and collections—the building blocks of a Swift application—but not enough to combine them together in interesting ways. In this chapter, we've gotten into the concepts of how to organize these types and their logic into meaningful and capable abstractions that can serve as the structure of an app.

We started in the comfort zone of object-oriented programming, building classes with properties and methods that would be perfectly recognizable to a Java 1.0 programmer from 1995. But, aware that toting around a bunch of state isn't always how we want to do things in the 21st century, we looked at Swift's functional programming–inspired alternatives for structuring our data. By using extensions and protocols, we can take simple enumerations and structures and make them as compelling as full-blown classes.

We've been able to do all this in the Xcode playground, which gives us a fine place to try out our Swift code. Now it's time to pick up our toys and move into developing actual iOS apps. In the next chapter, you're going to learn how to build actual iOS user interfaces and start building our real app.

As we go, we'll pick up a few more insights about Swift. If you find the language as compelling as we do, you may also be interested in Erica Sadun's book, *Swift Style [Sad17]*, which is all about the language itself and how to write clean, expressive code.

CHAPTER 4

Building User Interfaces

We'll kick things off with a little secret about iOS development, something it inherited from Mac development: *create the user interface first*. This seems totally backward for a lot of seasoned developers. A lot of us think through an application's requirements and immediately start thinking of our data models and strategies and...*nuh-uh*. Build the UI first. Build what users are going to see, what they're going to interact with, and start to understand how they'll experience it. Then figure out how the heck you're going to do that.

That philosophy is reflected in the tools provided for iOS development. If we built the user interface by writing code, it would be natural to code the functionality and then put buttons and views on top of it. Instead, the iOS SDK provides distinct tools for building the UI graphically and for coding its functionality. The tools let us see our interface first, and then make it work.

In this chapter, we're going to start building an app that will carry us through to submitting to the App Store, which we do in the penultimate chapter. And since iOS apps start with the user interface, that's *all* we're going to do in this chapter. We'll familiarize ourselves with the tools for building the UI, and then in the next chapter we'll start connecting it to code.

Creating Our First Project

Back in the first chapter, we used the AVPlayer to play some audio from the Internet. Building on that, we're going to spend most of the rest of the book writing a podcast client application. We'll fetch podcast feeds—XML files with descriptions of episodes and links to their audio files—download the audio, and play it. It's quite possible you already use one of the many popular iOS podcasting apps, such as Overcast, Pocket Casts, Castro, or Apple's own built-in Podcasts app.

Part of the appeal of developing a podcasting app is that it will do the kinds of things that nearly all iOS apps do: they request data from the Internet, model it in a way that's convenient for our program logic, present it in an attractive format for the user, and then let the user interact with it. For us, that'll be fetching and parsing podcast feeds, showing them in tables, and letting the user select shows and episodes. And in another app, those same general techniques might be how the user finds and purchases goods and services, interacts with social networks, researches information, and so on.

Also, we're going to have lots of screenshots from our favorite iOS and developer podcasts, so maybe you'll find a new show you like along the way. So let's get started.

To begin work on a new app, we need to create a project using the menu sequence File > New > Project (⇧⌘N). There's also a button on the Xcode greeting window for starting a project, so that's another way to do it.

When we create a new project, a window opens, and out slides a sheet that asks us what kind of project we want to create. This project template sheet, shown here, has a set of tabs for the various Apple platforms: iOS, watchOS, tvOS, macOS, and cross-platform. Within each tab, there are various starter project types split into sections like Application and Framework & Library. Since we're building an iOS application, we'll select the iOS tab and then look at the choices in the Application section. For our first example, we'll select Single View Application, and then click Next.

After we click Next, the sheet then asks us for details specific to the project, as shown in the following figure. Some of these change based on the project type; in general, this is where we need to provide names and other identifiers to the app, indicate which device formats (iPhone and/or iPad) it's for, and so on. For our app, here's how we should fill out the form:

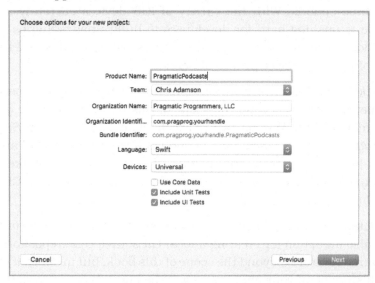

- *Product Name*: A name for the product with no spaces or other punctuation. Our product will be called PragmaticPodcasts here.

- *Team*: Once we've set up to run apps on physical iOS devices (which we'll do in *Running and Testing on the Device*, on page 108), this will be used to indicate which development team's identity is used when installing to the device. Until we're set up, however, this can be left blank.

- *Organization Name*: This can be a company, organization, or personal name, which will be used for the copyright statement automatically put at the top of every source file.

- *Organization Identifier*: This is a reverse-DNS style stub that will uniquely identify our app in the App Store, so if someone else submits a PragmaticPodcasts, the two apps won't be mistaken for each other because they'll each have a unique *Bundle Identifier*, which is the auto-generated fifth line of the form. If you have your own domain, you can use it for the company identifier; otherwise, just invert your email address, such as in com.company.yourhandle.

- *Language*: There are two choices for this pop-up menu: *Swift* and *Objective-C*. We've covered Swift for the previous three chapters, so let's choose that here.

- *Devices*: This determines whether the template should set us up with an app that's meant to run on an iPhone (and iPod touch) or iPad or be a "universal" app with a different layout for each. Not all templates offer all three options. With the variety of iOS devices currently available, Apple is pushing hard for developers to build universal apps that run and look good on a variety of screen sizes—all four sizes of iPhone and two of iPad—so select Universal here.

- *Check boxes*: Do not select Use Core Data, which is a data-persistence framework that is beyond the scope of this book. When we're done, feel free to move on to Marcus Zarra's excellent book, *Core Data in Swift: Data Storage and Management for iOS and OS X [Zar16]*. Go ahead and check both Include Unit Tests and Include UI Tests. These will make it easier to expose our app to automated testing, which we'll do in Chapter 6, *Testing the App*, on page 89.

After clicking Next, we choose a location on the filesystem for our project. There's also an option for creating a local Git source code repository for our files. Source control is beyond the scope of this book, but in short, if you want a local history of all your changes, select the check box. If you don't need a local repository, or (better yet!) if you plan to check your code into an external source control system such as GitHub later on, leave the box unselected.

Once we specify where the project will be saved, Xcode copies over some starter files for our project and reveals them in its main window.

The Xcode Window

Xcode 8 provides a single window for a project. This window provides our view into nearly everything we'll do with a project: editing code and user interfaces; adjusting settings for how the project is built and run; employing debugging tools; and viewing logged output.

The window is split into five areas, although some of them can be hidden with menu commands and/or toolbar buttons. These areas are shown in an "exploded" view in the figure on page 55.

The window is split up as follows:

Toolbar

The toolbar at the top of the window offers the most basic controls for building projects and working with the rest of the workspace. The leftmost toolbar buttons, Run and Stop, start and stop build-and-run cycles. Next are two borderless buttons collectively known as the scheme selector,

which chooses which "target" to run (currently PragmaticPodcasts) and in what environment (such as a simulated "iPhone SE," or the name of an actual iOS device connected to the Mac). Next comes an iTunes-like status display that shows the most recent build and/or run results, including a count of warnings and errors generated by a continual background analysis of the code. Further right, the Editor Mode buttons let us switch between three different kinds of editors, which we'll describe shortly. Finally, three View buttons allow us to show or hide the Navigator, Debug, and Utility areas. These areas are described next.

Navigator Area

The left pane (which may be hidden if the leftmost View button in the toolbar is unselected) offers high-level browsing of our project's contents. It has a mini toolbar to switch between eight different navigators. The File Navigator (⌘1) shows the project's source and resource files and is therefore the most important and commonly used of the eight. Other navigators let us perform searches (⌘3), inspect build warnings and errors, inspect runtime threads and breakpoints, and more.

Editor Area

The main part of the window is the Editor area. This view cannot be hidden. Its contents are set by selecting a file in the Navigator area, and the form the editor takes depends on the file being edited. For example, when a source file is selected, we see a typical source code editor; when a GUI file is selected, the Editor area becomes a GUI editor; and when an image file like a GIF or JPEG is selected, the Editor area displays the image.

The Editor Mode buttons in the toolbar switch the editor pane between three modes: *standard*, which is the default editor for the type of file that's selected; *assistant*, which shows related files side by side; and *version*, which uses source control to show the history of the file. In version mode, you can choose a side-by-side "comparison" of the local and previous versions of the file, a "blame" view that shows the committer of each line of code, or a log of commit comments alongside the code. The Editor area also contains a *jump bar*, a breadcrumb-style strip at the top that shows the hierarchy of the thing being edited; for a source file, this might read "project, group, file, method." Each member of the jump bar is a pop-up menu that navigates to related or recent points of interest.

By default, a new project comes up with its top-level settings selected in the Navigator area, which means that the Editor area defaults to showing settings for things like the app version number, the targeted SDK version and device families, and so on. There may also be a scary-looking "No matching provisioning profiles found" warning, which just means we're not set up to run our app on a real device yet; we'll deal with that in Chapter 6, *Testing the App*, on page 89.

Utility Area

The right side of the window is a Utility area that provides detailed viewing and editing of whatever is selected in the Editor area. It is split vertically into two parts: the *inspector pane* and the *library pane*. Depending on the file being edited, the toolbar atop this area can show different tools in its inspector pane. Basic information about a selected file and quick help on the current selection are always available. For GUI files, there are inspectors to work with individual UI objects' class identities (⌥⌘3), their settable attributes (⌥⌘4), their size and layout (⌥⌘5), and their connections to source code (⌥⌘6). We'll be using all of these shortly. At the bottom of the Utility area, a library pane gives us click-and-drag access to common code snippets, UI objects, and more.

Debug Area

The bottom of the window, below the Editor area and between the Navigator and Utility areas, is a view for debugging information when an app is running. Its tiny toolbar has a segmented button that lets us switch between the debugging-oriented *variables view* that allows us to inspect memory when stopped on a breakpoint, a textual *console view* of logging output from the application, or a split view of both. We'll make use of the right-side console view in a little bit, whereas the left-side variables view will be our focus in a later chapter.

So that's how Xcode presents our initial project to us, but what can we do? Well, there's a nice big Run button, and it's not like it's disabled. Let's try running the app. Make sure the scheme is some flavor of iPhone from the iOS Simulator section (and not iPad or the name of an actual device); in Xcode 8, our choices range from the iPhone 5 to the iPhone SE, with some different-sized iPhone 6 and 7 models in between. Click the Run button.

The Xcode status area will shade in with a progress bar that fills up as it builds all the files and bundles them into an app, and when it's done, it will launch the iOS Simulator. The Simulator is another macOS application, which looks and behaves more or less like a real iPhone or iPad. When our app runs in the Simulator, the main screen disappears and is replaced by a big white box that fills the Simulator screen. If the simulated iPhone screen is too big for your computer screen, use the Window > Scale menu (or keyboard short-cuts ⌘1 through ⌘5) to scale down the window to fit.

Building Our User Interface

That white box in the Simulator is our app. It's not much, but then again, we haven't done anything yet, so let's start building it. Press Stop in Xcode to stop the simulated app, and then take a look at the project in Xcode.

If the File Navigator isn't already showing on the left side of the project window, bring it up with the folder icon in the Navigator area (⌘1). The File Navigator uses a tree-style hierarchy with a blue Xcode document at the top, representing the project itself as the root. Under this are files and folders. The folder icons are *groups* that collect related files, such as the views and logic classes for one part of the app; groups don't usually represent actual directories on the filesystem. We can expand all the groups to see the contents of the project, as shown in the figure here.

Different project templates will set us up with different files. For the view-based app, we get two source code files in the PragmaticPodcasts group, along with a Main.storyboard, a LaunchScreen.storyboard, and an Assets.xcassets. These are the files we'll be editing. There are also a few helper files like Info.plist, but we won't need to edit them directly. The PragmaticPodcastsTests group is where we will write unit tests to validate our code, something we'll do in Chapter 6, *Testing the App*, on page 89. Ditto for PragmaticPodcastsUITests, which can test the purely UI parts of our app. Finally, the Products group shows the files our build will create: in this case, PragmaticPodcasts.app for the app, plus PragmaticPodcastsTests.xctest and PragmaticPodcasts-UITests.xctest for the runnable unit tests. Files shown in red indicate they haven't been built yet; PragmaticPodcasts.app is red in the preceding figure because, although we've run it in the Simulator, we haven't built it for the actual device yet.

Editing Storyboards with Interface Builder

We said at the outset that iOS development starts with the user interface. By focusing on what users see and how they interact with it, we keep our focus on the user experience and not on the data models and logic behind the scenes. We typically build our user interfaces visually and store them in *storyboards*. The project has one such file, Main.storyboard, so let's click it.

When we click Main.storyboard, the Editor Area switches to a graphical view called *Interface Builder*, or IB for short. In iOS, IB works with user interface documents called storyboards. Just like in movie-making, where a storyboard is a process used to plan out a sequence of shots in a movie or TV show, the storyboard of an iOS app shows the progression through the different views the app will present. The initial storyboard looks like the following figure.

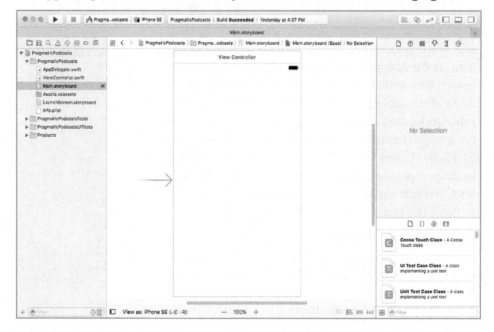

Our app uses a single view, so we follow the right-pointing arrow (which indicates where the app starts) into a rectangle that represents the visible area of the screen. This is our app's one view; if we were building a navigation-style app, there would be one view rectangle for each screen of the navigation. Click the view to show a header box with three icons. These are *proxy objects* that represent objects that will work with the view at runtime: a yellow circle *View Controller* that contains logic to respond to events and update the view; an orange cube *First Responder* that represents the ability to handle events; and an orange square *Exit*, used for when we back out of views in navigation apps (something we'll visit in a later chapter).

At the bottom left of the Editor area, next to the "View As:" label, IB shows a little view disclosure button. Click this to show and hide the scene list (shown here), which shows each "scene" of the story-board and its contents as a tree structure. Currently, our one scene has the proxy objects, and inside the view controller, we find two layout objects and a "view." This

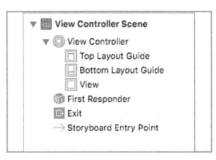

view is the big rectangle in the UI; as we add UI elements such as buttons and labels, the scene's tree list will show them as children of this view.

Speaking of the view, notice that it's a tall rectangle in more or less the shape of an iPhone SE screen (or whatever device is selected in the scheme selector). In the bottom of the Editor area, next to View As, notice the name of the model "iPhone SE." This is actually a button; click it to show a small gallery of the various iOS device sizes, from the huge iPad Pro 12.9" down to the little iPhone 4s. The currently selected device and its orientation (portrait or land-scape) will be shown in blue. If you choose an iPad model, the interface becomes a set of more detailed pop-ups; use the Device pop-up to get back to an iPhone model. Selecting different devices or orientations will change the size of the view rectangle in the content view, something that will be very important to us soon.

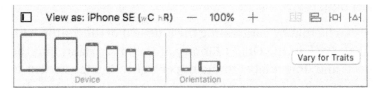

Next to the name of the device, there's a little legend that looks like "(w:C h:R)." These represent the *size class* of the device in that orientation. The labels "w"

and "h" represent "width" and "height," respectively, and the values "C" and "R" mean "compact" and "regular." "Compact" means an axis where we don't have a lot of space to work with, like the width of an iPhone in portrait orientation. We'll be able to use these later to customize our UI for different devices and orientations.

Adding UI Components

So let's start building our user interface. Since we already know how to make a media player, we'll build that scene first, and later we'll build scenes for listing podcasts and their episodes.

To add components to our storyboard, use the toolbar to show the Utility area on the right (if it's not already showing), and find the library pane at the bottom right. There's a mini toolbar here that should default to showing user interface objects; if not, click the little icon of a square in a circle (or press ^⌥⌘3). The bottom of the pane has a button to toggle between list and icon views for the objects, and a search filter to find objects by name. Scroll down through this pane to find the icon that just says Button; we can tap once on any of the objects to get its name, class, and description to appear in a pop-over. Drag the button from the Object Library into the upper left of the iPhone-sized view in IB. This will create a plain button.

It leaves a lot to the imagination, huh? Without the edge and background decorations of earlier versions of iOS, it doesn't necessarily look like a button at all. It could easily be mistaken for a text label.

That's somewhat by design. iOS' "flat" UI look has three stated themes: *deference*, *clarity*, and *depth*. The first of these, deference, means that the UI appearance focuses attention on our content rather than competing with a bunch of pseudo-realistic effects.

So maybe our problem is a lack of content. iOS expects us to tell the user what's going on in our app, and we're not holding up our end of the deal yet. Let's fix that. First, we'll say what the button does. Double-click the button to change its name to Play. Now it says what it does, but it still doesn't exactly feel button-y.

Maybe we can fix that by contrasting the blue text of the button with a plain label. Back in the Object Library at the lower right, find the Label object, and drag a label to the upper right. Change its text to "0:00." As you probably guessed, we will be using this to show the current time of the item that's playing.

Our user interface elements are kind of boring and small for a media player screen. That's because they're the default size, font, and color. We can change that easily enough. Select the button, and then bring up the Attributes Inspector in the right pane with the mini toolbar button that looks like the playhead of a value slider (or just use the keyboard shortcut ⌥⌘4). This brings up an inspector with many values we can change for the button: its color, font, title text, and more. Just use up and down arrows on the Font line to increase the size to 30.0. The larger text in the button won't fit anymore and will change to "…," so use the handles on the button to resize it until it says "Play" again.

Select the "0:00" label and change its font size to 30.0 as well. While we're working with labels, let's add another one for the current track's title. Drag a new label out from the library, and place it below the Play button. We can leave this label at the default size; just change the default text from "Label" to "Track Title." The view should look something like the following figure:

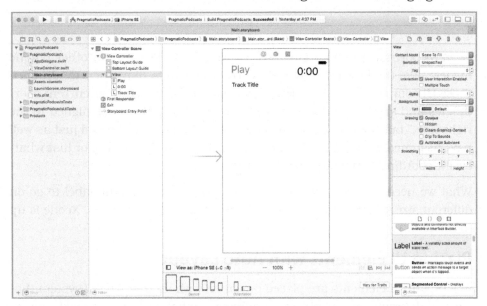

Go ahead and click the Run button to run this app again in the iOS Simulator. This launches our app in the simulated iPhone and shows our button and labels. Progress!

Alas, there's a catch. We've only been thinking about our user interface when the user is holding the phone in portrait view. What happens if the user holds it sideways? Let's find out. Rotate to landscape with Rotate Left and Rotate Right items in the Hardware menu (⌘← and ⌘→, respectively). The spacing between the components is the same, but now that's wrong, because the time label is no longer in the upper right—it kind of ends up in the middle of the screen.

Press Stop in Xcode, and let's look at the storyboard again. It turns out this is a problem we could have seen coming. Under View As, select the landscape orientation. The storyboard shows us what the UI looks like when it's sideways, as shown here:

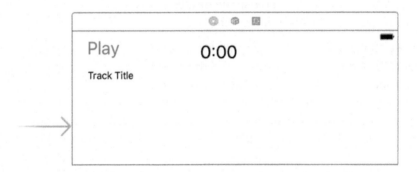

Even in portrait, the time label will be in the wrong place on other iPhone models, like the larger 7 and 7 Plus. The problem is that when we dropped these UI components in the view, Xcode could only know their current coordinates and sizes. We may have meant to say "keep the label aligned to the right side," but there was no way for Xcode to know that. It could just as well have assumed we wanted a constant distance from the button, or just whatever x-coordinate we happened to drag it to.

What we need now is a way to tell Xcode where we want the label to go on different size screens and in different orientations. Lucky for us, Xcode is up to the task.

Placing UI Elements with Auto Layout

In iOS, our UI elements are placed onscreen with an *auto layout* system that lets you determine where objects should go and how big they should be based on *constraints* that we set on them. This allows our interfaces to adapt to being rotated between portrait and landscape, and to handle the differing screen sizes of the 3.5-inch models (iPhone 4s), 4-inch models (iPhone 5s and

SE), the 4.7-inch iPhone 6s and 7, and 5.5-inch iPhone 6s Plus and 7 Plus. Constraints allow us to express what matters to us—the size of components, their alignment with or distance from other components, and so forth—and to let other factors vary as needed.

In this example, we want to put the Play button at upper left, with the track title label below it, and the current time label in the upper right.

Interface Builder puts a set of buttons, shown here, at the bottom right of the content area to give us access to Auto Layout features. These buttons display a pop-over or pop-up menu when tapped.

- *Update Frames*: This adjusts a view's position and/or size so it matches its constraints.
- *Stack button*: This button embeds one or more selected views into a *stack view*—a container for other views (and something we'll explore in a later chapter).
- *Align pop-over*: This lets us create constraints that align a view's edges or horizontal or vertical center with another view, or horizontally or vertically center it within its containing view (its *superview*).
- *Pin pop-over*: This lets us create constraints that specify a fixed value for spacing from one or more edges to another view (possibly the superview), and/or a fixed width or height.
- *Resolve menu*: The options here update the values of existing constraints to match the current position and size, or create any constraints that appear to be missing. We can also clear all constraints and start over with this menu.

With these tools, we can get our layout to look correct on any device and orientation, using three simple rules:

1. The Play button will always be at upper left (with a little margin padding from the top and left sides of the screen).

2. The current time label ("0:00") will be vertically aligned with the Play button, meaning it's always at the same height, and it will have a fixed distance from the right side. This will keep it consistently in the upper right.

3. The track title label will be left-aligned with the Play button, meaning their left sides will line up, while being placed a fixed distance below the button.

Laying Out the Play Button

We'll start with the Play button. Select it in the storyboard, and then click the Pin button (the third from left, easily recognized because it looks like a TIE Fighter from *Star Wars*.) This shows the pop-over in the following figure.

The top portion of this pop-over lets us "pin" exact distances from other UI components, or set exact values for width and height. In the top portion, our button is represented as a small square surrounded by braces on its top, bottom, left, and right. At the end of each brace, there's a combo-box menu saying which other component we want to set our spacing relative to, and how many points of distance we want.

Just below the braces, there's a check box called "Constrain to margins." Click that on, and then set the left and top distances to 0, and click each brace to make sure it's solid red. For the top distance, use the menu to verify that it says "Top Layout Guide" rather than "View," since this will help us deal with situations that take away space at the top of our UI (navigation bars, double-height status bars when a navigation app is running, etc.). If you don't see "Top Layout Guide" as an option, drag the button further down in the view and try again. When everything is set, click the Add 2 Constraints button at the bottom of the pop-over.

This may cause an orange box to appear near our button, possibly with orange braces that show numbers, when the label is selected. This is telling us that the label is currently misplaced relative to the constraints we just asked for. The box shows where the button should be if the constraints are applied, and any numeric values tell us how far off we are.

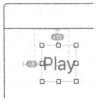

Click the Update Frames button (the leftmost of the five), or use its keyboard shortcut ⌥⌘=. This causes the button to jump to its correct position.

Laying Out the Time Label

Next up, let's fix the current time label. Select it and bring up the Pin menu again. We only want to pin one value this time: a distance of 0 to the margin on its right side. This will put a red box around the label when selected (as well as a red-arrow mini button next to View Controller Scene in the Document Outline pane). Red means that we don't have enough constraints. We've told Auto Layout where to put it horizontally—along the right edge—but not vertically.

We could pin the label to the Top Layout Guide, like we did with the Play button, but it would be nicer to align it to the Play button itself. That way, if we ever move the Play button, the current time label can move with it. So what we need is a constraint that applies to both of these components. Select both the Play button and the current time label via Shift-click, Command-click, or dragging a selection box over both of them (but not the track title label). Bring up the Alignment menu, shown in the figure.

The Alignment menu lets us create constraints between the two selected items, along with numeric values to "tweak" the alignment if needed. In this case, we want something that will line them up horizontally. Depending on relative sizes, aligning their tops or bottoms could work, and for two labels aligning baselines is often a good choice, but the safe option for now is to click the Vertical Centers button. So do that, and click the Add 1 Constraint button. Then, as before, use the Update Frames button to put the components in the right place, in accordance with our new constraints.

If we select either or both of these objects, they're now shown with blue lines indicating their layout constraints. Blue is good; it means there's no ambiguity, that there are enough constraints, *and* that they have been applied correctly.

Laying Out the Title Label

Let's finish up with the track title label. Make sure it's a safe distance below the Play button (drag it far enough down and Xcode will show blue lines to indicate the recommended spacing), select it, and bring up the Pin menu. We want it a fixed distance below the Play button, so put 8 for the top distance constraint, and check the pop-up menu to make sure that the Play button is checked (meaning that the 8 points will be relative to the Play button, not the Top Layout Guide or the parent view). Click Add 1 Constraint.

As before with the current time label, we are now under-constrained—we have a vertical position based on the Play button and its layout, but not a horizontal position. Again, we want to align this label to the Play button. Select both the track title label and the Play button, and bring up the Alignment menu. This time, choose Leading Edges. In this case, "leading" means the left side in left-to-right systems (like English), and right in right-to-left systems. Click Add 1 Constraint, and then clean up with Update Frames as before.

This looks fine, and has blue lines to indicate the title label has enough constraints, but there's actually a subtle bug. If we had a really long title, there is nothing to prevent the label from going off the right side of the screen. Often with labels, we want constraints on both sides to prevent this. Select the title label, bring up the Pin menu, and add a right constraint of 0, with Constrain to Margins still selected. This will stretch the handles all the way over to the right side, but the text should remain left-aligned inside the label.

Updating Frames Immediately

When using the Align or Pin menus, if you're sure you now have enough constraints, you can save the step of going to Update Frames afterwards. Instead, just above the Add *n* Constraints button, use the Update Frames pop-up menu to specify that either the selected items, or all views in the current container, should immediately update their frames as soon as the constraints are added.

This can be a great time-saver, or a source of horrible confusion—if you don't have enough constraints, or some of them are wrong, your selected item could appear in the wrong place, or even disappear entirely (perhaps because Auto Layout has decided to give it 0 width or height). If this happens, remember the first rule of Interface Builder: *Undo is your friend.*

Now we have a full set of constraints for each item in our UI. Let's try it out. Below View As, select the landscape orientation. The current time label will keep at the upper right as seen in the figure. The layout will also maintain its spacing and alignment to the edges when different iPhone models are selected from the Device section. And we can run the app again in the simulator and rotate the simulated device to our hearts' content.

Now imagine if we had to explicitly set each object's position and size in code: it would be a nightmare! With Auto Layout, we get to describe size, shape, and position with constraints, whereas, if we build our UI in code, we would be doing a bunch of math to set the position and size, using logic like "subtract the label's width from the superview's width minus the margin." For complex layouts on devices with different sizes and shapes, all of which can be rotated at any time, Auto Layout ends up being both easier and more dependable.

As layouts get more complex, Auto Layout has advanced features that we can use to help resolve complex situations. Each constraint has a priority value, so if we get into a case where conflicting constraints create an ambiguity, the Auto Layout system can compare priorities as a tiebreaker. It's also possible to create constraints in code, so if we did have to create an arbitrary number of views at runtime, we could still use Auto Layout on them and not resort to doing our own math to position them. It's a sophisticated system, but for starters, it's enough to just do the pinning and aligning supported by the storyboard UI.

Adding Images to the UI

Still, doesn't this look a little...*plain*? Those three labels at the top leave an awful lot of whitespace below them. And depending on the size of the device, that space could get really big—it will be a lot more noticeable on iPhone 7 Plus than iPhone SE.

Until we have more controls or displays that need space, one way we could use this space would be with an image. Most podcasts supply their own artwork, and later on when we're parsing podcast feeds, we can put an episode- or show-specific logo in this space. For now, we'll significantly beautify our app just by adding a generic image.

Image Views

In the Object Library, find the icon for an image view (it looks like a palm tree), and drag it to the empty space in the bottom of the scene. This will create a rectangle called UIImageView. This view will display any bitmap image we provide it with.

As you might recall from the last section, we will need to give the view some autolayout constraints if we want it to fill up the space below the title label and extending out to the sides and bottom of the scene. Select the UIImageView, click the Pin menu button to bring up the Auto Layout pop-over, and give it top, bottom, left, and right constraints of 0, with the Constrain To Margin check box selected. Click Add Constraints to finish with the pop-over, and then click Update Frames to apply the layout to the scene. This causes the image view to extend to the bottom and both sides of the scene.

Image Assets

Now we need some artwork. Later on, we'll download podcasts' logos from the Internet, but for now, we could really use a default; otherwise, this image view will be empty. Fortunately, we can add images directly to the app itself.

Back in the Project Navigator in the left pane, select the Assets.xcassets file. This kind of *assets file* is a collection of different kinds of image assets that will be included as part of our application: static images, app icons, 3D textures, etc. By default, it's empty but for an entry called AppIcon, which has a bunch of empty image wells; we will populate those much later, in Chapter 12, *Publishing and Maintaining the App*, on page 201.

Right now, what we want is a new image to be included with our app. At the bottom left of this view, click the Plus (+) button to bring up a pop-up menu, and choose New Image Set. This creates an entry in the list called "Image." If we select it, there are three image wells, labelled 1x, 2x, and 3x.

These wells represent the three pixel depths supported by iOS *Retina displays*, Apple's marketing term for displays of such a high resolution that the eye can't see individual pixels. On the first iPhones, there was one physical pixel for each virtual "point" in the coordinate system. Then the first Retina displays used four pixels for each point. This is represented by the "2x" (since the four pixels are arranged 2-by-2). Then with the large "Plus" models, we got an even higher resolution, indicated by the "3x".

For static images, we need to match pixel sizes to these multipliers. For example, if we want an image to appear as 100x100 on screen, then its 1x image file should actually be 100x100, but the 2x should be 200x200, and so on. If a given resolution isn't supplied, iOS will scale up or down from whatever image is available.

If you're working with our download code, you'll see that we have provided a generic podcast image at sizes 512x512, 1024x1024, and 1536x1536, as shown in the following figure. If you want to work with your own image or images, that's great; just drag them to the image wells to add them to the project.

Of course, the default name of Image is not great, since we might want to add more images to the app. In the asset list, select Image, and then click again to edit it. Change its name to default-logo. The asset library should now look like the following figure (minus 2x or 3x if you didn't have your own graphics for those sizes).

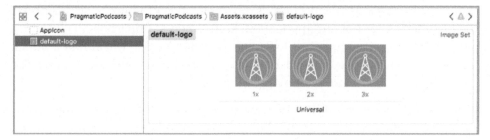

Populating the Image View

Now we can use this image in our UI. Go back to Main.storyboard, select the UIImageView, and bring up its Attributes Inspector ⌥⌘4. In the Image text field, type default-logo as shown in the following figure. Once you press Enter, the image view in the scene will immediately fill in with the image.

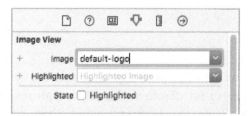

But there's a problem. Pretty much any layout of the view will be rectangular, and podcast artwork is typically square. In all likelihood, the image in the scene is being stretched vertically or horizontally to fill the entire view. We don't want that—we want it to respect its original aspect ratio—i.e., to stay square.

Still in the Attributes Inspector, look down a few lines and notice the pop-up menu for Content Mode. This defines how the contents of certain views, like image views, should be adapted to fit their size. The default choice is Scale To Fill, which stretches in both directions to fill the image view. Obviously, we don't want that.

There are two choices that perform scaling while respecting the image's aspect ratio. Aspect Fit will scale to fill either horizontally or vertically, while leaving empty space in the other dimension if necessary. Aspect Fill is similar, but it will fill both dimensions, by allowing part of the image to go beyond the image's boundaries if needed. We'd rather have empty space than risk cutting off parts of our image, so choose Aspect Fit. The image regains its proper shape.

There's one other problem, a fairly obscure one, but obvious if you used a big image like we did. Image views are a little weird with autolayout if you don't specify an explicit width or height—which we didn't, since we used constraints around the sides instead. Image views will try to honor the "intrinsic size" of their contents, so even if we want our 512x512 image to scale with Aspect Fit, the image view will try to get big enough to fit it. If you try switching the device type or orientation, the layout of the Play buttons and the labels may now be messed up.

The fix here is under the *Size Inspector*, the little ruler icon in the right pane's toolbar (also available with the shortcut ⌥⌘5). Scroll down and you'll see there are properties for Content Hugging Priority and Content Compression Resistance Priority. These refer,

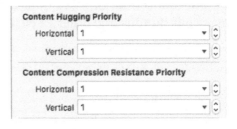

respectively, to how much the image view allows itself to be stretched or squished to suit other layout constraints. High values here mean the size of the contents' size always wins. We want the opposite of that, to always allow our image to be scaled, so set all of these values to 1.

With that fixed, the scene should now preview just fine for all devices and orientations, and you can run the app to see the default icon smartly using our whitespace in the bottom portion of the screen. Later on, we'll put each podcast's logo in here and it'll look really great.

What We've Learned

In this chapter, we've gotten out of the playground and into real app development. We created a new project in Xcode and looked at how its various parts are organized in the Xcode window.

Then we turned our attention to the user interface, since the best practice for iOS development is to start with the UI and then build out the logic and behavior behind it. Our UI is absolutely barebones at this point, but even this is enough to make us come to grips with the differing sizes and shapes of iOS devices and what happens when the user rotates the iPad or iPhone. To deal with this, we applied Auto Layout constraints to our UI elements, so they put themselves in sensible places depending on how much room they have to work with.

This chapter was a short diversion from our adventures in Swift in the first three chapters, and now it's time to bring it all together. In the next chapter, we will connect the UI we've built in this chapter to new code we'll write to make our buttons and other UI elements do their thing.

CHAPTER 5

Connecting the UI to Code

You've learned how to build user interfaces with storyboards and Interface Builder, and before that you used playgrounds to learn the ins and outs of the Swift programming language. But from where you stand right now, these two things have nothing to do with each other: you can't write code in a storyboard, and you can't drag and customize buttons and labels in a playground.

Obviously, there has to be some way to bring your two skill sets together, so you can bring a user interface to life and have your code do more than just produce log messages.

This chapter will let you close the loop by bringing these two worlds together. You'll connect user interface to code, so buttons can react to taps, and your code can update what's on the screen.

It's all about connections.

Connecting Actions

So how do we get a tap on the Play button to do something? After all, we've been creating the user interface in the Main.storyboard file, but it doesn't look like there's any place in this editor to start writing code.

In iOS, we use Interface Builder *connections* to tie the user interface to our code. Using Xcode, we can create two kinds of connections:

- An *outlet* connects a variable or property in code to an object in a storyboard. This lets us read and write the object's properties, like reading the value of a slider or setting the initial contents of a text field.

- An *action* connects an event generated by a storyboard object to a method in our code. This lets us respond to a button being tapped or a slider's value changing.

What we need here is an action connecting the button tap in the UI to a method in our code, which we'll write in a little bit. To create either kind of connection, we need to declare an IBOutlet or IBAction in our code, and then create the connection with Interface Builder. Fortunately, IB makes this pretty easy by giving us a way to combine the steps.

With the storyboard showing in the Editor area, go to the toolbar and click the Assistant Editor button (it looks like two linked circles). This brings up a side-by-side view with the storyboard on the left and a source file on the right. If there's not enough horizontal room on the screen to see things clearly, use the toolbar to hide the Utility area.

The pane on the right has a jump bar at the top to show which file is in the pane. After a pair of forward/back buttons, there's a button that determines how the file for this pane is selected: Manual, Automatic, Top Level Objects, and so forth. Set this to Automatic and the contents of the file ViewController.swift should appear in the right pane. We'll have more to say about why ViewController.swift is the file we need in the next few chapters, but for now, let's take the name at face value: this is the class that controls the view.

Xcode's template prepopulates ViewController.swift with trivial implementations of two methods: viewDidLoad() and didReceiveMemoryWarning(). We'll be adding a new method to this class.

Creating the action is pretty easy. Click to select the Play button in Interface Builder, and Control-drag a line over into the source code, anywhere between the set of curly braces that begin with class ViewController : UIViewController and end at the bottom of the file, and not within the curly braces of an existing method. Don't worry; a blue drop indicator and the tooltip "Insert Outlet, Action, or Outlet Collection" will appear only when we mouse over a valid drop zone. A good place to target is the line right before the final curly brace:

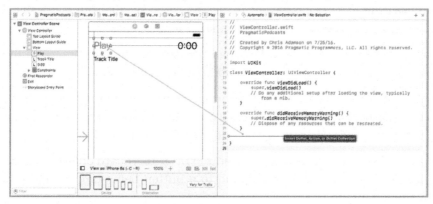

When we release the mouse in the source file, a pop-over asks us for the details needed to finish the method declaration. On the first line, change the Connection from Outlet to Action. This is important—for a button tap, we want a connection that goes from UI to code, and that's what an action is.

We need to give the method a name, so type handlePlayPauseTapped in the Name field. Next, the Type field determines what kind of object will be passed to the method as an argument identifying the source of the action. The default, Any, represents any type and works well enough, since we could reuse this method for other kinds of senders; the alternative would be to specify that the caller must be a UIButton. For the Event and Arguments fields we can take the default values. Click the Connect button to create the connection.

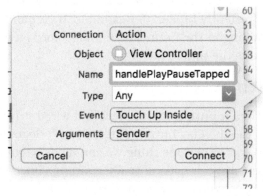

We're done with the Assistant Editor. Click the Standard Editor button in the toolbar to return to one-pane mode. Select ViewController.swift in the Navigator area, and you'll see that Xcode has stubbed out a method signature for us:

```
connecting/PragmaticPodcasts-5-1/PragmaticPodcasts/ViewController.swift
@IBAction func handlePlayPauseTapped(_ sender: Any) {
}
```

This method is marked with the @IBAction annotation, which allows connections of methods in code to UI objects in Interface Builder. Following the func keyword and the handlePlayPauseTapped method, the signature has _ to stifle the external parameter name, sender for the internal name, and Any for its type.

Xcode has also made a change to the storyboard, but it's not as easy to see. Switch to Main.storyboard and bring the Utility area back, if it's hidden. Click the Play button to select it. Then, in the Utility toolbar, click the little circle with the arrow (or press ⌥⌘6) to bring up the *Connections Inspector*. This pane shows all the connections for an object in Interface Builder: all the outlets from code to the object, and all actions sent by the object into the code. In this case, one connection appears in the Sent Events section, from "Touch Up Inside" to

"View Controller handlePlayPauseTapped." This connection, shown in the figure that follows, is editable here. If we wanted to disconnect it, we could click the little "x" button, and then reconnect to a different IBAction method by dragging from the circle on the right to the View Controller icon in the scene.

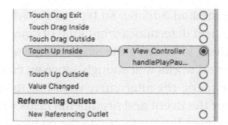

Honestly, we don't break and remake connections very often, but if a connection ever gets inadvertently broken (for example, by renaming the method in the source file), looking in the Connections Inspector is a good approach for diagnosing and fixing the problem.

Coding the Action

Now that we've added a button to our view and wired it up, we can run the app again. We can tap the Play button, but it doesn't do anything. Did we set up our connection correctly? One thing we can do as a sanity check is to log a message to make sure our code is really running. Once that's verified, we can move on to implementing our player functionality.

Logging

Back in Chapter 2, we learned about the print() function for logging messages to the Xcode console. We can use that in our action to just log a message every time the button is tapped, and thereby verify that the connections are working. Select ViewController.swift in the Project Navigator (⌘1) to edit its source code and rewrite handlePlayPauseTapped() like this:

```
connecting/PragmaticPodcasts-5-1/PragmaticPodcasts/ViewController.swift
@IBAction func handlePlayPauseTapped(_ sender: Any) {
  print("handlePlayPauseTapped")
}
```

Run the app again, and tap the Play button. Back in Xcode, the Debug Area automatically appears at the bottom of the window once a log or error message is generated, as seen in the following figure. Every time the button is tapped, another line is written to the log and shown in the Debug Area. If the Debug Area slides in but looks empty, check the two rightmost buttons at the bottom of the Debug Area, next to the trashcan icon; the left one enables a variables view (populated only when the app is stopped on a breakpoint), and the right (which we want to be visible) is the console view where log messages appear. Another way to force the console view to appear is to press ⇧⌘C.

So now we have a button that is connected to our code, enough to log a message that indicates the button tap is being handled. The next step is to actually make it play!

Connecting to a Player

We remember from *Getting Serious on the Playground*, on page 4, that the AV Foundation framework makes it pretty easy to play audio from a URL: we just create an AVPlayer from a URL, and tell it to play(). So let's do that here. The first thing we need to do is import the AV Foundation framework, so Xcode will let us use it in this source file. Add the import statement to the top of the file:

connecting/PragmaticPodcasts-5-1/PragmaticPodcasts/ViewController.swift
```
import AVFoundation
```

Now we can use an AVPlayer to play something when the user taps the Play button. We'll want the player to be around for as long as this view is on the screen, so let's make it a property of this class. Add this on a new line after the ViewController's opening curly brace:

connecting/PragmaticPodcasts-5-1/PragmaticPodcasts/ViewController.swift
```
private var player : AVPlayer?
```

We've made the player property an optional, since otherwise we'd have to have a player ready to go in the init(), and we want to let callers tell us what to play, when they're ready. So instead we'll allow the player to be nil at first.

How will we create a player? Well, what makes sense for callers? The job of this scene will be to just "play something." We could just let them call us with a URL, and we'll try to make an AVPlayer from that. So let's do exactly that by writing a new method:

connecting/PragmaticPodcasts-5-1/PragmaticPodcasts/ViewController.swift
```
func set(url: URL) {
  player = AVPlayer(url: url)
}
```

This method takes the URL that's passed in, tries to create an AVPlayer from it, and populates the player property.

When the rest of our app is able to parse podcast feeds and get episode URLs from them, it'll call this method to tell this scene what to play. That said, we'd like something to play with right now. For the time being, we'll hard-code a URL so we can get back to handling the tap on our Play button.

When Xcode created this ViewController.swift file for us, it stubbed out trivial implementations of a few methods. One of them is viewDidLoad(), whose contents look like this:

```
override func viewDidLoad() {
  super.viewDidLoad()
  // Do any additional setup after loading the view, typically from a nib.
}
```

In other words—and please ignore the business about "typically from a nib"— this means that this method will be called once our scene is loaded from the storyboard. viewDidLoad() is called only once and prior to the view actually appearing on screen. As the comment suggests, it's a great place to do initial setup. For us, it's where we can set our podcast URL, by calling the set(url:) method that we just wrote.

Remove the comment, and rewrite viewDidLoad() as follows:

```
connecting/PragmaticPodcasts-5-1/PragmaticPodcasts/ViewController.swift
Line 1  override func viewDidLoad() {
    2     super.viewDidLoad()
    3     if let url = URL(
    4       string: "http://traffic.libsyn.com/cocoaconf/CocoaConf001.m4a") {
    5       set(url: url)
    6     }
    7   }
```

Podcast URLs

For this example, we grabbed an episode URL from the CocoaConf Podcast, which has interviews with iOS developers, authors, and speakers from the CocoaConf conference tour (including the authors). If you want to check it out, visit http://cocoaconf.com/podcast/.

Of course, feel free to use an episode of your favorite podcast, if you know how to get the URL of an individual episode. If not, don't worry; we'll be digging deep into the contents of podcast RSS feeds in later chapters, and you'll see more URLs than you'll know what to do with.

On line 2, we call the superclass's implementation of the method, as we usually do in OO languages. Then on lines 3-4, we use the URL class's initializer that takes a string and use that to try to create a URL with the specified MP3 or AAC URL.

If the if let on lines 3-4 successfully created a URL, we'll make it to line 5, which calls our set(url:). We remember that calling that method will create our AVPlayer, and we will now be ready to play.

Now, *finally*, we're ready to do something interesting with the button tap. Go back to the handlePlayPauseButtonTapped() method, and replace the print() call with a more useful implementation:

connecting/PragmaticPodcasts-5-1/PragmaticPodcasts/ViewController.swift
```
@IBAction func handlePlayPauseTapped(_ sender: Any) {
  player?.play()
}
```

This uses the optional-chaining operator, ?, to say "if player is not nil, tell it to play()."

Network Security Concerns

We should be ready to go; when the view loads, it creates an AVPlayer, and when we get a button tap, we call play(). But try it by tapping the Run button. Spoiler alert: nothing happens when you tap.

Down in the console, you might notice that when the app comes up, there's a big error message:

```
App Transport Security has blocked a cleartext HTTP (http://) resource
load since it is insecure. Temporary exceptions can be configured via
your app's Info.plist file
```

Apps built for iOS 9 or later are controlled by *App Transport Security* (ATS), a feature introduced in iOS 9 to compel developers to adhere to safe, secure, and private networking practices. If you've heard the phrase "https everywhere," you get the gist: use secure connections wherever possible. Under App Transport Security, any attempt to load a plain http-style URL—like our podcast URL—fails immediately.

If we knew every podcast were reachable with an https:-style URL, or we were only playing media we hosted ourselves, we'd be fine. But we can't count on that.

App Transport Security allows us to carve out exceptions to its policies, and since we're still early in our study, we'll use the simplest means possible. ATS has a setting that basically means "allow everything," so that's what we'll use.

NSAllowsArbitraryLoads Considered Unsafe

The technique we're using—to just allow loading *anything*—will cause some pain when we submit the app to the App Store. The documentation even says:

> Setting this key's value to YES triggers App Store review and requires justification.

The main idea of App Transport Security is that for network resources that aren't or can't be https, we can carve out exceptions just for specific domains we know about in advance. But that won't work for a podcast app that needs to load whatever feeds the user asks it to load.

If it comes to it, we might be able to persuade Apple with a phone call or email. Another option, once we're parsing podcast feeds, is to only show podcasts with https:-style URLs that we know will work.

App Transport Security policies are still a work-in-progress. iOS 10 introduced a key called NSAllowsArbitraryLoadsInMedia that sounds like it fits our needs, but it is really meant for certain kinds of pre-encrypted video and doesn't actually let us load normal MP3s over plain http.

ATS exceptions are implemented on an app-wide basis, so they go in our apps' settings. We can see the custom properties for our app by clicking the Pragmatic Podcasts project icon at the top of the File Navigator, choosing the PragmaticPodcasts target, and selecting the Info tab. This view has settings for things like our app version and other metadata:

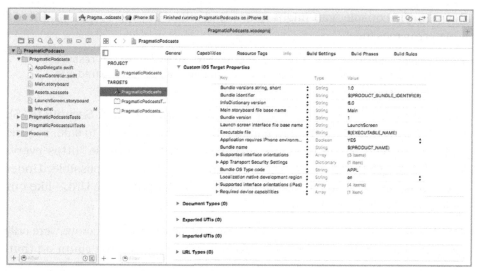

This is where the App Transport Security settings go, but this UI is hard to edit visually, and even harder to explain. (Trust us on this!) So instead, we'll go to the file where all these settings actually live. Under the Pragmatic Podcasts folder icon, select the Info.plist file. That shows the same metadata in the same hard-to-use interface. Right-click or Control-click Info.plist to expose a pop-up menu, and choose Open As Source Code. This lets us edit the raw XML.

Now, we can carve out our App Transport Security exception. Right before the </dict> at the bottom of the file, add the following:

```
<key>NSAppTransportSecurity</key>
<dict>
  <key>NSAllowsArbitraryLoads</key>
  <true/>
</dict>
```

What this does is basically turn off App Transport Security for the whole app. For now, this workaround gets us out of security jail.

Run the app again and tap the Play button. You should now be hearing the podcast start playing. Success!

Connecting Outlets

In fact, our player is so successful, there's no way to actually stop it in the app. Click the Stop button on the Xcode toolbar to kill the app.

Let's make our button both a Play and Pause button. To do that, we should only play() if the player isn't already playing. If it is playing, we need to pause.

A look at the AVPlayer documentation shows us the two pieces of information we need to make this work. First, in the "Managing Playback" section, right after play(), there's a pause() method. And just after that, there's rate, a Float that indicates how fast the media is playing, where 0.0 is paused and 1.0 is normal speed forward. This also means if we wanted to provide the popular "play podcast at one-and-a-half speed" feature, we could just set the rate to 1.5.

With rate and pause(), we can rewrite handlePlayPauseTapped() to properly support playing and pausing, as its name implies:

connecting/PragmaticPodcasts-5-2/PragmaticPodcasts/ViewController.swift
```swift
@IBAction func handlePlayPauseTapped(_ sender: Any) {
  if let player = player {
    if player.rate == 0 {
      player.play()
    } else {
      player.pause()
    }
  }
}
```

Run again, press the app's Play button, and once it's playing, press again to pause. We can now play and pause to our heart's delight.

This is great, but we're still not done: the button only ever says "Play." Wouldn't it be nice to have it say "Pause" when it's playing, so the button always represents what tapping it will actually do? Also, we have those other parts of the UI we've never filled in, like the current track label.

To do that, we need more connections. So far, we have an IBAction, a connection that goes from the UI to the code. Now we need to go from the code to the UI, to change the text of labels and buttons. For that, we need IBOutlets.

Creating and Coding Outlets

Recall that we talked about outlets back in *Connecting Actions*, on page 73. Whereas an action goes from a UI component in the storyboard to a method, an outlet goes from a property in our code to a UI component. The idea is that once we have outlets as properties, we can use them like any other variables: we can set their values, call methods on them, and so on.

We make an outlet the same way we made the action from the button: with a Control-drag from the storyboard to the source. To do that, switch to the Main.storyboard file, and then use the toolbar to switch to the Assistant Editor (the button with the two rings). Make sure the right pane is showing our ViewController.swift files; the first tab of its breadcrumb-style menus has an Automatic item that should do the right thing.

In the left pane, select the "Track Title" label, and Control-drag into the source code in the right pane. As you hover near the private var player : AVPlayer that we already created, the drag point will show a box that says "Insert Outlet or Outlet Collection," as shown in the figure. Release the drag here to create the outlet.

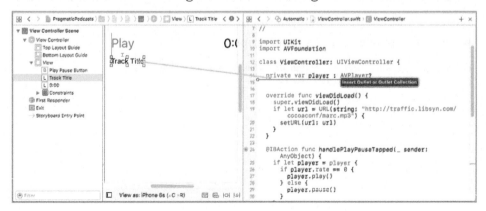

When you release the drag, a pop-up appears to fill in details of the connection. We saw this before when we created the button's action. We need to fill in these values and click Connect to actually create the outlet.

Leave Connection set to Outlet, and enter titleLabel for the name. Leave the Type as UILabel, make sure the Storage is Strong, and click Connect. This creates a new property in the ViewController.swift source file:

connecting/PragmaticPodcasts-5-2/PragmaticPodcasts/ViewController.swift
```
@IBOutlet var titleLabel: UILabel!
```

Now repeat this same process with the button: select it, Control-drag it into the source file, and create an outlet with the name playPauseButton and type UIButton. This should create the following line of code:

connecting/PragmaticPodcasts-5-2/PragmaticPodcasts/ViewController.swift
```
@IBOutlet var playPauseButton: UIButton!
```

Now we have properties for a UILabel and UIButton that we can call methods on, just like any other variables in our app. Let's start easy with the titleLabel.

We won't have a proper podcast episode title until later when we're parsing real podcast feeds. For now, we could just take the last part of the URL. Checking the documentation for the URL class shows that this is available as the property lastPathComponent. And if we look up UILabel, we find the way to change what it's showing is to set its text property. So now we have a simple way to update the UI. Rewrite set(url:) as follows:

connecting/PragmaticPodcasts-5-2/PragmaticPodcasts/ViewController.swift
```
func setURL(url: URL) {
  player = AVPlayer(url: url)
  titleLabel.text = url.lastPathComponent
}
```

Run the app again, and notice that as soon as it comes up, the title label shows the filename from the URL.

Looking good! We calculated a string in text (the lastPathComponent), and by just setting a property on an IBOutlet, we were able to update what the user sees in the UI. It'll be even better later when we can get a real title from the podcast feed. It's still good progress for now.

Speaking of getting data from the podcast feed, we also said in the last chapter that we were going to get each podcast's logo and put it in the image view. We're not ready to do that yet, but let's create the connection now, so it's ready to populate later. Control-drag from the image view into the source to create another outlet. This one can be called logoView.

connecting/PragmaticPodcasts-5-2/PragmaticPodcasts/ViewController.swift

```
@IBOutlet var logoView: UIImageView!
```

Constantly Changing Outlets

Of course, we still have the Play/Pause button that always says "Play." We need a way to fix that. The docs tell us that UIButton has a method setTitle(for:) that takes a string title and a UIControlState (so we could have, say, different titles for normal and disabled button states).

The question, actually, is knowing whether to set the title as Play or Pause, and when to change it. We could just do so in our button-tap handler, but that runs the risk of getting out of sync (for example, if we change the label because we think the audio is playing, but for some reason it failed to actually start playing). Also, that approach wouldn't automatically reset the button when the audio stops playing at the end of the file.

We want this button to use the playing state of the AVPlayer as its model, and for the player to tell us when it needs us to update the button.

If we look in the AVPlayer documentation, we find there's a discussion called "General State Observations," which says:

> You can use key-value observing (KVO) to observe state changes to many of the player's dynamic properties, such as its currentItem or its playback rate.

Perfect! Observing changes to the rate is exactly what we need. So, what the heck is KVO?

Key-value observing is a somewhat older Mac and iOS technology that implements an *observer pattern*. Interested objects can start observing a given property (if it supports KVO; not all properties do), and when it changes, they get a callback. We start observing by calling the addObserver() method on objects that support KVO, and when the value changes, we get a callback on a method called observeValue(forKeyPath:of:context:. In other words, we write a method with that signature, and it gets called automatically when the value we're observing changes.

So we start by telling the player that we want to observe its rate. We'll do this when we create it, in set(url:).

connecting/PragmaticPodcasts-5-2/PragmaticPodcasts/ViewController.swift
```swift
func set(url: URL) {
  player = AVPlayer(url: url)
  titleLabel.text = url.lastPathComponent
  player?.addObserver(self,
                      forKeyPath: "rate",
                      options: [],
                      context: nil)
}
```

The addObserver() call takes four parameters:

- observer: The object to call back to. In this case, it's self (that is to say, the ViewController class we're writing).

- forKeyPath: The property we want to observe, which is the player's rate.

- options: Behavior options for the callback, like whether both old and new values should be delivered.

- context: A C-style pointer that's not useful in Swift (it's left over from the Objective-C language that iOS and Mac apps originally used).

Why It's Called Key Path

The key path is interesting—and is named the way it is—because it lets us observe properties *of* properties. For example, the AVPlayer has a currentItem, which itself has observable properties like status. So we could observe changes to the status by using the key path currentItem.status. The keyPath, as it turns out, is a string representing a dot-separated path of properties.

KVO requires us to remove any observers we add, and failure to do so is a crashing bug. That will matter more later when this isn't the only scene in the app. For now, let's remove the observer when this object is purged from memory. When that happens, the *deinit* method—so named because it's the opposite of the init() that we're familiar with—is called. We typically put deinit() near the top of the class, after any init() overrides and before any instance methods, so do that here:

connecting/PragmaticPodcasts-5-2/PragmaticPodcasts/ViewController.swift
```swift
deinit {
  player?.removeObserver(self, forKeyPath: "rate")
}
```

Now we're finally ready to write our observer. This will be called any time the player's rate changes, giving us an opportunity to update our UI.

connecting/PragmaticPodcasts-5-2/PragmaticPodcasts/ViewController.swift

```
Line 1   override func observeValue(forKeyPath keyPath: String?,
       -                            of object: Any?,
       -                            change: [NSKeyValueChangeKey : Any]?,
       -                            context: UnsafeMutableRawPointer?)
     5   {
       -     if keyPath == "rate",
       -       let player = object as? AVPlayer {
       -       playPauseButton.setTitle(player.rate == 0 ? "Play" : "Pause",
       -         for: .normal)
    10     }
       - }
```

Lines 1-5 are the boilerplate for the method signature. Fortunately, you can just start typing observeValue and Xcode should offer you an auto-complete, which you can accept by just pressing the tab key (⇥).

What matters is how we respond to the event, starting on line 6 where we check to see that this is even the rate property that we're interested in (since *all* events this object is observing will call back to this same method). If so, then on line 7, we can try casting the sender to an AVPlayer by using an if let. Granted, we could just access self.player directly, but preferring to work with the information provided by the event is better practice.

Finally, we're ready to make use of our outlet to the button! On lines 8-9, we call the button's setTitle(for:) method to set the title for the .normal state. And the title we use is based on the rate of the player. If it's 0, we're paused and the button should say "Play." For any other value, the player is playing, so the button should say "Pause."

We're done with our KVO implementation, so click Run on the toolbar to try it out. When you tap the Play button, it should now update to be a Pause button as the audio starts playing, and vice versa. Pretty slick!

The last part of our UI that isn't wired up yet is the current time label. There are a couple ways we could implement that, but the cleanest will require learning a new coding technique, so we're going to put it off for a little bit.

What We've Learned

In this chapter, we've brought together many of the things we learned in the book up to this point. The first three chapters were all about writing code, and the previous chapter was about building user interfaces with storyboards and Interface Builder. By using connections—actions that connect UI components to methods, and outlets that connect properties in the code back to the UI—we have completed the loop. We can now create our UIs visually, and back them up with code.

By applying what we've learned, we now have a minimal audio player user interface with a working Play/Pause button, and a title label that updates itself when the player URL is set.

We've got a bunch more to do before we can ship our podcast player, but first we should take a step back. Our player app works for now, but how can we be sure it'll keep working, and that changes we make later won't break it? In the next chapter, we'll introduce Xcode's support for unit testing, and let Xcode verify that our code really works like we think it does.

CHAPTER 6

Testing the App

Now that we've tied our UI to our code, our simple app has some solid, if basic, functionality. Tap Play, it plays. Tap Pause, it pauses. Everything's good, and we can just start adding more features, right?

Well, how do we know that everything's "good"? We have run the app a few times, but have we really pushed the limits of the app? Have we really tried everything that anyone could possibly do to our app? How do we prove that our app is not going to crash before we ship it off to Apple?

And as we start adding features, what proves that those changes work, or that they're not going to have weird side effects that break the stuff that had been working? Do we only want to start testing the correctness of our code at the end, when we've got thousands of lines of code? Caring about the correctness of our code is something that should always be on our mind, not just in a deadline push to QA.

The way we deal with this is to use *unit tests*. In this chapter, we'll see how we can use our Swift programming skills to make sure that the rest of our code is doing what it is supposed to.

The Need for Unit Tests

Unit tests are exactly what they sound like. They are small, self-contained segments of code that test very small, targeted units of functionality. Rather than check to see if the whole application works, we can break the functionality into pieces to pinpoint exactly where errors and bugs are occurring.

Unit tests are designed to either pass or fail. Is this feature working the way you want it to, yes or no?

The Parable of the Dinosaur

Here is an example of unit testing gone bad.

In *Jurassic Park* (the book, not the movie), Dr. Grant asks the scientists how they can be sure that the dinosaurs are not breeding.

The scientists assure Dr. Grant that every precaution has been taken. They engineered the dinosaurs to all be female. They had the island blanketed with motion detectors to count each and every dinosaur every five minutes. They created a computer algorithm to check the number and types of dinosaurs found by the motion sensors, and the number only changed when a dinosaur died. There had been no escapes. They knew everything happening on the island, and they were completely in control.

Dr. Grant asks them to change the parameters of the computer program to look for more dinosaurs than they expected to have. The scientists humor Dr. Grant and change the algorithm to search for more dinosaurs. Lo and behold! There are more dinosaurs. After running the program several more times with increasing numbers, they eventually discover there are over 50 extra dinosaurs on the island. Oops!

The program had been set up with the expectation that the number of dinosaurs could only go down, never up. Once the program reached the number of dinosaurs it was expecting to find, it stopped counting, and the scientists never knew there was an issue. The program anticipated the outcome of dinosaurs dying or escaping the island but never the possibility that life could find a way.

Reasons We Unit Test

Bugs, like life, do find a way. The first thing to remember in computer programming is that the computer is stupid. The computer only does what you tell it to do. It can't infer what you meant. It is important to verify that you are giving the right directions to the computer, and the best way to do that is for us to test our apps.

One major reason to unit test an application is to eliminate crashes. The single biggest reason that most app submissions are rejected by Apple is because they crash. Even if Apple doesn't catch your crash, users have a talent for finding the one combination of things that will cause your app to crash. These are the users who tend to leave one-star reviews on the store, which is something we want to avoid if at all possible.

Unit tests also expose logic errors in our code. In the *Jurassic Park* example, the code being run had a logic error that prevented the scientists from discovering the problem until it was too late. We don't want that to happen to us.

Writing tests also helps us write our code. Have you ever started writing a piece of code only to figure out that one feature you spent days working on wasn't really going to work out in your project? By thinking critically about what specifically you want your application to do, you can avoid writing overly complicated and unnecessary code. Tests can inform the design of our code; they tell us what part of the code has what responsibilities, and how we recover if something unexpected happens.

Designing Good Unit Tests

Writing a unit test is not difficult. Writing a good unit test is another story altogether.

There are generally three types of unit tests:

- *Debugging:* These tests are built around bugs to ensure that when we change the code, these bugs do not reappear. Sometimes when we are coding, we make changes to the code that affect features we consider done or bugs that we have already resolved. Since we do not want to see that bug again, we need to write tests to make sure that the bug has not reappeared when we change anything.

- *Assert success:* We are testing to make sure we are getting a result we want.

- *Assert failed:* We are testing to make sure we are not getting a result we don't want.

You might wonder why you would need a test to assert failure. Isn't the point of testing to make sure that features we created work properly?

Think back to the *Jurassic Park* example. The scientists created tests to make sure they were finding all of the dinosaurs they were looking for. They asserted success once the number of dinosaurs they were looking for was reached.

Sometimes it is as important to write a test that we expect to fail to make sure that we are not getting a result we don't want. Had the scientists also included a failure assertion test, they would have discovered that they were getting results that made no sense: there are more dinosaurs in the park than there are supposed to be.

How Tests Work in Xcode

Built-in testing functionality was introduced in Xcode 5 and regularly improved since then. Apple based many of its testing functions on accepted and open source frameworks and has been working very hard to make testing a vital and useful tool in the developer utility belt.

We are going to go over several aspects of testing in Xcode in this chapter. Since we have spent a fair amount of time creating and developing the PragmaticPodcasts app, let's run it through some tests to see how it works.

Let's direct our attention to the File Navigator, shown in this figure. There is a group titled PragmaticPodcastsTests. Xcode has conveniently created this group and sample template class, PragmaticPodcastsTests.swift, for our first two tests. There is a second group, PragmaticPodcastsUITests, with a file PragmaticPodcastsUITests.swift; these are our user interface tests, which we'll try out later in the chapter.

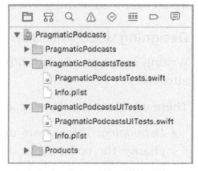

Before we move on to actually looking at the included test files, let's also look at the Test Navigator (⌘5). Rather than showing test files, this shows the tests themselves, and (if they've been run already) whether they passed or failed the last time they ran. This is another location in Xcode that makes it easy for you to get an overview of what tests you have and whether or not they are passing.

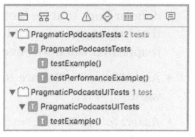

Click the PragmaticPodcastsTests.swift file in either the Project or the Test Navigator. There are four methods within this class: setUp(), tearDown(), testExample(), and testPerformanceExample(). Every test class that we create will have a setUp() and a tearDown() method. setUp() is used to instantiate any boilerplate code you need to set up your tests, and tearDown() is used to clear away any of the setup you needed to do for your tests. Whenever we find ourselves repeating code in multiple tests, it's a candidate for moving into setUp() and tearDown(). This is the principle of DRY: Don't Repeat Yourself.

Every test method we create will start with the word "test," just as the testExample() and testPerformanceExample() methods demonstrate. The first of these is an example of testing our app's logic, and the second tests its performance (that is to say, how long it takes to do something). Test methods take no arguments and return no value—this pattern, plus starting with "test," is how our tests are found and executed by the test engine. A test passes if it returns normally, and fails if it fails an assertion method before it returns.

For fun, let's just run the test included in the template. There are several ways to run our unit tests:

- Keyboard command: ⌘U
- Main menu: Product > Test
- Clicking the diamond icon next to either the test class or the specific test in Xcode

The first two ways of running tests run all of the tests, whereas the third way allows us to run selected tests. This is useful if we have one test that's failing and we want to focus on that one without having to run all the others.

Run the test in the manner of your choice. After the usual build activity, you'll see some messages like "Testing PragmaticPodcastTests" in the status bar, and then the "Test Succeeded" heads-up indicator will appear for a moment and then fade away.

Test Succeeded

Let's take a closer look at testExample().

testing/PragmaticPodcasts-6-1/PragmaticPodcastsTests/PragmaticPodcastsTests.swift
```swift
func testExample() {
// This is an example of a functional test case.
// Use XCTAssert and related functions to verify your tests
// produce the correct results.
}
```

The XCTAssert() method mentioned by the comment is provided by the import XCTest statement at the top of the file. It exists to tell the test engine whether a test has passed or failed. Let's try it out: on a new line in testExample(), add the following line, and then run tests again.

```swift
XCTAssert(false, "Pass")
```

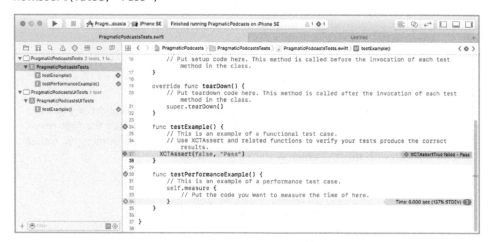

Oh no! The test stopped working! What happened?

Well, we just changed the conditions of the test. XCTAssert must pass a true condition in its first parameter for the test to pass. Since we programmed the condition to be false, the test fails and sends the string (which indicates what was *supposed* to happen) to the test engine, which shows up as an error bar next to the test method.

At first blush this might seem like a useless exercise. Why would we want to write a test that always fails when you run it?

We run a test that's designed to fail so that we verify that the testing framework itself is working properly. If we create nothing but tests that are supposed to pass, we can't know for certain that the tests are passing because the code is correct. There could be a problem with our test environment, and the tests would pass regardless. By prompting a failure, we now verify that when we write a test that passes, our code is, in fact, working correctly. As one wise person put it, "How do you know your smoke detector works if it never goes off?"

Where Assertions Come From

At this point you may be wondering where we got XCTAssert() and the other testing methods from. Xcode's testing framework is called XCTest and is built atop an older open source testing framework called OCUnit.

As we saw earlier, the method in XCTest to assert a true condition is XCTAssert(). The assertions all take the form of asserting that some condition is true, and failing the test if it is actually false. Different assertions make it easier to test numeric values, whether or not optionals are nil, and so on.

There are about twenty different assertion methods in the XCTest framework, but the ones we will be using most often are

- XCTAssert()
- XCTAssertFalse()
- XCTAssertEqual()
- XCTAssertNotNil()
- XCTAssertThrowsError()

There is a complete list of every assertion in the Xcode documentation, if you want to see how deep the rabbit hole goes. Search for "XCTest" and take the first result (the one whose icon shows four dots, which indicates the XCTest *framework*, rather than the icon with the "C," which is the XCTest *class*).

Creating Tests

Now that we know how to write tests—create a method with "test" in its name, and use XCTAssert-type methods to say what should be true during the test—let's put our existing functionality to the test.

We can start with the outlets that we created in the last chapter. Since the app launches and immediately loads our URL, we should see the last part of the URL as the titleLabel text, and the button should say "Play" or "Pause" based on the current player state.

In PragmaticPodcastsTests.swift, delete the provided testExample() and testPerformance-Example() methods, but leave setUp() and tearDown(), since we'll likely need them.

Our tests will need to access the outlets we're testing, and this presents a little bit of a hassle that we haven't had to consider before. Swift considers all the classes in the PragmaticPodcasts target to be one *module*, and classes in a module can see each other's properties and methods by default. However, PragmaticPodcastsTests is a different target and thus a different module, so it cannot see the methods or properties of our app's classes. We'll have to fix that before we can test anything.

We can declare different levels of access for our classes and their members. Swift has five levels of access, set by special keywords:

Access modifier	Visibility
public	Visible everywhere, but cannot be overridden
open	Visible everywhere, and can be overridden
internal	Visible within the same module, and can be overridden
fileprivate	Visible only within the class itself, and extensions in the same source file
private	Visible only within the class itself, and not visible to extensions

The default level of access is internal, so the files in the PragmaticPodcasts module can see each other's members, but PragmaticPodcastsTests can't. We could declare the members we want to test (the titleLabel and playPauseButton) as public, but there's a better way. The import directive can use a @testable keyword to open up internal members just for testing, and that's what we need.

Notice that at the top of PragmaticPodcastsTests.swift, there's already a @testable import set up for us:

testing/PragmaticPodcasts-6-1/PragmaticPodcastsTests/PragmaticPodcastsTests.swift
```
@testable import PragmaticPodcasts
```

This imports the PragmaticPodcasts module for use by the test class. By annotating it with the @testable keyword, we can access the properties and methods internal to the PragmaticPodcasts module, without having to make them public.

This will let our test code access the members of the ViewController class where we wrote all our functionality in the last chapter. Now let's write a test to let us look inside that class.

Writing the Unit Tests

For our first test, let's think of something easy. How about the title label that we wired up and coded in the last chapter? It seems like there should be a way to check that the string on that label is the last part of the URL that we're playing.

Reading the label's string will be easy. Actually, the trick will be how we get to the label. After all, look at the PragmaticPodcastsTests class—there's no reference to anything in the app we've written. How can we even access the label to test it?

When we run a test, the simulator launches the whole app, so it's possible for a test to ask the app itself about what it's showing. But for a test, we would like to test a scene in isolation—if we wrote a test that assumes the player is the only scene in the app, then as soon as we start building out the app with lists of episodes, the test will break.

Loading Storyboard Scenes

Fortunately, we can load any scene we like directly from the storyboard. All we have to do is give the scene a name in the storyboard. Open Main.storyboard, go back to our one media-player scene, and select its View Controller (either from the orange ball on the top of the frame, or from the Document Outline pane on the left). Now bring up the Identity Inspector (⌥⌘3) in the right pane. There is a field here called Storyboard ID. This is where we can enter a name. Type in PlayerViewController. It doesn't actually matter what name we use; we just have to remember to use this same name in our test class in the next step.

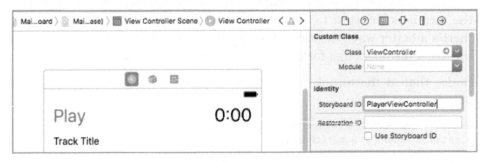

Now we can get this scene from within the test class, and from there, we'll get individual components like the title label and the Play/Pause button.

We're going to need to do this in any test we write, so getting the scene from the storyboard is something we should put in the setUp() method, rather than in each of the tests. We'll have setUp() populate a property, and then read from that property in each test. So right before the empty setUp() method, declare this property:

testing/PragmaticPodcasts-6-1/PragmaticPodcastsTests/PragmaticPodcastsTests.swift
```
var playerVC : ViewController?
```

Recall that we've been writing our UI code so far in a class called ViewController, so we're just creating a property of that type, called playerVC (to distinguish it from other view controllers we might test later). It has to be optional, because it can't be populated by the time the test class's init() runs, since the setUp() that will populate it is called *after* init().

Now we're ready to implement setUp(). We're going to rely on the UIStoryboard class, which can load a storyboard by name, and any scene within that storyboard by identifier. So here's how we'll do that:

testing/PragmaticPodcasts-6-1/PragmaticPodcastsTests/PragmaticPodcastsTests.swift
```
Line 1  override func setUp() {
     2    super.setUp()
     3    let storyboard = UIStoryboard(name: "Main", bundle: nil)
     4    guard let playerVC = storyboard.instantiateViewController(withIdentifier:
     5      "PlayerViewController") as? ViewController else { return }
     6    playerVC.loadViewIfNeeded()
     7    self.playerVC = playerVC
     8  }
```

Line 3 is where we load the storyboard, by passing the name of Main.storyboard (minus its filename extension) to the UIStoryboard. On lines 4-5, we call the instantiateViewController() method, passing in the PlayerViewController name that we gave the scene in the storyboard itself. This step is in a guard let, so if it fails—or if storyboard itself is actually nil because the previous step failed—we bail out without doing anything else.

On line 6, we know that playerVC is valid, but just having the view controller won't actually load up any of the UI components until we actually access them. The app would do this for us when it's running, of course, to put the components on the screen. Since our test won't be doing that, we can load it manually with loadViewIfNeeded(). Finally, on line 7, we assign the local playerVC to self.playerVC, the property that other methods in the class can see.

Using a Scene in a Test

Now that our scene is in the playerVC property, we can write test methods that use it. Let's write one now. Delete the testExample() and testPerformanceExample() methods, since we don't want them slowing us down doing nothing when we run tests.

Also, those test names aren't very descriptive. One common pattern for naming tests is to indicate the thing being tested, the state under test, and the expected behavior. So, we could say, "For the player's title label, once the URL is set, it should show the correct filename."

As a test, this will be the method testPlayerTitleLabel_WhenURLSet_ShowsCorrectFilename(). So let's write this method. All it has to do is load the scene and then look at the string in the label.

```
testing/PragmaticPodcasts-6-1/PragmaticPodcastsTests/PragmaticPodcastsTests.swift
Line 1  func testPlayerTitleLabel_WhenURLSet_ShowsCorrectFilename() {
     2    guard let playerVC = playerVC else {
     3      XCTFail("Couldn't load player scene")
     4      return
     5    }
     6    XCTAssertEqual("CocoaConf001.m4a", playerVC.titleLabel.text)
     7  }
```

Our method declaration on line 1 uses our very descriptive method-naming scheme, saying exactly what we're testing, under what conditions, and what should happen. For the moment, the URL is set in viewDidLoad(); later on, when we're parsing podcast feeds, we'll take that out and the test will need to be rewritten to set the URL. Of course, having tests that break when we make major changes like that is exactly what we want, right?

On lines 2-5, we use a guard let to collect the playerVC that we populated in setUp(). If this didn't work and playerVC is actually nil, then falling into the else should cause us to immediately fail the test, which we do with the XCTFail() on line 3.

Finally, the moment of truth. On line 6, we can get the titleLabel from the playerVC and inspect the label's text property. Is it the CocoaConf001.m4a filename from the URL like we expect? XCTAssertEqual() will determine if we pass or fail.

Go ahead and run this test, either by clicking the diamond to the left of func testPlayerTitleLabel_WhenURLSet_ShowsCorrectFilename() (once Xcode figures out that this really is a test method and puts it there), or by clicking the test in the Test Navigator (⌘5). The simulator will launch, you'll see some activity in the Xcode status bar, and then you should see the "Test Succeeded" overlay that appears for a few seconds and fades out, along with the diamond next to the test method filling in with a green checkmark.

◈   func **testPlayerTitleLabel_WhenURLSet_ShowsCorrectFilename() {**

Interacting with the System Under Test

One thing that makes our test really simple is the fact that it's totally passive: all we have to do is read a value and assert that it's the right thing. It's actually more common to have to set things up a little.

Consider our Play/Pause button. We could write a test to make sure it says "Play" easily enough, but we also want to know that it says "Pause" once it's playing. This will test that fancy KVO stuff we wrote in the last chapter.

But to get the player playing, we need to actually *press* the Play/Pause button or do something equivalent. Can a test do that? Well, think back to how we set up the connections: a tap on the button calls the method handlePlayPause-Tapped(). So we can just call that same method from a test, like this:

testing/PragmaticPodcasts-6-1/PragmaticPodcastsTests/PragmaticPodcastsTests.swift
```
Line 1  func testPlayerPlayPauseButton_WhenPlaying_ShowsPause() {
     2    guard let playerVC = playerVC else {
     3      XCTFail("Couldn't load player scene")
     4      return
     5    }
     6    playerVC.handlePlayPauseTapped(self)
     7    XCTAssertEqual("Pause",
     8                  playerVC.playPauseButton.title(for: .normal))
     9  }
```

Our testPlayerPlayPauseButton_WhenPlaying_ShowsPause() starts with the same guard let as in the previous test, either fetching the playerVC or failing the test immediately. On 6, we effectively "tap" the Play/Pause button by calling the same method that real button taps do. The only difference is that for the sender parameter, we send self, the test class itself. That method takes an AnyObject for this sender parameter, and never uses it, so this is fine.

Now that we've "tapped" the Play/Pause button, we want to check its title. Recall that in ViewController.swift, we set the title with setTitle(for:), which took a title string and a button "state," which for us is .normal. So to get the title, we can use a UIButton method called title(for:). And that's what we do on lines 7–8, asserting that the value we get back from the playPauseButton's title is Pause.

Run this test by itself, or click the diamond next to the class name to run all tests on the class. Everything passes, and now we see how to interact with the player scene—or to use testing jargon, the *system under test*—before we assert what we expect its values to be.

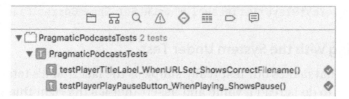

Testing Asynchronously

We've learned how to test that parts of our user interface show what they're supposed to, and that's really useful. However, the whole point of this scene is to play an audio file, and we would also like to get some test coverage of that functionality. In other words, when we call handlePlayPauseTapped(), what proves that anything is playing?

Back in the ViewController class where we have all the controller logic for the scene, we had an AVPlayer that's responsible for playing the audio. It has a currentTime() method that tells us how far into the current media item it has gotten. So this seems straightforward: we write a test to tap the Play button, then check that the current time isn't 0.

First things first...back in ViewController.swift, we declared the player to be private. Good for encapsulation, but bad for testing, since the test class won't be able to access it, even with our existing @testable import PragmaticPodcasts declaration. So go back to that class and remove the private keyword, so the declaration looks like this:

testing/PragmaticPodcasts-6-2/PragmaticPodcasts/ViewController.swift
```
var player : AVPlayer?
```

Back in PragmaticPodcastsTests.swift, we're now ready to write our test. When we ask for the player's current time, we'll get back a struct of type CMTime. That comes from the Core Media framework, so we need to add an import statement to our test class:

testing/PragmaticPodcasts-6-2/PragmaticPodcastsTests/PragmaticPodcastsTests.swift
```
import CoreMedia
```

Our test is almost identical to checking the Play button's title, except now we're going to check the player's current time and make sure it's not zero. The CMTime is picky about timekeeping, and that makes its docs hard to read at first, but it has a convenience property called seconds that is just a Double, and that's good enough for us. All we care about is that it's not 0. So here's our test:

testing/PragmaticPodcasts-6-2/PragmaticPodcastsTests/PragmaticPodcastsTests.swift

```swift
func testPlayerCurrentTime_WhenPlaying_IsNonZero() {
  guard let playerVC = playerVC else {
    XCTFail("Couldn't set up test")
    return
  }
  playerVC.handlePlayPauseTapped(self)
  XCTAssertNotEqual(0, player.currentTime().seconds)
}
```

Click the diamond next to the testPlayerCurrentTime_WhenPlaying_IsNonZero() method declaration, and like usual Xcode builds our test code, we see some activity in the status window…and the test fails. Wait, what?

```swift
func testPlayerCurrentTime_WhenPlaying_IsNonZero() {
  guard let playerVC = playerVC, let player = playerVC.player else {
    XCTFail("Couldn't set up test")
    return
  }
  playerVC.handlePlayPauseTapped(self)
  XCTAssertNotEqual(0, player.currentTime().seconds)
}
```
⊗ XCTAssertNotEqual failed: ("0.0") is equal to ("0.0") -

Making Tests Wait

What happened? Well, try running the app again and not just the tests. After you tap the Play/Pause button, the title changes immediately, but it takes a second or two for the audio to load and start playing. But from the test's point of view, as soon as it calls handlePlayPauseTapped(), the player object is ready to be tested. What's happening is that we are testing too soon. We need a way to wait before we run our test.

What we need is *asynchronous testing*, the ability to test things that happen at unpredictable times. If we wanted to test that 2 + 2 == 4, or that a string has a certain value, we could do that right away, because the value would be there right when we asked for it. That's what we've been doing all along. But with the AVPlayer, we don't know when (or if) its contents will start playing. Asynchronous testing lets us test these kinds of unpredictable events.

The way to deal with these situations is a testing class called XCTestExpectation. An XCTestExpectation is an object that describes an event that we expect to happen at some point in the near future. We tell the test how long it can wait, and then perform test assertions elsewhere—in parts of the code that run asynchronously—finally notifying the expectation when we're done. And if we don't do so in time, that's considered a failure.

Joe asks:
What the Heck Is an "Expectation Object"?

There is a wonderful quote by the late John Pinette that goes, "Salad isn't food. Salad comes with the food. Salad is a promissory note that food will soon arrive."

Expectation objects are like salad. They are not the test; they are the promise to your program that something is going to happen a little later.

If you went to a restaurant and got a salad, and then waited for an hour for food that never arrives, you would realize something is terribly wrong. You were set up to expect that another part of your meal was coming, and if it never arrived, your meal would be a failure.

That, in a nutshell, is how asynchronous testing with expectation objects works.

Back in the PragmaticPodcastsTests class, the first thing we will do is create an XCTestExpectation property:

testing/PragmaticPodcasts-6-2/PragmaticPodcastsTests/PragmaticPodcastsTests.swift
```
var startedPlayingExpectation : XCTestExpectation?
```

This expectation object will start as nil (which is why it has to be an optional), and we will populate it when we start the test. When we know the player's current time is greater than zero, we can tell it that we're done by calling its fulfill() method.

So our new approach is going to be to create the expectation, start playing, periodically check on the player, and when we find playback has started, fulfill the expectation. We'll also have a timeout to fail the test if we don't call fulfill() in a certain amount of time.

Using a Timer

To periodically check on the player, we have a few options. Probably the simplest is to create a Timer, which is an object that can repeatedly call one of our methods on a schedule we set. We'll want to hold on to the timer as a property, so that we can turn it off when we don't need it anymore:

testing/PragmaticPodcasts-6-2/PragmaticPodcastsTests/PragmaticPodcastsTests.swift
```
var startedPlayingTimer : Timer?
```

So using a timer to periodically check on the player, here's what our new testPlayerCurrentTime_WhenPlaying_IsNonZero() is going to look like (this will pop up one error as you type; we'll fix it in a minute):

testing/PragmaticPodcasts-6-2/PragmaticPodcastsTests/PragmaticPodcastsTests.swift

```
Line 1  func testPlayerCurrentTime_WhenPlaying_IsNonZero() {
   -      guard let playerVC = playerVC else {
   -        XCTFail("Couldn't set up test")
   -        return
   5      }
   -      startedPlayingExpectation = expectation(description:
   -        "player starts playing when tapped")
   -      startedPlayingTimer =
   -        Timer.scheduledTimer(timeInterval: 1.0,
  10          target: self,
   -          selector: #selector(timedPlaybackChecker),
   -          userInfo: nil,
   -          repeats: true)
   -      playerVC.handlePlayPauseTapped(self)
  15      waitForExpectations(timeout: 10.0, handler: nil)
   -    }
```

There are a bunch of new things to unpack in here, so let's take it slowly. On lines 6-7, we call the method expectation() from our superclass, XCTest, to create an expectation with the given description. We assign this to the property we created earlier, startedPlayingExpectation. This is what we have to fulfill() before a timeout in order to pass the asynchronous test.

Lines 9-13 are where we create the Timer. By using the scheduledTimer() method, we create a timer that can fire on a regular interval. We have to provide five parameters to create a timer like this:

- timeInterval: How often, in seconds, the timer should call back to us. Getting called every 1.0 seconds should be frequent enough for a unit test.

- target: An object to call back to. We want the timer to call back to this test itself, so we use self.

- selector: A method on the target to call. We describe the method as a *selector*, which is the method's name and any named arguments written in a specific format. This line will currently produce an error, as Xcode realizes we haven't written this timedPlaybackChecker() yet.

- userInfo: An object we want the Timer to deliver to the selector on each callback. We don't need one, so this can be nil.

- repeats: A Bool indicating whether we want the Timer to keep firing until we stop it, or once and never again. true means we want it to keep firing.

Next, we virtually tap the button handlePlayPauseTapped() as before. But we don't immediately test anything. Instead, on line 15, we call the XCTest method waitForExpectations(). This puts the test on hold for the given timeout period, and allows the system under test to achieve the expected state and call fulfill() on all expectations created in the test. If the expectations aren't fulfilled before the timeout—10.0 seconds in our case—the test fails.

Our final step is to create the timedPlaybackChecker() that we told the Timer it could call back to. This method will be called every 1.0 seconds, and needs to check to see if the player has actually started playing. If it has, it should fulfill the expectation created back in the test.

testing/PragmaticPodcasts-6-2/PragmaticPodcastsTests/PragmaticPodcastsTests.swift

```
func timedPlaybackChecker(timer: Timer) {
  if let player = playerVC?.player,
    player.currentTime().seconds > 0 {
    startedPlayingExpectation?.fulfill()
    startedPlayingTimer?.invalidate()
  }
}
```

A method called as a Timer callback, like our timedPlaybackChecker() here, always takes a single argument: the Timer that's calling into it. Our timed update is pretty simple: we use an if let to get the player, then we check if its currentTime() (in seconds) is greater than 0. If that's true, then we can fulfill() the expectation, which will cause the testPlayerCurrentTime_WhenPlaying_IsNonZero() test (where waitForExpectations() is still pending) to finally pass. As a bit of cleanup, we also call invalidate() on the Timer, which causes it to stop running.

So try out our new and improved testPlayerCurrentTime_WhenPlaying_IsNonZero() test. You'll notice that the test run takes a little longer compared to the earlier version that failed quickly, and you'll probably actually hear a little bit of the podcast audio before the timer realizes that playback has begun and ends the test.

Now we are passing our test and proving that even tricky asynchronous behaviors like waiting for media to download and start playing can be exposed to unit tests!

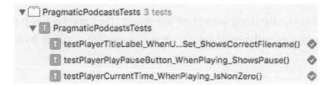

The Best Test Is a Reproducible Test

 To keep things simple, we haven't changed the code of the ViewController class, which currently depends on downloading an MP3 from the Internet in viewDidLoad(). That means that tests performed when the computer is offline will fail.

Later on, we'll be removing that code, and callers will set ViewController's URL themselves. At that point, it would be better if the tests provided a known-good MP3 in the Xcode project itself. That way, the test could get a URL of this embedded file (see the Bundle documentation if you want to know how this works) and set that on playerVC prior to doing asserts or checking expectations. That way, we would remove a big external dependency and have a greater confidence in our tests.

User Interface Testing

It's great that we now have the ability to automatically test our app's logic. If we inadvertently make a breaking change, or our assumptions get broken (like if our sample podcast feed disappears), then we'll discover it the next time we run our test suite.

However, one thing we haven't really exposed to testing is the user interface. If we broke the connection from a button to the method it calls, we would never know, because we test the method, not the button itself.

Testing user interfaces has always been really hard to do, which is why a lot of people don't do it! The testing culture is much stronger among web developers—where you can always post the same HTTP request and scrape the HTML you get back from a server—than among desktop and mobile developers.

Fortunately, Xcode has a powerful tool for testing user interfaces themselves. Let's try it out.

Recording a UI Test

We currently test the functionality of the Play/Pause button, but not the button tap itself. Let's see how we can make sure that it's still connected and does what it's supposed to.

In the Project Navigator, notice that after the PragmaticPodcastsTests group we've been working with, Xcode also created a PragmaticPodcastsUITests group, with a single file, PragmaticPodcastsUITests.swift. Select this file and notice that it has setUp() and tearDown() methods like before, although their contents are different from what we saw in the regular unit test files. There's also an empty testExample() method, with a comment to get us started:

testing/PragmaticPodcasts-6-3/PragmaticPodcastsUITests/PragmaticPodcastsUITests.swift
```swift
func testExample() {
  // Use recording to get started writing UI tests.
  // Use XCTAssert and related functions to verify your tests
  // produce the correct results.
}
```

"Use recording"? How do we do that? Notice that at the bottom of the content pane (either above the Debug Area or at the bottom of the window if that's now showing), we have a circular red button. That, as you might suspect, is the Record button. To see how it works, put the cursor inside the testExample() method and start a blank line. Now click the Record button.

This launches the app in the Simulator. After a few seconds, once the app is up and running, tap the Play button. If the Xcode window isn't covered up, you may notice that code is being written inside the testExample() for us. Once the audio starts playing, click the Pause button. A few more lines of code get written for us. This is actually all we need to record for now, so click the Record button again to stop the UI recording. Then stop the Simulator with the Stop button on the top toolbar as usual.

Take a look inside testExample() to see what the recorder has written for us:

testing/PragmaticPodcasts-6-3/PragmaticPodcastsUITests/PragmaticPodcastsUITests.swift
```swift
Line 1 func testExample() {
     2   XCUIDevice.shared().orientation = .portrait
     3   let app = XCUIApplication()
     4   app.buttons["Play"].tap()
     5   app.buttons["Pause"].tap()
     6 }
```

The code here is recognizable as Swift, even if the classes are not. And that makes sense because we're not writing code to create the UI here; we're using code to discover what's on screen at a given time. The XCUIApplication object created on line 3 is a sort of proxy that lets us discover what's going on in the app. We'll use this to query for onscreen UI elements.

On line 4, our recorded code asks the XCUIApplication for an array of all buttons currently on screen, and to find the one called Play. The first part of this expression is of type XCUIElement, and it works as a sort of query. If it resolves to exactly one object, we can programmatically tap() it. If there are zero or more than one matching buttons, an error occurs and our test fails. So already we have a test that would notice if we accidentally deleted the Play/Pause button or gave it the wrong title.

This is a nifty way to discover our UI at runtime, and if our app had different controls to interact with yet, recording would show us how to access them. We can also write this logic by hand, or clean it up after the recorder is finished: for example, we can access buttons by index rather than by name, if that makes more sense to us.

Writing UI Tests

Still, this isn't much of a test; there's no condition that we're testing to be true or false. If we click the diamond next to testExample() or run all the tests with ⌘U, this test will pass, because there's nothing to make it fail. So let's figure out what we want to test.

Let's think about our previous unit tests: when we tap the Play button, its title should change to Pause. So that's something we can test for after performing the tap.

This is pretty easy: the XCUIElement expressions that the recorder creates for us have an exists property, which is true if there is one and only one matching view. So, once we tap, it should then be possible to find exactly one button named Pause. And to make a real test of it, we can just XCTAssert() that it exists.

Start a new test method called testUI_WhenPlayTapped_UpdatesTitles(), and implement it as follows:

```
testing/PragmaticPodcasts-6-3/PragmaticPodcastsUITests/PragmaticPodcastsUITests.swift
Line 1  func testUI_WhenPlayTapped_UpdatesTitles() {
2    let app = XCUIApplication()
3    app.buttons["Play"].tap()
4    XCTAssertTrue(app.buttons["Pause"].exists)
5    XCTAssertTrue(app.staticTexts["CocoaConf001.m4a"].exists)
6  }
```

Line 2 is the same as in the recorded test: it creates a local variable, app, to represent the XCUIApplication app-proxy object. Line 3 is also the same as before, and programmatically taps the Play button for us.

The magic is on line 4. We ask the app to look through its array of buttons for one titled Pause, and then to call the exists() method to provide a true/false value for whether we found the button. By wrapping this in XCTAssertTrue(), we have a test: if the button isn't found, the test fails. For good measure, line 5 does a similar assert with expected contents of the title label (notice that we access labels via the staticTexts member of XCTUiApplication).

And if this test method does fail, that means we have to figure out what went wrong—perhaps we broke the action to get the tap, the outlet to access the button, or our nifty KVO code that actually changes the button title. At any rate, if we do break something in the storyboard or the code, we'll find out about it as soon as we run the UI tests again.

Click the diamond next to testUI_WhenPlayTapped_UpdatesTitles(). We see the app run in the Simulator, and back in Xcode we see the green checkmark that means our test passed.

◈   `func testUI_WhenPlayTapped_UpdatesTitles() {`

One thing to notice about UI tests is that they really run in the simulated app as-is, as opposed to the unit tests where we loaded a specific scene from the storyboard. That's actually a good thing. Once we have multiple scenes—a table of podcasts, a table of episodes, and then the player—we would want to tap the same controls that go between those scenes to make sure that those user interactions work as expected.

> ## Xcode Testing and Continuous Integration
>
> Obviously, it would be burdensome if the only way to run unit tests and UI tests was through the Xcode UI. That would be completely impractical for automated testing, in which the tests are run automatically by a server, usually after a developer has checked in his or her changes.
>
> Fortunately, our tests aren't limited by the Xcode UI. Xcode provides a command-line executable, xcodebuild, which can perform many of Xcode's functions programmatically, including building projects and running their tests. Combined with a scripting language, this gives us all we need to run our tests automatically. In fact, this is how popular continuous integration systems like Jenkins interface with Xcode.
>
> For those who prefer an all-Apple solution, OS X Server offers *Xcode bots*, which are Xcode-savvy services for building and testing Xcode projects. There's more information about bots in the "Xcode Server and Continuous Integration Guide" in the Xcode documentation.

Running and Testing on the Device

Automating our tests and testing the user interface will eliminate a lot of problems that can come up in our app. But we still have another big blind spot: what if the app behaves differently in the iOS Simulator app than it would on a real device?

This is not idle speculation. Macs are often (but not always!) more powerful than iOS devices, so apps can run faster in the Simulator than on real iOS hardware. A mouse or trackpad pointer is more precise than a finger touch, so running in the Simulator might also blind us to usability problems in the app. And there is some functionality that simply doesn't exist in the Simulator: the Simulator won't pretend that the Mac's built-in webcam is either of the iPhone cameras, and we can't tilt our laptop back and forth to test motion-sensing code.

To have full confidence in our app, we need to run it on the device. Let's close out the chapter by doing that.

Preparing the Device

To start with, we need an iOS device running the current version of iOS, since this is what our app expects to run on. If your device is running something older, you can go to the app target, find the iOS Deployment Target under Build Properties, and set that to a lower version than the default.

Connect the device to the Mac with its USB cable. The first time you do this, Xcode may present a dialog asking if you want to use the device for development; be sure to approve this.

Once the device is connected, it will appear in the scheme selector above the various simulated devices, but as being "unavailable." Running on the device will take a little more work than just plugging in the cable.

Preparing a Developer Account

Apple doesn't let just anyone run anything on a device. Prior to Xcode 7 and iOS 9, putting our own code on an iOS device required being a member of the developer program. That's a bridge we'll cross much later (in Chapter 12, *Publishing and Maintaining the App*, on page 201), but in the meantime, it's now possible to get our app running on our device with just a little fuss.

To put an app on a device, Apple wants to know who we are and what we're doing. That's always been the case; what's different in the last few years is that they'll let pretty much anyone do it, not just paid-up members. Either way, the first step is to sign into Xcode. Open Xcode's preferences (⌘,) and select the Accounts tab. Click the + to add an Apple ID, and sign in with your credentials (the same ones used for the Mac App Store to download Xcode in the first place).

Just signing in isn't enough. Select the project in the Project Navigator, select the PragmaticPodcasts target, and click the target's General tab. There, you'll see a warning that there are "No code signing identities found." *Code signing* is the process of using cryptographic techniques to provably verify that a known developer is the one installing the app to the device, and therefore the operation can be allowed. Fortunately, we don't have to do the underlying math; there's a handy Fix Issue button. Go ahead and click it.

If all goes well, this will use our Apple ID from the Accounts tab to download and set up the needed credentials to allow us to put apps on the device. We'll talk more about how these actually work later, in Chapter 12, *Publishing and Maintaining the App*, on page 201. Fixing the issue may also make you choose a Development Team; there should only be one, with your Apple ID name followed by (Personal Team), so use that.

When the issues are resolved, the warning in the target about signing identities becomes a pop-up with a choice of Team. Also, the device will be available in the scheme selector, without the (Not Available).

Xcode and iOS Versions

 If your device still isn't available in the scheme selector, make sure you have the latest release of Xcode. Releases of iOS and Xcode usually go out in lock-step, even for point releases, so you need Xcode 8.1 to run on iOS 10.1, Xcode 8.2 to run on iOS 10.2, and so on.

Select this destination and run the app as usual (be sure to unlock the screen first, since Xcode can't enter your PIN for you). After a short delay in which Xcode rebuilds the app for the device's CPU (which is different than the Simulator's, after all), it copies the app across the USB cable, onto the device.

The first time you run it, there's one more wrinkle: Xcode trusts you and the device, but the device may not trust you. This shows up as an Xcode error sheet saying "process launch failed; Security." If this happens, open the Settings app on the device itself, and select General. You'll see a new section called Profiles & Device Management, and, within it, the section Developer App, which shows your Apple ID. Click this, and, on the screen that follows, tap to trust apps from your Apple ID, as shown in the figure.

With this last security issue resolved, running the app in Xcode will make it run on our device and behave just like before. At least we hope it does! If it doesn't, then we have a device-specific issue. And in cases where behavior differs between device and Simulator, the device always wins, since that's what our users will run the app on. In fact, it's so important to focus on the device that the testing techniques we've learned throughout the chapter all work on the device, too; just choose a device in the scheme selector before running the test.

What We've Learned

In this chapter, we took a break from adding features to our very simple app, and adopted techniques to make sure those features keep working.

We have explored Apple's built-in unit testing suite, XCTest, for testing both application logic and user interface. We also saw how to test the user interface and how it interacts with our code. And to top it off, we ran the app on the device, so we'll see exactly what the users will when they run it on their iPhones and iPads.

You now have the tools to go forth into the world and test your apps so that you can be sure your users won't have to deal with a crash or erroneous behavior.

Looking at our app, though, there's one piece of the player UI we've never really done anything with: the current time display. We could have implemented that with a Timer, which we learned about in this chapter, to check on the playback time and update the label. But there's actually a more elegant approach to handling asynchronicity, and that's what we'll focus on in the next chapter.

CHAPTER 7

Handling Asynchronicity with Closures

Our player UI can play and pause audio, update the button label based on whether audio is playing or paused, and show a title. And in the last chapter, we exposed that functionality to unit testing, to make sure it keeps working. But there's one part of the UI we still haven't implemented: the label that shows the current playback time.

Thing is, time can be a real challenge for software. It's easy to write a series of instructions and have them executed in order. It's harder when things naturally happen at unpredictable times that we have to respond to, or when we want something to happen in the future, or if we have to respond to something and then do something.

We've seen two of iOS's older approaches to this: Timers to do work in the future (possibly repeatedly), and key-value observing (KVO) to respond to changes in supported properties. But both require somewhat clunky schemes to call back to designated objects, with special conventions for method names or parameter lists. It would be nice if there were something cleaner, so we could just say, "Every half-second, *do this*," or "When something special happens, *do that*."

Lucky for us, this cleaner approach—a Swift type that itself contains executable code—already exists, and we're going to put it to work in this chapter.

Understanding Closures

So let's think about the time display for our media player. Whenever media is playing, we want to periodically get the current playback time, and show that in the label as minutes and seconds...maybe hours, too, for those podcasts that won't wrap it up already. (You know who you are!)

In *Using a Timer*, on page 102, we learned how to use the Timer for our asyn-chronous tests, and it seems like that would work here, too. We could create a timer to periodically check on the player, get its current time, and update the label. That's fine, of course, although maybe a little wasteful if it keeps running when playback is paused, and there's extra code to write if we have to create a new timer when we start playing and destroy it when we pause.

Thinking about it, though, we didn't need a timer to change the Play/Pause button: that was based on an event we could observe from the player itself with KVO. So it's reasonable to think that AVPlayer could offer something appropriate for a playback time display.

If we look in the AVPlayer documentation, we find there's a discussion called "Timed State Observations," which says:

> KVO works well for general state observations, but isn't intended for observing continuously changing state like the player's time. AVPlayer provides two methods to observe time changes:

See? Just what we need! The section goes on to explain there are two methods to add these kinds of time observers—one for continuous observation, and another just for specific times, like reaching the end of the playing item. The first is what we need, so follow the link to the documentation for addPeriodic-TimeObserver(forInterval:queue:using:). Now let's look at the declaration to see how we call it:

```
func addPeriodicTimeObserver(forInterval interval: CMTime,
  queue: DispatchQueue?,
  using block: @escaping (CMTime) -> Void) -> Any
```

What...the...heck?

OK, let's step back. This takes three arguments, and the first two are easy enough to understand: a CMTime with external name forInterval, and an optional DispatchQueue (whatever that is!) called queue. And the return type is an Any, so that's fine.

Obviously, the weird part is that third parameter, with external name using and internal name block. What's weird is its type: @escaping (CMTime) -> Void.

Set aside the @escaping for a moment, and consider what's left: (CMTime) -> Void. With the types on both sides of the arrow, that looks like a function or method declaration, right? Parameter types on the left, return type on the right?

That's pretty much what it is, in fact. This is the syntax for a *closure*, a self-contained block of functionality. Closures can take arguments, do work, and return a value...just like the functions and methods we're already used to.

But it's not that closures are a variation on functions; in fact, it's the other way around. Swift functions and methods are just special cases of closures! A closure is just some code represented as an object, and thus a function is a closure with a name, and then a method is a function associated with an instance of some type.

But closures are important because, as a Swift type, they can also be passed as parameters, stored in variables, and returned by functions and methods. We can pretty much do the same things with closures as we already do with Ints, Strings, and objects.

And using it as a type is what addPeriodicTimeObserver() is offering: we pass in a closure to be executed periodically—say, once every half-second—and the code in that closure gets repeatedly executed on that schedule. We don't have to use some special method name and parameter list like KVO's observeValue(forKeyPath:of:change:object:), and as a bonus, AVPlayer only calls this method when the media is playing.

Closures are perfect for our time label, so let's see how to use them.

Coding with Closures

To try out closures, we are going to call addPeriodicTimeObserver(forInterval:queue: using:), passing in a closure to call repeatedly when our podcast is playing. There's a little housekeeping we have to do for this approach: the docs say that the return value is an object of type Any that we will eventually provide to removeTimeObserver() to stop our updating. So, with the other properties near the top of ViewController.swift, add a property where we can hold on to this object. It'll need to be an optional, since we won't actually create it until long after init() is done.

closures/PragmaticPodcasts-7-1/PragmaticPodcasts/ViewController.swift
```
private var playerPeriodicObserver : Any?
```

We already cleaned up the player's KVO observer for the Play/Pause button in deinit(), so let's clean up this playerPeriodicObserver there, too, by adding the following:

closures/PragmaticPodcasts-7-1/PragmaticPodcasts/ViewController.swift
```
if let oldObserver = playerPeriodicObserver {
  player?.removeTimeObserver(oldObserver)
}
```

Notice that since playerPeriodicObserver is an optional, and removeTimeObserver() takes a non-optional parameter, we carefully unwrap with an if let.

A Simple Closure

Now we're ready to add the periodic observer. We'll do that in set(url:), where we currently create the player and set up the observer. For the moment, let's just log a message in the closure, before we worry about updating the UI.

```
closures/PragmaticPodcasts-7-1/PragmaticPodcasts/ViewController.swift
Line 1  let interval = CMTime(seconds: 0.25, preferredTimescale: 1000)
    2   playerPeriodicObserver =
    3     player?.addPeriodicTimeObserver(forInterval: interval,
    4                                     queue: nil,
    5                                     using:
    6       { currentTime in
    7         print("current time \(currentTime.seconds)")
    8     })
```

Because addPeriodicTimeObserver() wants a CMTime to indicate how often we want our closure to run, we create one on line 2. Without getting too deeply into the Core Media framework, the idea of a CMTime instance is that it uses a timescale to represent how accurately it's keeping time. We don't need it to be super-accurate for a UI display, so we'll just update every quarter-second, keeping track of time in 1000ths of a second.

Lines 2-8 are one big call to addPeriodicTimeObserver(). Line 3 specifies the 0.25-second interval we just created. For the queue on line 4, the docs say we can pass nil for the default behavior, so that's what we'll do for now.

Finally, we have the using parameter on line 5. This takes our closure, which runs from lines 6 to 8. To write a closure, we use the syntax:

```
{ paramName1, paramName2, ... -> returnType in code... }
```

Simply put, the contents of a closure are a list of parameters, the arrow with a return type (omitted if none), the in keyword, and then executable code, all inside curly braces. We can choose whatever names we like for the parameters; in this case, the actual type of currentTime was defined as CMTime back in addPeriodicTimeObserver()'s declaration of its own using parameter.

So the closure receives a single parameter that we've called currentTime. To keep things simple, we'll just print() it, in seconds, on line 7.

Run the app, and click the Play button. In the console area at the bottom of the Xcode window—bring it up with ⇧⌘C or View > Debug Area > Activate Console, if it doesn't appear automatically—you'll see the log messages appear every 0.25 seconds or so as shown in the figure at the top of the next page. Hit Pause, and they'll stop, and then resume when you tap Play again.

```
current time 0.0
current time 0.0
current time 0.250194205
current time 0.501078072
current time 0.750126422
current time 1.001095203
current time 1.251089769
current time 1.50009547
```

So, we're off and running, literally. We now have a simple block of code that will be called every 0.25 seconds when the podcast episode is playing. As a bonus, there's far less boilerplate than we had from setting up callback methods for KVO or Timers. Another advantage in Swift is that a closure can be created pretty much anywhere—in free functions, or methods on enums or structs, for example, whereas the callback approaches we saw earlier only work with full-blown objects.

Updating the Label from the Closure

Now we're ready to have our closure actually update the label with the current playback time. First things first, though: we don't currently have an outlet to the label, and we need one in order to change its text from code. We'll wire up a connection just like we did with the other UI elements.

Switch to Main.storyboard and select the 0:00 label. Bring up the Assistant Editor with the "two rings" toolbar button, or ⌥⌘↩. Make sure that ViewController.swift comes up as the Automatic selection in the right pane, and then Control-drag from the 0:00 label in the storyboard to the properties in the code. When you end the drag, a pop-up appears to fill in the details; give it the name timeLabel, and make sure the connection is "outlet," the type is UILabel, and the storage is "strong," and then click Connect.

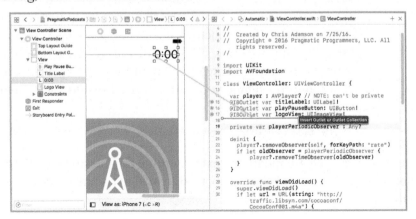

Now we're ready to populate this label. Switch back to the Standard Editor (⌘↵) and return to ViewController.swift. Go down to the closure in set(url:). We could write all our label-updating code inside the closure, but we're already indented pretty far, so putting a bunch of code here is going to be kind of ugly. Instead, replace the print() line with the following method call:

closures/PragmaticPodcasts-7-1/PragmaticPodcasts/ViewController.swift
```
self.updateTimeLabel(currentTime)
```

For the moment, this is going to bring up an error because we haven't written the updateTimeLabel() method yet. But, more importantly, notice how we use self here. The closure has access to any variables currently in scope when the closure is created. Since self is available anywhere in the class, the closure can see it. Other variables local to set(url:), like url or interval, could be called too, if they were useful inside the closure. We call this *capturing* the variable.

Capture and Escape

The idea of a closure "capturing" a variable also explains the @escaping we saw back in the definition of addPeriodicTimeObserver(). This keyword is a signal that the closure will be held on to by the method or function receiving the closure, which in turn means that variables referenced by the closure will live on past the lifespan of the function call that receives the closure—addPeriodic-TimeObserver() in this case—even a local variable that would otherwise disappear.

There's a corresponding @noescape that means variables captured by the closure *won't* be used after the function call that takes the closure. This lets the compiler make certain optimizations that aren't possible if the variable is going to hang around.

@escaping is by far the more common scenario, and it has an important side effect. When we refer to properties or methods from inside the closure, we explicitly have to use self, as we do here, to acknowledge that we know we're capturing self. Forgetting self in a closure is an easy mistake to make, but it's also easy to correct: you'll see an error telling you that you need to add self to "make capture semantics explicit."

🔘 Call to method 'updateTimeLabel' in closure requires explicit 'self.' to make capture semantics explicit

---

Now let's get this label to update its text by writing the missing updateTimeLabel() method. There's nothing closure-y about this; it's just some math and string formatting:

```
     closures/PragmaticPodcasts-7-1/PragmaticPodcasts/ViewController.swift
Line 1  private func updateTimeLabel(_ currentTime: CMTime) {
    2    let totalSeconds = currentTime.seconds
    3    let minutes = Int(totalSeconds / 60)
    4    let seconds = Int(totalSeconds.truncatingRemainder(dividingBy: 60))
    5    let secondsString = seconds >= 10 ? "\(seconds)" : "0\(seconds)"
    6    timeLabel.text = "\(minutes):\(secondsString)"
    7  }
```

To format the string, we convert the CMTime into a total number of seconds, and then divvy that into minutes and seconds. The minutes are easy (just divide by 60), but the seconds are a little more obscure: Swift 3 eliminates the modulo operator (%) seen in many other languages, and instead requires us to use a method called truncatingRemainder(), as seen on line 4. With minutes and seconds computed, we figure out if the seconds need a leading "0" (line 5), and then set timeLabel's text to a colon-separated string.

And that's it! Run the app again, tap Play, and watch as the time counter counts up along with our playback.

We know from our earlier log statements that it doesn't bother updating when we're paused, and if we had a slider to skip around the podcast, the label would stay updated, since it's getting a new currentTime every quarter-second.

Care and Feeding of Closures

We're going to see closures in several more places in the iOS SDK, so it's a good idea to make sure we're fully comfortable with them before we move on.

Trailing Closure Syntax

One little change we can make right off the bat will make our code easier to read. In Swift, if the last argument to a method or function is a closure, we can omit its label and put it directly *after* the closing parenthesis of the declaration. In other words, if we start with this:

```
function(param1: foo, param2: { bar in
  ...
})
```

We can instead write:

```
function(param1: foo) { bar in
  ...
}
```

This is much easier to read and eliminates the weird trailing }) when the closure and parameter list end. We'll use this syntax from here on out.

Closures and Memory Management

Our code has a more serious and very subtle problem. Back in *The Swift Programming Language*, on page 11, we discussed how Swift deals with the memory management of reference types—as opposed to structs, enums, and the numeric types, which are all value types—with a system of "reference counting."

The way reference counting works is that each object is created with a reference count of 1. Objects are freed from memory if their count ever goes to 0. For example, if the code that creates an object doesn't do anything with it by the time it goes out of scope, the reference count will go down by one, reach 0, and the object will be destroyed.

For throwaway objects referred to by local variables within a method, that's fine. And when we want to hold onto an object for longer, we can assign it to a property. The property assignment increments the reference count, so it stays around as long as the property needs it to. Adding the object to a collection like an array also increments the reference count, so it works the same way.

It's a pretty good system, because it's faster and more deterministic than the popular system of garbage collection used in other languages: memory can be reclaimed immediately when it's not needed, and the CPU doesn't have to go out and look for unreferenced objects it can free.

But there's a fairly big problem with reference counting: what happens when two objects refer to each other? Consider the diagram pictured here, where object A has a reference count of 1, because some other object has it as a property or in a collection. If object A creates object B and holds on to it with a property, B's reference count is 1. If B then adds a reference back to A, A's reference count becomes 2.

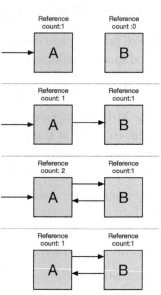

Now imagine the object originally referring to A removes its reference (or is freed from memory itself). With nothing else referring to A, we should expect it to be cleaned up, which will nil out any properties as it deinits, thereby freeing up B. However, *this can never happen*. A cannot be freed because it still has a reference count of 1, and that's because it is a property of B. But B cannot be freed either, because A has a reference to it, so B's reference count will never go to 0.

This is called a *reference cycle*, and it is a serious problem because it means our app will consume more and more memory for no good reason, since we're unable to free objects that we don't actually want around anymore.

We've unwittingly walked into this situation ourselves: player is a property of our ViewController, and it has the closure we passed to it for the periodic observer. However, that closure has a reference to self, which is the ViewController. Therefore, reference counting can't free either object: ViewController forces the player to remain in memory, and the closure we passed to the player keeps the ViewController in memory.

The way to break a retain cycle is to have different kinds of references. In Swift, these are *strong* and *weak*, where strong is the default and what we've been using all along. The difference is that a weak reference *does not increment the reference count*. It still points to the other object, but it doesn't force it to stick around in memory. If the referred-to object has its reference count go to 0, the weak reference just becomes nil.

Let's think about this in our A and B example. A creates B as before, but B creates a weak reference back to A. This means that A's reference count remains at 1, even after B adds it as a (weak) property. So when the one object that was referring to A drops its reference, A's reference count becomes 0. Because it's 0, A can now be freed from memory. In A's deinit(), all of its properties are nil'ed out, reducing their reference counts by 1. That means B's reference count is now 0, and it, too, can be freed.

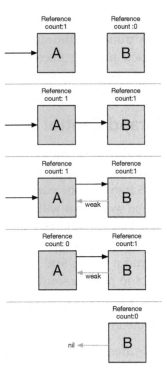

So how do we fix our code? For a property, we can declare it to be weak simply by putting the weak keyword before the var, just like we do with other annotations like @IBOutlet. But for us, the problem is the self that is captured by the closure, so it's not clear where we declare it to be weak.

The solution is that the closure syntax also allows us to provide a *closure list*, indicating the memory-management for variables being captured by the closure. This list appears in square braces, prior to the closure's parameters, like this:

```
{ [weak capturedVar1, ...] paramName1, ... -> returnType in code... }
```

So combining this fix, and the trailing closure syntax mentioned at the beginning of this section, here's the final version of how we create the closure and pass it to player:

closures/PragmaticPodcasts-7-1/PragmaticPodcasts/ViewController.swift
```
playerPeriodicObserver =
  player?.addPeriodicTimeObserver(forInterval: interval,
                                  queue: nil)
  { [weak self] currentTime in
    self?.updateTimeLabel(currentTime)
}
```

Notice that inside the closure, our reference to self now has the optional-chaining operator (?). That's because making self a weak variable necessarily forces it to become an optional—the main selling point of a weak variable is that it can become nil if it has to, and "can become nil" is the very definition of an optional.

And with this change, our memory leak is now fixed. It wouldn't have caused any trouble in the single-screen app we have now, but later on when we create a new player screen each time we play an episode, we would be piling up these scenes in memory, one after another, with no way of freeing them up...possibly leading to slow-downs or even a crash.

Grand Central Dispatch

Now that we know closures, we know how to wrap up little blocks of code and pass them around as objects. Beyond AV Foundation, we'll find that many iOS frameworks work with closures. One of the most popular idioms is to do some work that will take an unpredictable amount of time, and then when it's done, it can call a closure we provide to finish up. This is the *completion handler* pattern, and it's frequently used for things like network access: like "Send a tweet, and when it goes through, call my closure that updates the UI and plays a sound."

This also raises an interesting question: *just who's executing our closures anyway?*

Closures play an important role in solving one of the biggest problems on a platform like the iPhone and iPad. All currently available iOS devices have multiple CPU cores, meaning they can perform multiple tasks at the same time. However, we often think of our code as running in a single straight line of execution. If all our code runs in lock-step order, it seems it'll have to be on one CPU core. So what's the other one going to do?

In iOS (and macOS, for that matter), Apple's solution is a system called *Grand Central Dispatch.* The idea of GCD is that there are multiple processing *queues* that take units of work to execute, in order. As a low-level system technology, iOS can examine how many cores the device has and how busy they are, and mete out the work evenly, so we don't tax one core while leaving the other idling.

And the units of work that the queues manage…are closures!

GCD Queues

Consider the following figure:

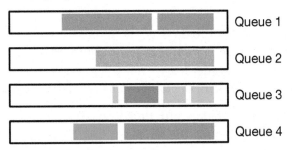

This is a hypothetical arrangement of GCD queues. There don't have to be exactly as many as there are CPU cores. In fact, an app often has twenty or more queues by default. In the diagram, each colored block is code to be executed, and they flow through the queues left-to-right. Some queues are specific to background tasks like network I/O or audio, while others are utility queues that take whatever work they're given. So imagine the work our app is doing is represented by the blue blocks on queue 1. And then the blocks with other colors are tasks the system performs by itself: downloading mail, playing music, and what have you.

But let's also say we have some extra work we want performed in parallel with our app's main tasks. That's the blue block on queue 4. We've actually already been exposed to this idea of choosing a queue to perform additional work for our app. When we called the AVPlayer's addPeriodicTimeObserver() to add the closure to update the time label, the second parameter was called queue. The documentation says:

> A *serial* dispatch queue onto which block should be enqueued. Passing a concurrent queue is not supported and will result in undefined behavior.

> If you pass NULL, the main queue (obtained using dispatch_get_main_queue()) is used.

There's a little jargon here to untangle. A *serial* queue always executes its closures in order, and only one can be running at a time. With a *concurrent* queue, it's possible two or more of its closures could be running at once.

Then there's the *main queue*. This is super important, because the main queue is responsible for all UI in an iOS app. The main queue's only job is to look for user input (touches, rotations, or shakes) and update the user interface. It runs this loop over and over, many times a second, so it's vitally important that we don't do long-running, slow work on the main queue, which would appear to the user as slowdown or janky animation, as needed refreshes of the UI get delayed.

It's possible to take this advice too far in the wrong direction. For instructional purposes, we're going to do exactly that.

Bad Idea Department

 What we're about to do is going to make our app buggy. We'll fix it in the next section. But if you want to take a pass on coding these steps and just leave everything working as-is, that's totally fine. We'll revert these changes at the end of the chapter anyway.

Passing nil for the queue makes our timed observations occur on the main queue, the one that refreshes the UI. Let's say, in our naive can-do spirit, that we want to run our closure on a different queue. We can totally do that; we just have to specify the queue to use, either by creating our own GCD queue or by asking iOS to give us a utility queue.

To get a utility queue, we call Dispatch.queue and pass in a *quality-of-service* argument. This argument is of type DispatchQoS and ranges from high-priority values like userInteractive to "we'll get around to it" priorities like background.

Let's try it! We just change the value we pass to queue, but to help find it in the code, here's the entire call that sets up the periodic observer on the player.

closures/PragmaticPodcasts-7-2/PragmaticPodcasts/ViewController.swift

```
Line 1 playerPeriodicObserver =
    2   player?.addPeriodicTimeObserver(forInterval: interval,
    3                                   queue: DispatchQueue.global(qos: .default))
    4   { [weak self] currentTime in
    5     self?.updateTimeLabel(currentTime)
    6 }
```

The only difference is line 3, where we use Dispatch.queue() to get a default-quality queue.

Now, we optimistically believe this will make our app faster and better, because we've taken work off the main queue. Try running it and see what happens when you press the Play/Pause button.

Well, that didn't go so well, did it?

Instead of seeing any visible improvement in our app, it is clearly *worse*. The time label goes several seconds without updating. Worse, we are now seeing errors in the console pane (⇧⌘C), and they're pretty scary looking:

```
2016-08-29 20:02:58.211 PragmaticPodcasts[13002:5709690] This application is
modifying the autolayout engine from a background thread after the engine
was accessed from the main thread. This can lead to engine corruption and
weird crashes.
```

First, hats off to the Apple engineer who wrote this log statement. "Weird crashes" is exactly what we want to avoid in our app. (Weird Crashes would also be a great name for an all-developer rock band or karaoke posse, but that's another story.)

But what have we done, and how do we fix it?

GCD and the Main Queue

When we said earlier that the main queue is responsible for handling user-input events and updating the user interface, we left out a key caveat: it is the *only* queue that should *ever* do that stuff.

The UI can be fast because its code can assume that it won't be accessed by two closures running concurrently on different queues. We just broke that assumption.

So, the rule is clear: *never touch the UI from a queue other than main.* That means no setting text on labels, no setting titles on buttons, no changing background colors or font sizes or anything like that, unless you're on the main queue.

And usually, it's not a problem. When a button is tapped and calls our code, that's on the main queue, because it's the main queue that's looking for button taps and other touch events in the first place.

But we also mentioned previously that there are some iOS APIs that do weird things with closures, like making a network call and running our closure when it's done. Those APIs don't use the main queue, because they don't want to block the main queue on something that takes a long time like network access or file I/O.

In a case like that, there must be a way to safely update the UI, even if our code isn't on the main queue. That's the situation we're in now, so let's look at the solution.

Along with allowing us to create queues or look up system queues, GCD also lets us send work to certain queues. The DispatchQueue type has several related methods named async() or sync() (or variants on these terms) that take a closure that uses no parameters and doesn't have a return value. This closure is then executed on that queue. The difference is that sync-style calls put the work on the other queue and wait for it to finish, while the async sends the work to the other queue and then unblocks the current queue immediately.

The following figure shows this arrangement, with a global queue using Dispatch.main.async() to put work onto the main queue.

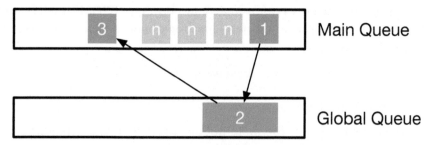

The trick of moving work off of and back onto the main queue involves three steps:

1. Our app's code ("1") is running on the main queue and creates a closure ("2") for a background task, which it puts on a global queue. The main queue can then immediately continue to start processing user input again or performing other app code (the blocks marked "n").

2. The code on the global queue runs for however long it needs; this is why putting work on other queues is great for long-running and unpredictable things like downloading data from the network. When it's done and needs to update the UI, it creates another closure ("3") and sends it back to the main queue.

3. The UI-updating closure reaches the front of the main queue and is executed, allowing it to update the UI.

So with that in mind, we'll rewrite how we set up our periodic observer. In this version, our code to create the periodic observer is "1" in the diagram, the observer itself is "2," and updating the time label is "3."

```
     closures/PragmaticPodcasts-7-2/PragmaticPodcasts/ViewController.swift
Line 1  playerPeriodicObserver =
    2     player?.addPeriodicTimeObserver(forInterval: interval,
    3                                     queue: DispatchQueue.global(qos: .default))
    4     { [weak self] currentTime in
    5       DispatchQueue.main.async {
    6         self?.updateTimeLabel(currentTime)
    7       }
    8  }
```

The change here is lines 5-7, and it's really simple. All we've done is take our one line of UI code (the call to self?.updateTimeLabel()) and wrap it in a brand-new closure that we then send to the main queue. We do that by identifying the queue we want (Dispatch.main) and then calling its async() method.

Notice we're again using the trailing-closure syntax; this could also be written as Dispatch.main.async(execute: { ... }), but that's a lot uglier.

Anyway, the point is we have addressed our bug by doing right by the main queue; our modification to the timeLabel is now explicitly performed on the main queue. Run it again and everything works smoothly, with no pauses and no scary error messages.

Of course, this was a case of getting ourselves in trouble just to prove a point. The approach we used in the beginning of the chapter was the right one: send nil for the queue, and AVPlayer will do the work of running our closure on the main queue (or, in terms of the diagram, "3" is put directly on the main queue by the AVPlayer and there is no closure "2"). Feel free to undo the changes we made in this section to get back to that point. The downloadable sample code for all later chapters will do so as well.

Where this technique is truly useful is in dealing with long-running tasks like network access. It's a very common pattern to download data on a background queue, let that take however long it needs (without blocking the main queue), and, only when it's done, create another closure to update the UI and send it back to the main queue. That's exactly what we'll be doing in the next few chapters.

What We've Learned

In this chapter, we looked at the last of the major Swift types: closures. A closure is a type that contains executable code, capturing any variables that are in scope at the time of the closure's creation and are used in its code.

With the ability to treat executable code as just another "thing" that we pass around in our app, we open up new ways to express ourselves, and allow ourselves to use powerful and cleaner asynchronous APIs in the iOS frameworks than were possible with callback-driven approaches like Timers and key-value observing.

We used a closure to update the player's time label at specific intervals, and also investigated UIKit's paramount rule about accessing the user interface only from the main GCD queue.

Now that we have a functional player scene and the ability to handle asynchronous code, it's time for our podcast app to start getting real. In the next chapter, we'll go out to the network, pull down real podcast feeds, and parse them into native Swift types.

CHAPTER 8

Loading and Parsing Network Data

All this time, we've sort of been working our podcast app backwards: instead of parsing a feed, finding episodes, and playing one, we started with the player. This gave us a chance to play around with building user interfaces, but now it's time to do the heavy lifting.

Think about what a podcast app does: it goes out to the network and fetches a list of episodes for one or more podcast feeds. Each of those must contain the metadata (titles, dates, etc.) and a URL for the audio. This metadata is in some structured form—by convention, podcasts use XML with a specific set of tags—so the client needs to *parse* this data, looking through the structured data for the parts it needs. From that, it can build a user interface showing the podcast feeds, and let the user interact with it.

In this chapter, our task will be to download a podcast feed from the network, and to parse its contents into a format that's convenient for our Swift code to work with. We'll see what the iOS SDKs offer for each of these tasks and what parts we have to handle ourselves.

Fetching Network Data

There are actually lots of APIs in iOS that can download data from a network connection. We're going to focus on one that is the most useful for our current app and is the preferred networking API for most use cases: the *URLSession*. Like its name suggests, it's a class for interacting with a URL for some period of time.

It's also very flexible: URLSession can download or upload data, can work with password-protected resources, can download to disk or store in memory, and caches data it has already fetched (provided the server indicates that data is still valid). With proper care and feeding, a URLSession can download data while the app is in the background, so the app will have fresh content when fore-grounded again.

We'll start using URLSession by downloading a podcast feed and inspecting its contents. That'll help us figure out what to do next.

Creating a New Class

We're going to create a new class to download and parse podcast feeds, which brings up a question we've put off for a long time: *How do we create new files in Xcode?* So far, everything we've done has gone in the ViewController.swift that controls the player UI.

Of course, as a common task, creating files in Xcode is easy. Select ViewController.swift in the Project Navigator (⌘1), just to ensure that our new file will be in the same group, under the PragmaticPodcasts folder icon. Now do File→New→File…, or just ⌘N. This brings up a sheet of file templates.

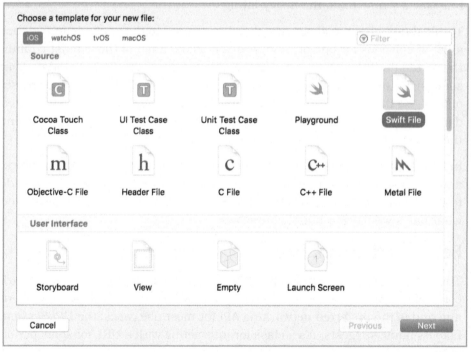

A set of small tabs at the top shows the SDK (iOS, watchOS, tvOS, macOS) we're browsing; make sure it says "iOS." The main part of the sheet shows different document types in sections: source files, user interface files, resources, and so on. Among source files, our most common options are to use a *Cocoa Touch Class*, if we know we're subclassing something built into the iOS SDK, or *Swift File*, if we want an empty Swift file. Choose "Swift File" and click Next. A file-navigation sheet will fly in to let us name the file and specify where it should be saved. The default location is fine, so just give it the name PodcastFeedParser.swift, and click Create.

This will create the file, add it to the PragmaticPodcasts group, and select it for editing. Since we asked for a plain Swift file, it's empty but for a header comment with a default copyright message, and the usual import Foundation directive.

Coding the New Class

So, how are we going to do this? We called our file PodcastFeedParser, so that implies we could take a podcast feed, parse its contents, and then let a caller access the results somehow. For technical reasons we'll explain later, this will need to be a class (rather than, say, a struct with methods or extensions). So let's start by stubbing out an empty class:

`network/PragmaticPodcasts-8-1/PragmaticPodcasts/PodcastFeedParser.swift`
```
class PodcastFeedParser {

}
```

Now, since we will always be working with podcast feed URLs, let's create an init() method that takes a URL:

`network/PragmaticPodcasts-8-1/PragmaticPodcasts/PodcastFeedParser.swift`
```
init(contentsOf url: URL) {
```

As a reminder, this syntax gives our init()'s one parameter an outer name of contentsOf and an inner name of url. So callers will use let parser = PodcastFeedParser (contentsOf:someURL), while inside the initializer, we'll work with url, not contentsOf. The idea is to make the inner and outer names appropriate to the contexts they're used in.

Now how do we do anything with the URL? This is where the URLSession comes in. Take a look at its documentation and see that it has two initializers: one that takes a configuration, delegate, and delegateQueue, and another that only takes the configuration. We'll use the easy one-parameter version for now, but do note the "queue" argument: this lets us determine which queue will execute any code we provide to the session. What's interesting is that the behavior here is the opposite of what we saw in *GCD and the Main Queue*, on page 125, with the AVPlayer; with URLSession, sending nil means "choose a *background* queue for me." That's good for keeping networking tasks from interfering with the main queue's UI work, but it does mean we won't be able to touch the UI directly in our network code.

Begin the init() implementation by creating the URLSession, like this:

network/PragmaticPodcasts-8-1/PragmaticPodcasts/PodcastFeedParser.swift
```
let urlSession = URLSession(configuration: .default)
```

This uses the default configuration for the session, as opposed to options better suited for things like downloading a URL directly to the filesystem.

Now that we have a session, what do we do with it? URLSessions let us create *tasks* to do things with them, like load data to memory or start streaming URL contents. There's a whole separate URLDataTask class that we could set up, but there's a convenience method that takes a URL to load and a closure to receive the results. The signature of the closure receives three optionals: a Data with the received data, an URLResponse with metadata like HTTP headers, and an Error if something went wrong.

Since the last argument is a closure, we can use the trailing-closure syntax to skip the closure's variable label (completionHandler) and just start writing the call like this:

network/PragmaticPodcasts-8-1/PragmaticPodcasts/PodcastFeedParser.swift
```
let dataTask = urlSession.dataTask(with: url) {dataMb, responseMb, errorMb in
```

Putting Mb, for "maybe," on the end of the variable names for the closure arguments is a convention we like for working with optionals, especially since the closure's parameter syntax doesn't include the type, so we don't have a visual reminder that the first argument is a Data?, not just Data, the non-optional type.

This closure will be called when all the data from the URL has been received, or if we fail with an error. Let's just consider the success case for now. If we used a valid URL and have network access, dataMb will be populated. Let's try unwrapping it and see what we get:

network/PragmaticPodcasts-8-1/PragmaticPodcasts/PodcastFeedParser.swift
```
  if let data = dataMb {
    print ("PodcastFeedParser got data: \(data)")
  }
}
```

That second closing curly brace ended our closure, completing the urlSession. dataTask(with: url){ … line. So we've used the URLSession to create a URLDataTask, and told the task what to do when it's done. All that's left now is to actually start the task. The superclass, URLSessionTask, defines all the start-stop sort of functionality, but there's not actually a "start" method. Instead, since a task may be pause()d, we use the corresponding resume() task to start or restart loading the URL. So we can finish our initializer like this:

network/PragmaticPodcasts-8-1/PragmaticPodcasts/PodcastFeedParser.swift
```
  dataTask.resume()
}
```

Now all we have to do is call this. Eventually, we're going to load the podcast feed when the app starts up, so instead of going back to the player class, switch to the file AppDelegate.swift. This file was provided for us by Xcode and contains methods that are called at various points in an app's life cycle: when it starts up, when it's backgrounded or foregrounded, when it receives a push notification, etc.

Find the method application(didFinishLaunchingWithOptions:), and before its final return true, add the following lines:

network/PragmaticPodcasts-8-1/PragmaticPodcasts/AppDelegate.swift
```
if let url = URL(string: "http://cocoaconf.libsyn.com/rss") {
  let parser = PodcastFeedParser(contentsOf: url)
}
```

This looks to see if the provided string is a valid URL—feel free to copy over the URL from your favorite podcasts in iTunes, if you like. If it is valid, we use the URL to initialize the PodcastFeedParser class we just created. For the moment, we're not going to do anything with parser, so don't worry when the little yellow warning icon pops up to tell you that the value isn't being used.

Run the app, and keep your eyes on the debug console (⇧⌘C). You should see our single print() line's output:

```
PodcastFeedParser got data: 100373 bytes
```

OK, cool! We're getting data! 100,373 bytes, in fact (or however much was in the URL you loaded). But it would be nice to actually see the podcast XML so we can figure out how to write the parser.

Data is not a type that says much about its contents. How could it? We could have downloaded text, images, media; all that Data says is that it has a bunch of bytes. Still, since we expect a podcast feed to have XML contents, we can try turning it into a string. There's a String initializer that takes a Data, plus a hint as to how the data is encoded (ASCII, UTF-8, etc.). So back in PodcastFeed-Parser.swift, replace the print() line with the following:

network/PragmaticPodcasts-8-1/PragmaticPodcasts/PodcastFeedParser.swift
```
if let dataString = String(data: data, encoding: .utf8) {
  print ("podcast feed contents: \(dataString)")
}
```

Run the app again, and you'll see a huge dump of XML in the console (we've cleaned it up a little for the book's formatting):

```
podcast feed contents: <?xml version="1.0" encoding="UTF-8"?>
<rss version="2.0" xmlns:atom="http://www.w3.org/2005/Atom"
  xmlns:cc="http://web.resource.org/cc/"
  xmlns:itunes="http://www.itunes.com/dtds/podcast-1.0.dtd"
  xmlns:media="http://search.yahoo.com/mrss/"
  xmlns:rdf="http://www.w3.org/1999/02/22-rdf-syntax-ns#">
  <channel>
    <atom:link href="http://cocoaconf.libsyn.com/rss" rel="self"
       type="application/rss+xml"/>
    <title>CocoaConf Podcast</title>
    <pubDate>Tue, 12 Jul 2016 15:43:32 +0000</pubDate>
    <lastBuildDate>Wed, 31 Aug 2016 05:50:12 +0000</lastBuildDate>
    <generator>Libsyn WebEngine 2.0</generator>
    <link>http://cocoaconf.com/podcast</link>
    <language>en-us</language>
```

...and so on. Great job! We've fetched our first podcast feed.

Now to figure out what's in it!

Mapping XML to Swift Types

This is all we need to do to download data from the network. Not bad, right? Problem is "data" is all we have. Literally, we've got a Data object that's about 100 KB. How is this going to do us any good?

What we need to do now is to figure out what parts of this data are useful for our app, and then after that, we can figure out how to get those parts out.

If we look at that String we made from the data, we can clearly see a structure:

- There are a number of tags at the beginning of the file that describe the podcast itself: its title; a link to the podcast's home page; some iTunes-specific metadata like itunes:image and itunes:author; and so on.

- After this, there is a series of item tags, each of which describes one episode. An item includes a title, more iTunes-unique tags like itunes:duration and itunes:explicit, and, most importantly, an enclosure tag that provides the URL of the audio, its MIME type (usually audio/mpeg), and a file duration.

Not everything in the feed is going to be useful to our app, even if we were making a really elaborate podcast client. Moreover, the current format—a single 100 KB Data object—is totally inconvenient for our application. We may be able to turn it into a String, but we're not going to search through a monster string every time we want to do something with the data.

We need to figure out what parts of this data are useful to our app, and then parse the XML to provide us with just that data, as easier-to-use Swift types.

What would be good to have? Let's start with the feed first, before we get individual episodes. The useful parts of the metadata—things we can imagine showing in a UI—include the title, description, author, artwork, and a link to the podcast's home page.

OK, let's make a Swift type for that. In the project navigator, use New File (⌘N) to create another new file, using the plain "Swift File" template. Name the file PodcastFeed.swift. We will only need to set these values once, while we're parsing them, so this type can be a struct, rather than a class that would be better suited for maintaining state.

Write the PodcastFeed type as follows:

network/PragmaticPodcasts-8-2/PragmaticPodcasts/PodcastFeed.swift

```
import Foundation

struct PodcastFeed {

    var title : String?
    var link : URL?
    var description : String?
    var iTunesAuthor : String?
    var iTunesImageURL : URL?

}
```

We've made all the members optional. Parsing will take a while, and we wouldn't want to have to hold on to all of these values somewhere else until we're ready to do an "init everything all at once" type of setup, which we'd have to do if they were concrete types. Besides, some podcasts might not populate some of these tags, particularly the iTunes-specific ones.

While we're at it, let's think of what we would want for a podcast episode. This will be both something we show in a list of episodes, and the object we pass to our player. So it obviously needs the URL from the enclosure, along with a title. Maybe the other fields will be useful later (like the publication date for sorting, or the duration if we're going to show that in the player UI). But for now, let's keep things really simple, and add more later if we need to. Create PodcastEpisode.swift, and write it like this:

network/PragmaticPodcasts-8-2/PragmaticPodcasts/PodcastEpisode.swift

```
import Foundation

struct PodcastEpisode {

    var title : String?
    var enclosureURL : URL?
    var iTunesDuration : String?
    var iTunesImageURL : URL?

}
```

Now we know *what* we're going to parse from the XML data. The big question is...*how?*

Parsing XML

We've downloaded the XML as a Data object, and created two structs to hold the useful parts of that data. Now the question is how we go through the data to populate those structures. The way we do this is to use a parser, an object that understands the syntax and structure of XML. The parser can walk through the tree-structured XML data and expose its element names, attributes, text, parent-child attributes, and so on.

As we might expect from a modern computing platform, the iOS SDK does have built-in parsing for XML, in the form of Foundation's XMLParser class.

XMLParser is an *event-driven* parser, rather than a document-oriented parser like you might be used to from working with the DOM of a web page. The difference is that instead of parsing and delivering an entire document model all at once, an event-driven parser fires off events as it goes. Our code can be notified when the parser starts or ends XML elements, encounters text or CDATA, stops on an error, and so on.

The trick is to act only on the events relevant to our needs and build up a data model that makes sense for our app—that is to say, using the PodcastFeed and PodcastEpisode types we just created.

Setting Up the XMLParser

Looking at the XMLParser docs, there are init()s that take URLs and Data, which is great, since our URLSession downloads the podcast feed to a Data. But there doesn't seem to be anything about parsing the XML elements themselves.

The way it works is that the parser has a delegate property of type XMLParserDelegate. Look up XMLParserDelegate and that's where we find all the methods about starting and ending elements, finding text, and so on. Notice also that XML-ParserDelegate is a protocol—the idea is that we implement this protocol in one of our classes and assign it to the protocol's delegate property, and it gets callbacks as the parser does its work.

This is a lot like the target-action pattern we saw with key-value observing back in *Constantly Changing Outlets*, on page 84. Here the pattern is called *delegation*. The idea is that when the parser doesn't know what to do at some point (for example, when it encounters a new XML element), it can *delegate* that work to another object. Delegation is an older pattern in iOS, but we still see it in many of the frameworks.

Alternatives to XMLParser

One thing we need to admit up front is that XMLParser is pretty terrible to use with Swift. It's an old class that was designed to work well with Objective-C, the original language for macOS and iOS development. If podcast data were JSON, we could use the somewhat more modern JSONSerialization API, and for data that's under your control, that's a good reason to prefer JSON to XML.

In the wild, there are third-party alternatives to XMLParser. Janie even wrote her own Swift wrapper around the C-based libxml2 (see http://redqueencoder.com/wrapping-libxml2-for-swift/ for details).

Often, developers who want to add third-party code to their apps will use *dependency managers*, applications that download external code libraries, along with any code those libraries need. For iOS development, the two most popular dependency managers are CocoaPods (https://cocoapods.org) and Carthage (https://github.com/Carthage/Carthage). This makes it easier to include a third-party XML parser with your code and keep it up to date.

We'll stick with just the built-in iOS APIs in this book, but when you need something that the SDK doesn't provide—or doesn't do well—you may want to look around for better options.

First thing we'll want to do is declare that the PodcastFeedParser class we've been working in can be the delegate. Unfortunately, if we just append : XMLParserDelegate to its declaration, we get an error that it doesn't conform to NSObjectProtocol. Unfortunately, the XMLParser API is so old that any delegate has to be a subclass of NSObject, so change the class declaration like this:

network/PragmaticPodcasts-8-2/PragmaticPodcasts/PodcastFeedParser.swift
```
class PodcastFeedParser : NSObject, XMLParserDelegate {
```

Now that we're a delegate, we can start parsing. Rewrite the init() method as follows (we're only changing a few lines, as described after the listing).

network/PragmaticPodcasts-8-2/PragmaticPodcasts/PodcastFeedParser.swift
```
Line 1  init(contentsOf url: URL) {
   -      super.init()
   -      let urlSession = URLSession(configuration: .default)
   -      let dataTask = urlSession.dataTask(with: url) {dataMb, responseMb, errorMb in
   5        if let data = dataMb {
   -          let parser = XMLParser(data: data)
   -          parser.delegate = self
   -          parser.parse()
   -        }
  10      }
   -      dataTask.resume()
   -  }
```

> \!/
> ⍨   **Joe asks:**
>
> # Why Does an XMLParserDelegate Need to Be an NSObject?
>
> An essential part of how delegate protocols work is that the class calling back to the delegate (XMLParser, in this case) needs to be able to discover whether a given delegate method has or hasn't been implemented, since we're free to ignore any delegate methods that aren't useful to us. If the delegate method exists, it gets called; if not, the parser continues on.
>
> This is an example of *language dynamism*, the ability to perform certain tasks at runtime that more static languages perform at compile time. In some languages, you can invoke a function by just providing its name as a string, but in something like C, a function is basically a memory address, and must be figured out at compile time. Swift *can* be somewhat dynamic, but dynamism is not as baked into the language and basic types as it was in Objective-C, which the older iOS APIs were built around. Swift prefers figuring things out at compile time—which tends to produce safer and faster code—and this makes it a more static language than Objective-C.
>
> So the trade-off is that for using something like XMLParser, we can't use Swift types like structures, enumerations, or even basic classes: we have to subclass the legacy NSObject to pick up those dynamic behaviors.

Lines 6-8 replace the dataString we were logging earlier. On line 6, we create the XMLParser, and then set its delegate to self on line 7. Then we can kick off the parser on line 8 by calling its parse() method.

The only other change is that since we're referring to self *inside* the init() that creates self, we need to add the explicit call to super.init() on line 2, so that self already exists before we capture it in the closure.

Go ahead and run this and...well...nothing happens! The player UI just comes up as usual. The XMLParser actually has parsed the podcast feed, but since we haven't implemented any of the delegate methods, the parser never called back to our code. Let's try adding something simple. After the end of the init() method, but still inside the class, add a trivial implementation of the XMLParserDelegate method parserDidStartDocument().

network/PragmaticPodcasts-8-2/PragmaticPodcasts/PodcastFeedParser.swift
```swift
func parserDidStartDocument(_ parser: XMLParser) {
  print ("parserDidStartDocument, " +
  "currently on line \(parser.lineNumber)")
}
```

Run again, check the console at the bottom of the Xcode window, and you should see:

```
PragmaticPodcasts[6520:2911015] parserDidStartDocument, currently on line 1
```

And there we go; we are now parsing XML. Now to pull out the parts we want.

Parsing XML Elements

So now that we are downloading the podcast feed and have a parser set up, how do we pull out the title, description, and other fields that will go into our PodcastFeed and PodcastEpisode structures?

Let's think about how the XMLParserDelegate works. Looking at the documentation, it can call us when it starts an element, ends an element, and gets characters (text) inside an element. It's a little primitive, but it does give us everything we need. Here's a strategy:

1. When the parser starts an element that we care about, initialize a "current element text" property.

2. When the parser gets characters, append them to the current element text.

3. When an element ends, look at its name to see which field of our structure it goes with, and write the current element text to it.

To take it easy at first, we'll start with populating the PodcastFeed, before we move on to building individual PodcastEpisodes. In our PodcastFeedParser.swift, start by declaring two variable properties.

network/PragmaticPodcasts-8-2/PragmaticPodcasts/PodcastFeedParser.swift
```
var currentFeed : PodcastFeed?
var currentElementText: String?
```

These properties represent a PodcastFeed we're creating, plus the current element property that we strategized previously. We'll reset the currentFeed when we start parsing a new document, so let's rewrite the parserDidStartDocument() delegate method to do that:

network/PragmaticPodcasts-8-2/PragmaticPodcasts/PodcastFeedParser.swift
```
func parserDidStartDocument(_ parser: XMLParser) {
  currentFeed = PodcastFeed()
}
```

So far, so good. Next, we'll implement the "start element" callback.

Autocomplete Is Your Friend

Some of the methods in the iOS SDK have really verbose signatures, like the one we're about to write, parser(didStartElement:namespaceURI:qualifiedName:attributes:). Worse yet, with a delegate, if we misspell anything, our method won't be called—the XMLParser will just fail to find the method under its correct spelling and move on, assuming our delegate didn't implement it.

So here's a great way to deal with that: let Xcode's autocomplete write the method signature for you. Just start writing any part of the method name, and a pop-up list will show the possible completions. You don't have to start with the func keyword, or even the actual beginning of the method name, "parser." As shown in the screenshot, you can just start typing didStart, and every possible completion with those characters in that order will appear in the pop-up. Then just click or arrow-and-tab to accept the correct completion.

One important point is that autocomplete only works with methods and functions that the compiler would know about and that are legal at your cursor's current position. In other words, if you started typing the name of an AVPlayer method and it didn't show up in the list, you might be missing import AVFoundation in that file, which would prevent autocomplete from knowing about its classes and methods.

network/PragmaticPodcasts-8-2/PragmaticPodcasts/PodcastFeedParser.swift

```swift
func parser(_ parser: XMLParser, didStartElement elementName: String,
            namespaceURI: String?, qualifiedName qName: String?,
            attributes attributeDict: [String : String] = [:]) {
  switch elementName {
  case "title", "link", "description", "itunes:author":
    currentElementText = ""
  case "itunes:image":
    if let urlAttribute = attributeDict["href"] {
      currentFeed?.iTunesImageURL = URL(string: urlAttribute)
    }
  default:
    currentElementText = nil
  }
}
```

There are three things we might want to do here, based on the elementName, so we deal with them in a switch:

- If the element is one whose text we want to capture, we set currentElementText to an empty string, which we will append later as we receive text callbacks.

- If the element is itunes:image, then the URL we want is available from the tag's attributes, so we try to grab it from attributeDict.

- Any other cases are tags we don't care to parse, so we nil out currentElementText, as a sign we can use later to tell our parser to not bother with this element's text.

Next, we'll deal with text inside an element. That means that if we're currently parsing a title element whose markup looks like this:

```
<title>CocoaConf Podcast</title>
```

Then the text in this case is CocoaConf Podcast. But we have to be careful. The documentation for parser(foundCharacters:) reads:

> Sent by a parser object to provide its delegate with a string representing all or part of the characters of the current element.

The important part here is "all or *part of* the characters." It's not guaranteed we'll get the string all at once. We could receive it over the course of several callbacks. And that means we need to gradually build up currentElementText over the course of however many times parser(foundCharacters:) is called:

network/PragmaticPodcasts-8-2/PragmaticPodcasts/PodcastFeedParser.swift
```swift
func parser(_ parser: XMLParser, foundCharacters string: String) {
  currentElementText?.append(string)
}
```

Notice the use of the optional-chaining operator, ?. If currentElementText is nil— as it is for all the tags we aren't interested in parsing—this line will quietly do nothing.

Finally, our third step is to implement the element-did-end method, using the currentElementText to populate the corresponding field of the currentFeed. This delegate method is parser(didEndElement:namespaceURI:qualifiedName:), another long signature that you'll probably want to use autocomplete for, rather than writing by hand.

network/PragmaticPodcasts-8-2/PragmaticPodcasts/PodcastFeedParser.swift
```swift
func parser(_ parser: XMLParser, didEndElement elementName: String,
            namespaceURI: String?, qualifiedName qName: String?) {
  switch elementName {
  case "title":
    currentFeed?.title = currentElementText
  case "link":
    if let linkText = currentElementText {
```

```
      currentFeed?.link = URL(string: linkText)
    }
  case "description":
    currentFeed?.description = currentElementText
  case "itunes:author":
    currentFeed?.iTunesAuthor = currentElementText
  default:
    break
  }
}
```

Our implementation is basically one big switch statement, switching on the various elementName values we care about, and either assigning the currentElementText value to the struct fields directly, or converting them to URLs as needed.

This is all we need to parse the information at the beginning of the feed. We might as well stop before parsing any of the episodes—something we'll tackle in the next section—particularly because they use some of the same element names we're currently handling, but for different purposes. So go up to the did-StartElement we wrote earlier, and add another case to the switch, prior to the default:

network/PragmaticPodcasts-8-2/PragmaticPodcasts/PodcastFeedParser.swift
```
case "item":
  parser.abortParsing()
  print("aborted parsing. podcastFeed = \(currentFeed)")
```

The idea here is that the first time we encounter an element named item, we know it's an episode, so we abort parsing (for now, anyways) and log what we've received so far. Look in the console and you should see output like this:

```
PragmaticPodcasts[8393:3720948] aborted parsing. podcastFeed =
Optional(PragmaticPodcasts.PodcastFeed(title: Optional("CocoaConf Podcast"),
link: Optional(http://cocoaconf.com/podcast), description: Optional("The
CocoaConf Podcast features members of the iOS and OS X community offering
tips, insight, facts, and opinions for other iOS and OS X developers. You\'ll
recognize many of the voices from the popular CocoaConf conference series."),
iTunesAuthor: Optional("Daniel H Steinberg"), iTunesImageURL: nil))
```

So we're now populating our PodcastFeed structure from the contents at the top of the XML feed. All we have to do now is get the individual episodes, and we'll finally have a complete data model for our podcast app.

Marking Sections of Code

 When we're editing source, the jump bar at the top of the content pane shows a series of pop-up menu items. Going left to right, they become more specific: the current project (click to see its targets); the group folder for the current source file (click to see

Marking Sections of Code

other groups); the source filename (click to see other files in the group); and finally, the property, method, or function that the cursor is currently in (click to jump around to other methods).

As source files grow, this last one can become a huge list of method names, so long that it becomes unreadable. One way to clean it up is to add special comments. If you add //MARK: and some text, it creates a section header. For example, to create the image seen here:

we just used the following syntax on a line by itself:

```
// MARK: - XMLParserDelegate implementation
```

The hyphen after the colon is optional; it creates a divider line. You can also use the syntax //TODO: or //FIXME: to create reminders for yourself that will appear in this pop-up menu.

Combining XML Parsers

Once the parser gets through the XML tags describing the podcast feed as a whole, it gets into a series of <item> tags that describe individual episodes. If we think of the XML as a tree structure, the contents of each episode are one level down from the top-level metadata. Let's look at what an episode item looks like in the XML (we've added some line breaks and omitted a huge block of HTML in the <description>tag to fit the book's formatting):

```
<item>
        <title>Episode 1: The Pilot Episode</title>
        <pubDate>Tue, 27 May 2014 16:50:00 +0000</pubDate>
        <guid isPermaLink="false">
                <![CDATA[https://www.signalleaf.com/podcasts/CocoaConf-Podcast/
                5384fccb9caead020000000f]]></guid>
        <link><![CDATA[https://www.signalleaf.com/podcasts/CocoaConf-Podcast/
                5384fccb9caead020000000f]]></link>
```

```
<itunes:image href=
        "http://static.libsyn.com/p/assets/5/f/d/1/
        5fd1ec09a6797067/podcast-icon-1400x1400.jpg" />
<description>...</description>
<enclosure length="25453104" type="audio/x-m4a"
        url="http://traffic.libsyn.com/cocoaconf/
        CocoaConf001.m4a?dest-id=305853" />
<itunes:duration>29:07</itunes:duration>
<itunes:explicit>no</itunes:explicit>
<itunes:keywords />
<itunes:subtitle><![CDATA[In which we begin]]></itunes:subtitle>
</item>
```

As it is, the parser will descend into each of these tags and keep emitting its element-started and -ended callbacks. So we'd get a didStartElement for the <item> tag, and then another for its first child, like the episode's <title>.

We could let the parser keep going like this, digging deeper and deeper into the XML tags' hierarchy. But this will get hard to code after a while, because some tags—like title or description—are used for different purposes depending where in the tree structure we are. That means some of the cases in our switch might need their own switches or if-elses to figure it all out. For example, case "title" would then have to have some logic for "is this the title of an episode or the whole podcast?" That could get really ugly fast.

What works better, actually, is to have multiple XMLParsers. That's what we're going to do next.

Parsing Podcast Episodes

First, though, since we know we need to store the parsed episodes somewhere, let's switch over to PodcastFeed.swift and add an array to hold them:

network/PragmaticPodcasts-8-3/PragmaticPodcasts/PodcastFeed.swift
```
var episodes : [PodcastEpisode] = []
```

Next, we'll create a new class that knows how to parse episodes. Do File→New→File... and once again choose an iOS "Swift File" from the template sheet. Name it PodcastEpisodeParser.swift.

We've called this class a "parser," but really all that matters is that it can implement the XMLParserDelegate protocol.

network/PragmaticPodcasts-8-3/PragmaticPodcasts/PodcastEpisodeParser.swift
```
class PodcastEpisodeParser : NSObject, XMLParserDelegate {

}
```

The reason this class needs to also implement the XMLParserDelegate protocol is the crucial trick of iOS XML parsing: we're going to pass the delegate from one object to another during the parsing process, and it's going to work like this:

1. When the PodcastFeedParser starts an item (i.e., an episode), create a Pod-castEpisodeParser and make it the XMLParser's delegate.

2. The PodcastEpisodeParser is then responsible for populating the fields of a PodcastEpisode.

3. When the PodcastEpisodeParser reaches the end of an item, reassign the XML-Parser's delegate back to the PodcastFeedParser, which can then collect the completed PodcastEpisode and add it to the feed's array.

Let's start putting the pieces in place. In our empty PodcastEpisodeParser.swift, add two new variables: one for the PodcastFeedParser that creates the episode parser, and one for the episode that will be built up.

network/PragmaticPodcasts-8-3/PragmaticPodcasts/PodcastEpisodeParser.swift
```
let feedParser : PodcastFeedParser
var currentEpisode : PodcastEpisode
```

Those are non-optional properties, so they'll give an error for a moment, because they haven't been initialized by the end of init(). Good thing we're ready to write the init():

network/PragmaticPodcasts-8-3/PragmaticPodcasts/PodcastEpisodeParser.swift
```
init(feedParser: PodcastFeedParser, xmlParser: XMLParser) {
  self.feedParser = feedParser
  self.currentEpisode = PodcastEpisode()
  super.init()
  xmlParser.delegate = self
}
```

Providing this one init() means the only way to create our parser is by providing the feed parser that we can return the delegate to when we're done, and the XMLParser itself, which we need only so we can reassign its delegate. The practical upshot of this is that as soon as the feed parser creates the episode parser, the latter will be all set to parse out the contents of the <item> tag.

As before, we need to build up a string of the current element's text, so add that as a property.

network/PragmaticPodcasts-8-3/PragmaticPodcasts/PodcastEpisodeParser.swift
```
var currentElementText: String?
```

Now we're ready to get started with our delegate callbacks as before. One thing that's different is that the URL of the podcast episode is not in its own tag. Instead, it is an attribute of the <enclosure> tag. The started-element call-back is the only time we get a look at a tag's attributes, so we'll want to grab the URL attribute then.

network/PragmaticPodcasts-8-3/PragmaticPodcasts/PodcastEpisodeParser.swift

```swift
func parser(_ parser: XMLParser, didStartElement elementName: String,
            namespaceURI: String?, qualifiedName qName: String?,
            attributes attributeDict: [String : String] = [:]) {
  switch elementName {
  case "title", "itunes:duration":
    currentElementText = ""
  case "itunes:image":
    if let urlAttribute = attributeDict["href"] {
      currentEpisode.iTunesImageURL = URL(string: urlAttribute)
    }
    currentElementText = nil
  case "enclosure":
    if let href = attributeDict["url"], let url = URL(string:href) {
      currentEpisode.enclosureURL = url
    }
    currentElementText = nil
  default:
    currentElementText = nil
  }
}
```

Our switch statement here has four cases:

- For tags that we need to populate in PodcastEpisode, which is currently only title and itunes:duration, reset the currentElementText to an empty string.

- If and when the itunes:image element is encountered, get its href attribute, and save it as the iTunesImageURL property.

- Similarly, when the enclosure element is encountered, find the url attribute, and save it to the currentEpisode.

- As with the feed parser, for tags we don't care about, nil out the currentElementText, so that appending characters do nothing. Notice in the cases where we get our contents from an attribute, we don't want to collect any textual contents of the tag, so we nil out currentElementText there too.

Now we can move on to collecting the text of elements we care about, which is exactly as before:

network/PragmaticPodcasts-8-3/PragmaticPodcasts/PodcastEpisodeParser.swift

```swift
func parser(_ parser: XMLParser, foundCharacters string: String) {
  currentElementText?.append(string)
}
```

The last delegate callback method we need to implement is when the element ends. In the feed parser, this was where we would store the contents of currentElementText. For the episode parser, this is also the time we will look for the end of the <item> tag itself, which is our signal to hand control back to the feed parser.

network/PragmaticPodcasts-8-3/PragmaticPodcasts/PodcastEpisodeParser.swift

```
Line 1  func parser(_ parser: XMLParser, didEndElement elementName: String,
   -                namespaceURI: String?, qualifiedName qName: String?) {
   -      switch elementName {
   -      case "title":
   5        currentEpisode.title = currentElementText
   -      case "itunes:duration":
   -        currentEpisode.iTunesDuration = currentElementText
   -      case "item":
   -        parser.delegate = feedParser
   10       feedParser.parser(parser, didEndElement: elementName,
   -                          namespaceURI: namespaceURI, qualifiedName: qName)
   -      default:
   -        break
   -      }
   15 }
```

The handling of title is similar to how we stored the fields in the feed parser, so the real difference here is how we handle the ending of the item itself. On line 9, we reset the XMLParser's delegate back to the feedParser, so it (and not this episode parser) will get the subsequent callbacks for later contents of the XML.

Then, on lines 10-11, we manually call the feed parser's did-end-element method. With the episode parser's work done, this gives the feed parser a chance to collect the parsed episode.

Using the Episode Parser

That's it for the PodcastEpisodeParser. Now we just have to create and use it from the feed parser. Switch back to PodcastFeedParser.swift, and start by creating a property for the episode parser:

network/PragmaticPodcasts-8-3/PragmaticPodcasts/PodcastFeedParser.swift

```
var episodeParser : PodcastEpisodeParser?
```

Next, in parser(didStartElement:namespaceURI:qualifiedName:), take out the case that aborted parsing when we first start an item, and instead use the opportunity to create the PodcastEpisodeParser:

network/PragmaticPodcasts-8-3/PragmaticPodcasts/PodcastFeedParser.swift
```
case "item":
  episodeParser = PodcastEpisodeParser(feedParser: self,
                                       xmlParser: parser)
  parser.delegate = episodeParser
```

This is the first step of our original plan: passing the XMLParser's delegate to the episode parser, so it starts getting the callbacks as elements are encountered. We've written all the episode-parsing logic, and when it's done, it re-points the delegate back to the feed parser and manually calls the did-end-element method. Now, we need to grab the completed episode and add it to the array of episodes. So add a case in parser(didEndElement:namespaceURI:qualifiedName:) to handle that:

network/PragmaticPodcasts-8-3/PragmaticPodcasts/PodcastFeedParser.swift
```
case "item":
  if var episode = episodeParser?.currentEpisode {
    if episode.iTunesImageURL == nil {
      episode.iTunesImageURL = currentFeed?.iTunesImageURL
    }
    currentFeed?.episodes.append(episode)
  }
  episodeParser = nil
```

Notice we do one other thing here: if the episode did not find an episode-specific iTunesImageURL, we assign it the feed's iTunesImageURL, if any. That way, we should pretty much always have an image to show in our UI.

Finally, since we took out the one logging statement that showed whether or not any of this worked, let's log the currentFeed that we end up with when we reach the end of the document:

network/PragmaticPodcasts-8-3/PragmaticPodcasts/PodcastFeedParser.swift
```
func parserDidEndDocument(_ parser: XMLParser) {
  print ("parsing done, feed is \(currentFeed)")
}
```

We are finally done! Run the app again, and look in the console for the results of our parsing. You should see something like this (we've reformatted the output for the book and cut it off after the first few episodes):

```
parsing done, feed is Optional(PragmaticPodcasts.PodcastFeed(title:
Optional("CocoaConf Podcast"), link:
Optional(http://cocoaconf.com/podcast), description:
Optional("The CocoaConf Podcast features members of the iOS and OS X
community offering tips, insight, facts, and opinions for other iOS and OS X
developers. You\'ll recognize many of the voices from the popular CocoaConf
conference series."), iTunesAuthor: Optional("Daniel H Steinberg"),
iTunesImageURL:
Optional(http://static.libsyn.com/p/assets/5/f/d/1/5fd1ec09a6797067/
```

```
podcast-icon-1400x1400.jpg), episodes: [PragmaticPodcasts.PodcastEpisode(title:
Optional("Episode 22: Anastasiia Voitova"), enclosureURL:
Optional(http://traffic.libsyn.com/cocoaconf/anastasiia.mp3?dest-id=305853),
iTunesDuration: Optional("29:01"), iTunesImageURL:
Optional(http://static.libsyn.com/p/assets/5/f/d/1/5fd1ec09a6797067/
podcast-icon-1400x1400.jpg)), PragmaticPodcasts.PodcastEpisode(title:
Optional("Episode 21: Marc Edwards"), enclosureURL:
Optional(http://traffic.libsyn.com/cocoaconf/marc.mp3?dest-id=305853),
iTunesDuration: Optional("01:00:01"), iTunesImageURL:
Optional(http://static.libsyn.com/p/assets/5/f/d/1/5fd1ec09a6797067/
podcast-icon-1400x1400.jpg)),
...
```

Notice this includes the metadata for the podcast itself in the first few lines, and then the properties we parsed for each episode: title, enclosure URL, duration, and image.

What have we accomplished? We started with a Data object that was mostly XML syntax and many tags that aren't useful to our app. At the end of the parse, we have Swift objects that contain just the data that we need to show a podcast feed's metadata and its individual episodes in our app. With those URLs, we can use our player scene to present and play any episode of the podcast.

What We've Learned

In this chapter, we dug into one of the most common tasks for any iOS app: fetching data from the network and parsing it into native Swift types. We started by using URLSession to fetch the contents of a URL into a Data object, on a queue of our choice (or, by default, a background queue) so that network activity doesn't block the main queue that updates the user interface.

Next, we took this data and ran it through the XMLParser, the event-driven parser built in to iOS. While having to manually handle the start, end, and contents of each tag as it's parsed is rather burdensome, it does let us sift through the XML for just the pieces we want (and saves the memory hit of creating an entire DOM that we might only want a tiny fraction of).

We've just scratched the surface of how apps interact with back-end services. When you're ready to dig further into the topic, Pragmatic Programmers has a whole book available on the topic: *iOS Apps with REST APIs [Mou16]* by Christina Moulton.

Now that we have a PodcastFeed object with an array of PodcastEpisodes, we're ready to present the actual podcast feed in our app's user interface. In the next chapter, we'll see how UIKit tables provide the natural interface for doing just that.

CHAPTER 9

Presenting Data with Tables

So many of the iOS apps we use every day are built around the concept of "lists of things." Twitter apps show lists of tweets, sports apps show lists of games and their scores, and streaming media apps show lists of episodes that are available for playback. Most of the time, the contents of these lists have been downloaded from the Net.

And if that sounds suspiciously like where we are with our podcast app, well, it should. What we are doing is the bread and butter of much of iOS development: get a list of available "things" from the Net, show them in a list to the user, and let the user pick one. In the last chapter, we handled the downloading part, and in the next chapter we'll do the picking. Right now, we want to show the list. And to do that, we're going to use one of the most common UI elements in iOS: the *table view*.

Tables on iOS

Coming from the desktop, one might expect a UITableView to look something like a spreadsheet, with rows and columns presented in a two-dimensional grid. Instead, the table view is a vertically scrolling list of items, optionally split into sections.

The table view is essential for many of the apps that ship with the iPhone, as well as popular third-party apps. In Mail, tables are used for the list of accounts, the mailboxes within each account, and the contents of each mailbox. The Reminders app is little more than a table view with some editing features, as are the alarms in the Clock app. The Music app shows lists of artists or albums, and within them lists of songs. Even the Settings app is built around a table, albeit one of a different style than is used in most apps (more on that later).

To add a table to an iOS app, we use an instance of UITableView. This is a UIScrollView subclass, itself a subclass of UIView, so it can either be a full-screen view unto itself or embedded as the child of another view. It cannot, however, have arbitrary subviews added to it, as it uses its subviews to present the individual cells within the table view.

The table has two properties that are crucial for it to actually do anything. The most important is the dataSource, which is an object that implements the UITableViewDataSource protocol. This protocol defines methods that tell the table how many sections it has (and optionally what their titles are) and how many rows are in a given section, and it provides a cell view for a given section-row pair. The data source also has editing methods that allow for the addition, deletion, or reordering of table contents.

The second important property to know about is the table's delegate, an object implementing the UITableViewDelegate protocol, which provides method definitions for handling selection of rows and other user interface events.

These two roles are performed not by the table itself—whose only responsibility is presenting the data and tracking user gestures like scrolling and selection—but by some other object, often a view controller. Typically, there are two approaches to wiring up a table to its contents:

- Have a UIViewController implement the UITableViewDataSource and UITableViewDelegate protocols.

- Use a UITableViewController, a subclass of the UIViewController that is also defined as implementing the UITableViewDataSource and UITableViewDelegate protocols.

It's helpful to use the second approach when the *only* view presented by the controller is a table, as this gives us some nice additional functionality like built-in pull-to-refresh, or scrolling to the top when the status bar is tapped. But this approach prevents having subviews other than the table, like an overlaid progress bar or spinner while we're loading, or maybe an ad view below the table.

Creating Table Views

To present our podcast feeds, we need to create a table view and then code up an implementation of UITableViewDataSource that uses our parsed PodcastFeed—specifically, its list of episodes—to populate the table.

To create a view, we need to go to Main.storyboard. Here we have the one scene for the player, which we worked on for a few chapters. The table of podcast

The Model-View-Controller Design

The careful apportioning of responsibilities between the view class and the controller comes from UIKit's use of the *model-view-controller* design pattern, or MVC. The idea of this design is to split out three distinct responsibilities of our UI:

- *Model*: The data to be presented, such as the array of episodes
- *View*: The user interface object, like a text view or a table
- *Controller*: The logic that connects the model and the view, such as how to fill in the rows of the table, and what to do when a row is tapped

This pattern explains why the class we've been doing most of our work in is a "view controller"; as a controller, it provides the logic that populates an onscreen view, and it updates its state in reaction to user interface events. Notice that it is not necessary for each member of the design to have its own class: the view is an object we created in the storyboard, and the model can be a simple object like an array. At this point in our app's evolution, only the controller currently requires a custom class. Still, some developers prefer the clarity of each role having its own class, so sometimes you'll see a class that exists only to implement UITableViewDataSource for a given table.

episodes is going to be a new scene, and in the next chapter we will connect the two scenes.

Creating Tables in Interface Builder

Every scene has some kind of view controller as its root object. Recall that our player scene is built around a class just called ViewController— yeah, we'll want to change that at some point—and so now we need a new view controller to begin our episode list scene. Visit the Object Library at the bottom of the Utilities pane on the right (show it with View→ Utilities→Show Object Library or ^⌥⌘3, if it's absent), and notice all the yellow circle icons. These are the view controller icons, and they include several specific types, like those for tabs or split views. All we need is the plain UIViewController, shown as a dashed box inside a solid yellow circle.

To create the new scene, drag this icon into an empty space in the storyboard (i.e., not in the existing player scene). As you do, the dragged image will turn into the outline of an entirely new scene. You can put it anywhere in the storyboard you like, but it'll be easier for the next chapter if you put it to the left of the existing player scene.

This scene is completely empty by default. Since the point of the scene is to show a table of our podcast episodes, we'll add a table view to it. In the Object Library, find the icon for the table view; it's a gray box with four equally sized rectangles inside it (you can click the icon once to show a descriptive pop-up and confirm you've chosen the correct icon). Drag this icon into the new scene.

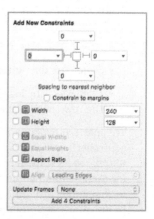

The table view appears inside the scene as "Table View / Prototype Content" and has an arbitrary size. Since it starts out with no constraints, Interface Builder has no idea where it should go or how big it should be inside this scene. Select the table view and go down to the auto layout Pin Menu icon at the bottom right. It's fine for this table view to fill the entire scene, so turn off "Constrain to margins" and set the top, bottom, left, and right constraints to 0. For the top and bottom, use the pop-up menu on the size to ensure the constraint is going to the top or bottom "layout guide" and not the "view"; this will be important in the next chapter when we add a navigation bar. When ready, click the Add 4 Constraints button at the bottom of the pin pop-up. Then, to perform the layout, click the Update Frames button (the leftmost of the layout buttons).

We have one more storyboard task for the moment: we will now want the app to start with our table of episodes, not the player. The current first scene is indicated by an arrow pointing to its left side, and that's currently the player scene. To change this, select the view controller of our table scene, either by its yellow ball icon at the top of the scene, or from the document outline on the left. Bring up the Attributes Inspector (⌥⌘4) on the right, and look for a check box called Is Initial View Controller. Select this box, and an arrow appears to the left of our table scene (and disappears from the player scene), indicating that our app will now start with the episode scene. Your storyboard should look like the following figure.

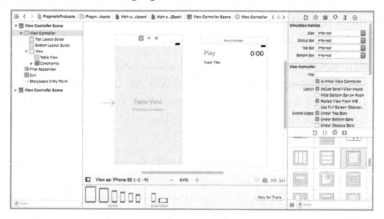

Now, let's start giving this table some content.

Connecting Tables to Code

As we mentioned earlier, every scene in a storyboard corresponds to one view controller. Recall that a view controller is an object that provides the logic of what should go in the view, and how it should respond to user input, network activity, and other events. We already have one view controller providing the logic of the player scene, still with its default name of ViewController (yes, we'll want to change that eventually).

To create the logic that will populate our table with podcast episodes, we need a new view controller class, one that's specific to this scene. In the file navigator, select the PragmaticPodcasts group (the folder) or any of the files in it, and select File→New→ (⌘N) to create another new file. This time, choose the Cocoa Touch Class template, and when the options sheet comes up, change Subclass to UIViewController and give the file the name EpisodeListViewController.swift. Click Next to save the new file in the same folder as all our other source files.

Class:	EpisodeListViewController
Subclass...	UIViewController
	☐ Also create XIB file
Language:	Swift

The file will be created with stub implementations of a few methods we don't need right now, like viewDidLoad() and didReceiveMemoryWarning(), which you can either ignore or delete for now.

With the class created, we actually need to turn our attention back to the storyboard. We need to tell our new table scene that this is the class to use for its view controller. That way, it will be able to make connections like IBActions and IBOutlets. In the storyboard, select the table scene's view controller (the yellow ball icon) again, and this time, go to the Identity Inspector (⌥⌘3).

As its name implies, this is where we can tell Interface Builder what a given storyboard object really *is*. Notice that at the top of the inspector, there is a field for Class, currently with the placeholder text UIViewController. This means that if we run the app now, the scene will be created with a generic view controller. But we want to associate the scene with our new class. So, type EpisodeListViewController into the field; it should autocomplete. This will change the name of the scene in the Document Outline on the left to Episode List View Controller.

Now that the storyboard knows to associate this scene with our class, we can start making connections. Bring up the Assistant Editor via the toolbar button with the linked rings or ⌥⌘↩. The EpisodeListViewController.swift file should appear in the right pane. Select the table view (either within the scene or from the Document Outline on the left), and Control-drag into the space between the class's opening and closing curly braces. Release and fill out the pop-up with connection type Outlet, name table, type UITableView, and storage Strong. Click Connect to create the connection in the source file.

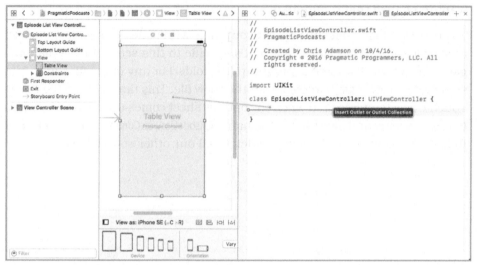

The other thing we said was important about tables was their dataSource and delegate properties. These provide the table with its contents, and special UI behaviors like section headers and footers, selection behavior, and so on. These properties are defined in the protocols UITableViewDataSource and UITableViewDelegate, and since our view controller class will be implementing them, we should declare that. In the EpisodeListViewController.swift file—you can edit it in the right pane of the Assistant Editor if it's still showing—change the class declaration as follows:

tables/PragmaticPodcasts-9-1/PragmaticPodcasts/EpisodeListViewController.swift
```
class EpisodeListViewController: UIViewController,
UITableViewDataSource, UITableViewDelegate {
```

For the moment, this will show an error icon in the gutter, since we haven't yet implemented the required UITableViewDataSource methods.

Now we can connect the table's dataSource and delegate properties to the view controller. In the storyboard scene, Control-click the table, so a black heads-up display (HUD) showing its connections pops up (you can also use the Connections Inspector, ⌥⌘6, which we've used before). Locate the circles next to dataSource and delegate, and drag a line from each of them to the view controller's icon (the yellow ball), either in the Document Outline on the left or at the top of the scene.

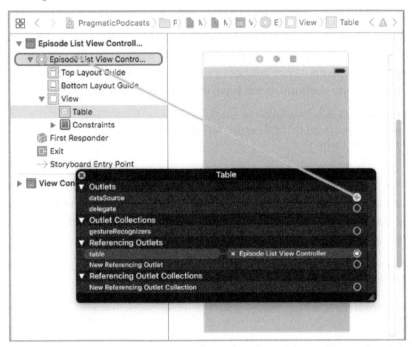

With these few steps, the table now knows to call into our EpisodeListViewController to get its contents. All we have to do now is to actually implement the methods that provide those contents.

Populating Table Data

To provide table contents, we need to have some kind of data model. The contents of this model will be what we use to implement the methods that provide the number of rows and what to put in each cell. The model can be as simple as an array, or it can be its own class if it does a lot of work, which might make us want to move that work out of the controller.

For our first table, we'll keep things simple: we'll just have an array of Podcast-Feeds. So, in EpisodeListViewController.swift, add a property for it:

tables/PragmaticPodcasts-9-1/PragmaticPodcasts/EpisodeListViewController.swift
```
var feeds : [PodcastFeed] = []
```

Despite adding this property, we still have an error in our code, because we have not implemented the required methods of UITableViewDataSource. That's what we're going to do next.

UITableViews present their data as sections and rows. A section can have a header and/or footer, and any number of rows. To keep things simple for our app, we'll put each podcast in its own section, and the rows in each section will be episode titles.

The required methods in UITableViewDataSource are tableView(numberOfRowsInSection:) and tableView(cellForRowAtIndexPath:). To have a table with more than one section, we also need to implement numberOfSections(in:), so let's start there. Since the table will have as many sections as we have PodcastFeeds in our array, this one is easy:

tables/PragmaticPodcasts-9-1/PragmaticPodcasts/EpisodeListViewController.swift
```swift
func numberOfSections(in tableView: UITableView) -> Int {
  return feeds.count
}
```

Next, we need to say how many rows are in each section. If we had four episodes in our first podcast feed, and ten in the second, then our first section should have four rows, and the second ten. We provide this part of the model in tableView(numberOfRowsInSection:).

tables/PragmaticPodcasts-9-1/PragmaticPodcasts/EpisodeListViewController.swift
```swift
func tableView(_ tableView: UITableView,
               numberOfRowsInSection section: Int) -> Int {
  return feeds[section].episodes.count
}
```

So far, so good. Now we just need to create a table cell and return it in tableView(cellForRowAtIndexPath:). This method gets passed an IndexPath, which was originally meant as a way to represent a path through tree structures (like "the root's second child, then the third child of that, then the first child of that…"). UIKit gives it a second purpose by defining the properties section and row, so that a two-item IndexPath can represent a unique section-and-row member of a table.

Beyond dealing with the path, the other task that's new to us is returning a UITableViewCell. This is another kind of view, which by default offers a plain text label and an image view on the left. Certain styles also offer a second "detail" table. So our job is to create a label and set its contents before we return it. Here's our very simple first version of that:

tables/PragmaticPodcasts-9-1/PragmaticPodcasts/EpisodeListViewController.swift
```swift
func tableView(_ tableView: UITableView,
               cellForRowAt indexPath: IndexPath) -> UITableViewCell {
  let episode = feeds[indexPath.section].episodes[indexPath.row]
  let cell = UITableViewCell(style: .default, reuseIdentifier: nil)
  cell.textLabel?.text = episode.title
  return cell
}
```

The error shown in the gutter should disappear, now that we have implemented the required methods. We can run the app at this point, and it will show a table, although it's currently empty, because we haven't sent the results of our feed parser to the table. That's our last big step to bring together the work of our last few chapters.

Bringing It All Together

Our table's contents come from the feeds property. Any time that property changes, we should update our table contents. We can do that by calling the table's reloadData() method, which will force a complete update of all the table's contents. So, rewrite the property to add a didSet:

```
tables/PragmaticPodcasts-9-1/PragmaticPodcasts/EpisodeListViewController.swift
var feeds : [PodcastFeed] = [] {
  didSet {
    DispatchQueue.main.async {
      self.table.reloadData()
    }
  }
}
```

Notice that this uses DispatchQueue.main.async and a closure to ensure that the reload is performed on the main queue. As explained in *GCD and the Main Queue*, on page 125, any code that touches UIKit—which we do by reloading the table—needs to do so on the main queue, and we have no guarantee that whatever code is setting the feeds property is doing so on the main queue, so it's on us to take care of this.

Now, who's going to set this property, and how? Recall that our parser takes an unknown amount of time to finish its work—it is downloading from the Internet after all—but when it does, it calls parserDidFinishDocument(), where we're currently just logging an "I'm done" type message. This would be when we want to take the parsed feed and pass it to the table. But the parser doesn't know about the table, and it shouldn't anyways. The parser should just know about parsing.

We could give the parser a general-purpose way to do something at the end of the document. It could generate an event that another object could respond to, but let's do something a lot more Swift-y. Go to PodcastFeedParser.swift and add the following property near the top of the class:

tables/PragmaticPodcasts-9-1/PragmaticPodcasts/PodcastFeedParser.swift

```
var onParserFinished : (() -> Void)?
```

Yes, seriously. Take a look. This is a variable called onParserFinished, whose type is (() -> Void)?. That's an optional of a closure that takes no arguments and returns no value. The idea here is that whoever creates the parser can provide a closure to be executed when the parser finishes. It's inside this parser that we can update the table, while keeping the parser itself blissfully unaware that the table even exists.

For this to work, we need to not only have this closure, but we need to actually execute it. Fortunately, it's as easy as making a function call since, after all, functions are just a special type of closure in the first place. Rewrite parserDidEndDocument() like this:

tables/PragmaticPodcasts-9-1/PragmaticPodcasts/PodcastFeedParser.swift

```
func parserDidEndDocument(_ parser: XMLParser) {
  onParserFinished?()
}
```

In other words, if the onParserFinished optional is non-nil (as determined by the optional-chaining operator, ?), then just go ahead and call it.

Now, let's use our new closure. Switch over to AppDelegate.swift. This is where we currently have a call to our parser in application(didFinishLaunchingWithOptions:). Go ahead and take that out, because we don't need it anymore.

We need our parser to run after we know the app has launched *and* the user interface has loaded. One place we can do that is farther down in this file, in the method applicationDidBecomeActive(). This method is called anytime the app's UI comes to the foreground—so, both at launch, and if we background the app and then bring it to the foreground again. That sounds like a reasonable place to reload our podcast feed for now.

For this final step, we want to load our podcast feed and then use the onParserFinished closure to send the result to the table. A good question here is: how do we get to the EpisodeListViewController? As it turns out, the application object passed into this method gives us a path to find it.

```
tables/PragmaticPodcasts-9-1/PragmaticPodcasts/AppDelegate.swift
Line 1  func applicationDidBecomeActive(_ application: UIApplication) {
   -      if let url = URL(string: "http://cocoaconf.libsyn.com/rss"),
   -        let episodeListVC = application.keyWindow?.rootViewController
   -          as? EpisodeListViewController {
   5        let parser = PodcastFeedParser(contentsOf: url)
   -        parser.onParserFinished = { [weak episodeListVC] in
   -          if let feed = parser.currentFeed {
   -            episodeListVC?.feeds = [feed]
   -          }
  10        }
   -      }
   -    }
```

There's a lot going on here. Let's look through the pieces:

- On line 2, we use an if let to try to create a URL for our podcast feed, as we've done before.

- The if let continues on line 3, where we ask the application for its keyWindow, which gives us a top-level reference to the app's UI. The keyWindow has a rootViewController, which is whichever scene we set to be the "initial view controller," as we did earlier in the chapter. Assuming the storyboard is set up correctly, this if let will let us cast the result to our EpisodeListViewController type (line 4).

- We create a PodcastFeedParser on line 5.

- On line 6 we begin a closure, which will be set as the parser's onParserFinished property. We want to capture episodeListVC weakly so that we don't create a retain cycle where this closure and the view controller cause one another to hang around in memory forever.

- Inside the closure, we unwrap the parser's feed to make sure we got something (line 7), and if successful, we make a one-member array of it and set that as the EpisodeListViewController's feeds (line 8). Recall that we put a didSet on the feeds property, so this will kick off a reload of the table.

And finally, here we go: *run the app.* The app comes up in the simulator, briefly shows an empty table, and then populates itself with the parsed list of episodes. We can scroll the table up and down to see all the episodes and select individual rows, although this doesn't do anything (yet).

After a couple chapters' work, here is our payoff: we are downloading a podcast feed from the network, parsing the data we need from it, and using those results to populate the user interface. Soon we'll connect the rows to the player from the earlier chapters, and we'll have a functioning podcast player app.

Customizing Table Appearance

So, we now have our live podcast data in the table, which is a great accomplishment. But...it does look kind of plain. Everything's black and white, the fonts are kind of "meh," and most of the titles are getting cut off.

We can do a few things with the table to make it look a lot better, so let's end the chapter by doing that.

Section Headers

One easy thing we can do is to provide section headers. After all, we organized the data as one podcast per section, with all the episodes for a podcast as the section's contents. Once we have multiple sections, we're going to want a visual separation.

We can provide section headers and footers through the table's delegate. To this point, we've focused on our table's data source, which provides the table's contents. By contrast, the delegate customizes the table's appearance and its user interaction. For headers that appear above a section (and footers below), the delegate offers two methods: one that just returns a string for a header, and another for a whole customized view.

Let's take the simple approach: by implementing tableView(titleForHeaderInSection:), we can just provide the title that we parsed from a given podcast's feed. Add the following method in EpisodeListViewController.swift:

tables/PragmaticPodcasts-9-1/PragmaticPodcasts/EpisodeListViewController.swift
```
func tableView(_ tableView: UITableView,
               titleForHeaderInSection section: Int) -> String? {
  let feed = feeds[section]
  return feed.title
}
```

This one is dirt simple: we need to return a string, so we get the PodcastFeed that corresponds to the section index, and just return the title we parsed. Run this and see the results:

Try scrolling the table around a little. Notice that the section header "sticks" to the top of the table view. Once we have a second section, scrolling will cause it to replace the first section's header, so there's always an on-screen indication of what we're looking at. Simple change, nice readability boost.

Custom Table Cells

The header is nice, but the biggest problem with our table is that the cells are very plain and don't contain much of the information we parsed for each episode. Each cell only shows a title, and even that is cut off. We have got to do better.

Fortunately, we can. In the last section, we created plain, default UITableViewCells and populated those. There's another option: create custom cells in the storyboard, and populate those.

Go to Main.storyboard and select the table. Bring up its Attributes Inspector (⌥⌘4), and notice the first section has a pop-up called Content. This determines if our table is made up of Dynamic Prototypes or Static Cells. The differ-
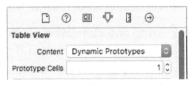
ence is that the dynamic style is populated at runtime—as we're doing by filling in the table with podcast data—while static table cells are used for creating a fixed number of cells in the storyboard for use in things like menus.

The next line down is Prototype Cells and has a text field that's currently set to 0. Change it to 1 and watch what happens: the table gets a single table cell as a subview. This is the cell we're going to customize.

First, though, we need a custom subclass of UITableViewCell that this prototype cell can be an instance of. Do File→New→File to create a new file. On the sheets that follow, choose Cocoa Touch Class, call it EpisodeCell, make it a subclass of UITableViewCell, and save it to the default directory with all our other files.

That's all we need the source for right now, so go back to Main.storyboard, and select the cell. Go to the Identity Inspector (⌥⌘3) and change the class to be the EpisodeCell class we just created.

Now, let's think about the cell's appearance. We would do well to have our episode titles use multiple lines if needed, and show some of the other fields we parsed for the episode.

We're obviously going to need a bigger cell. Select the table, and go to the Size Inspector (the ruler icon in the right pane, also ⌥⌘5). The first entry here is for the default height of each row, currently 44. That's not going to fly; set it to 100.

This enlarges the prototype cell in the table, big enough that we can start adding some subviews to it. We'll drag in three from the Object Library, starting with the image view, which is the gray icon with a palm tree:

1. Drag an image view into the left side of the cell. Use the pin pop-up to set its height and width to 80, and pin its left side spacing to be 10 points from its container, the Content View. Add these constraints, then open up the align pop-up and add a vertical centering constraint. Use the Update Frames button to clean up the size and position of the image view.

2. Drag a label to the top and right of the image view. Using the pin menu, give it 8 points of space on the left and right. Then, use Shift-click or Command-click to select both this label and the image view, bring up the align pop-up, and add a Top Edges constraint. Type over the default Label text to rename it Title.

3. Drag one more label to the bottom and right of the image view. Again, use the pin menu to give it 8 points of space on its left and right. Then, select this label and the image view, bring up the align pop-up, and create a Bottom Edges constraint. Rename the label Duration.

That improves our layout, but we can also punch up the appearance of the labels. Select the Title label and bring up the Attributes Inspector. First, set its Lines to 2, so we have more room to work with before we have to truncate the string. Then, try setting Color to something other than plain old black (we've used a purple for the screenshots). Finally, choose a different font. You can use one of the "dynamic type" system fonts like Title 3 or Headline for a font that will grow or shrink based on the user's accessibility settings, or just pick a specific custom font by name and size. Customize the Duration label too, maybe making it distinct from the title label (we used a smaller, orange, italic font).

When you're done, the layout should look something like the following figure:

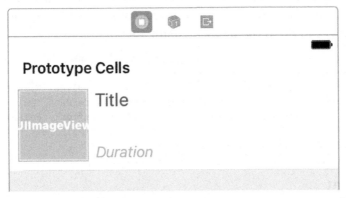

Next, we need connections from these subviews into the EpisodeCell class. Select the cell and bring up the Assistant Editor with the toolbar button, making sure that the storyboard is in the left pane and EpisodeCell.swift is in the right. You should be able to Control-drag as usual to make connections from the storyboard objects to the source file. Name the connections artworkImageView, titleLabel, and durationLabel as appropriate, so we end up with the following properties in EpisodeCell.swift:

tables/PragmaticPodcasts-9-2/PragmaticPodcasts/EpisodeCell.swift
```
@IBOutlet var artworkImageView: UIImageView!
@IBOutlet var titleLabel: UILabel!
@IBOutlet var durationLabel: UILabel!
```

When Assistant Editor Fails

 Sometimes, even when you select the right object in the storyboard in the left pane of the Assistant Editor, and its custom class is set correctly, Xcode doesn't show the corresponding source file in the right pane. We figure it's a bug. When this happens, the best option is to switch from Automatic to Manual in the breadcrumb bar at the top of the right pane, and use its pop-up menus to navigate to the EpisodeCell.swift class.

We're almost done in the storyboard and can switch out of Assistant Editor back to Standard Editor. There's one more important thing to do: select the cell itself and bring up the Attributes Inspector. Notice the second entry is Identifier; this is a string that we use from code to fetch this one cell we've just customized. Enter EpisodeCell for the identifier.

OK, payoff time. Switch back to EpisodeListViewController.swift. We need to rewrite tableView(cellForRowAtIndexPath:). Our previous version created a UITableViewCell and set its one text label's contents. The new version will get the custom cell we just created, and fill in the fields by using its outlets.

```
tables/PragmaticPodcasts-9-2/PragmaticPodcasts/EpisodeListViewController.swift
Line 1  func tableView(_ tableView: UITableView,
    2                     cellForRowAt indexPath: IndexPath) -> UITableViewCell {
    3    let episode = feeds[indexPath.section].episodes[indexPath.row]
    4    let cell = tableView.dequeueReusableCell(withIdentifier: "EpisodeCell",
    5                                            for: indexPath) as! EpisodeCell
    6    cell.titleLabel.text = episode.title
    7    cell.durationLabel.text = episode.iTunesDuration
    8
    9    return cell
   10  }
```

Line 3 is the same as before: get the PodcastEpisode from our feeds array that this row represents. The big change is lines 4-5. This uses the UITableView method dequeueReusableCell(withIdentifier:forIndexPath:) to load a cell we have associated with the table via the identifier string (EpisodeCell) that we just set in the storyboard. Because we already set its class in the storyboard with the Identity Inspector, we can safely use as! EpisodeCell to force it to our custom class. And since the custom cell class has outlets for titleLabel and durationLabel, we can set their contents from our PodcastEpisode.

We're going to put off the image for a moment, so go ahead and run it now to see how we're doing. With the larger cell height, custom fonts, colors, and multiline labels, we're already looking a *lot* better.

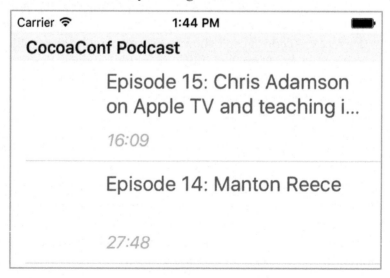

Loading Images in Table Cells

Now, to deal with our image view. At first glance, there's a pretty straightforward way to load its image. The UIImageView has an image property that is a UIImage. Combine this with the fact that it's possible to load an image from a Data object, and that we can fill a Data with the contents of a URL. That gives us a naïve way to fill it (but don't actually do this, because it's really bad):

```
cell.artworkImageView.image =
  UIImage(data: try Data(contentsOf: episode.enclosureURL!))
```

The reason this is bad is what we talked about in *Grand Central Dispatch*, on page 122: this call performs the entire download on the main queue, blocking all UI until it completes. Worse, it does so for every cell. So not only would it take a long time to load the table, but as soon as we scroll, it would slow down each time a new cell needs to appear from the top or bottom. So obviously this approach won't work.

We did learn in the last chapter about URLSession and how it can perform downloads off of the main queue. This seems like it should be the answer, but with table cells, it's actually a little trickier.

Notice the method we use to get our cell from the storyboard is called dequeueReusableCell(withIdentifier:forIndexPath:). If you're curious about the whole "dequeue" part, you're right to be. Here's the story: creating table cells is expensive, and when you're scrolling quickly through a long table, you don't want things to slow down to create cells that are just going to fly by in an instant anyways. So once a cell scrolls off the top or bottom of the table, it is actually stored for potential reuse.

When we call the dequeue method, the table looks to see if it has a used table cell for us to reuse, and only creates a new cell from the prototype in the storyboard if it doesn't. Reusing cells this way makes things go a lot faster.

But when we throw asynchronicity into the mix, as GCD necessarily does, things can get screwy. Consider this scenario:

1. We start populating a cell for podcast episode foo, by setting its labels and starting to download its artwork.

2. But we're scrolling and the cell goes offscreen before the image load finishes.

3. We need a cell for episode bar, so we set its labels and start to download its artwork.

4. We stop scrolling, so the cell stays onscreen. Let's say that bar's artwork is a really small file or it's on a faster server, so it loads pretty quickly. In fact, it finishes before foo's image does.

5. foo's image finally finishes downloading, and it sets the image on the cell. Unfortunately, the cell is now being shown with bar's labels, and we're showing the wrong image.

So if we want to load the episode image asynchronously, how do we avoid this problem? It seems like we could fix the problem on step 5 by making sure the cell is still expecting image data for this URL, and not set the image view if it's not.

So, let's literally do exactly that. Switch to EpisodeCell.swift and add the following property:

tables/PragmaticPodcasts-9-3/PragmaticPodcasts/EpisodeCell.swift
```
var loadingImageURL : URL?
```

We will set this when we start loading an image, and check it again when we're done.

Now, go back to EpisodeListViewController.swift. In tableView(cellForRowAtIndexPath:), right after setting the labels and before returning the cell, add the following (this is the last block of code in this chapter, promise!):

tables/PragmaticPodcasts-9-3/PragmaticPodcasts/EpisodeListViewController.swift
```
Line 1  cell.artworkImageView.image = nil
    -   if let url = episode.iTunesImageURL {
    -     cell.loadingImageURL = url
    -     let session = URLSession(configuration: .default)
    5     let dataTask = session.dataTask(with: url) { dataMb, responseMb, errorMb in
    -       if let data = dataMb, url == cell.loadingImageURL {
    -         DispatchQueue.main.async {
    -           cell.artworkImageView.image = UIImage(data: data)
    -         }
   10       }
    -     }
    -     dataTask.resume()
    -   }
```

On line 1, we clear out any image previously set for this cell. Next, on line 2, we make sure we even parsed an iTunesImageURL at all. If so, 3 sets the cell's loadingImageURL to this URL; if the cell gets reused, this will be overwritten. Then, on lines 4-5, we create a URLSession and its URLSessionDataTask to download the URL data.

When the download finishes, line 6 checks to see that the data task actually did receive data, and that the cell's iTunesImageURL still matches the url that the task started with. If they don't match, the cell was reused and the data task has old data we don't want to use anymore, so we bail. But if they do match, we put ourselves on the main queue (line 7) so that we can populate the image of the artworkImageView (line 8).

Well, that's some pretty twisty code, but does it work? Give it a shot: run the app.

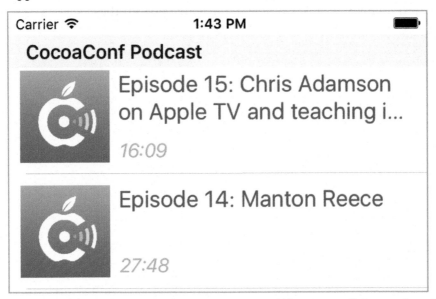

We have images! And, just as importantly, we still have speed! Swipe the table up and down and you should see it still scrolls quickly, loading images when it can, but not stopping the UI to do so.

What We've Learned

In this chapter, we learned about, arguably, the most essential UI element in all of the iOS SDK: the UITableView. By connecting a table view to a data source, we can create scrolling tables with our app's data and present it in a familiar, convenient form to the user. And we're not exaggerating when we say that downloading data from the Internet and putting it in table views is the bread and butter of many, if not most, iOS apps. Whether you're looking at podcast episodes, tweets, airline flights, sports scores, documents to open, or what have you, it's table views all the way down.

We also learned that the basic presentation offered by tables is pretty bare-bones, so we can perk things up with UITableViewDelegate functionality, or create custom table cells with our own layouts and designs.

Our sample app has taken a huge step forward, combining the downloading and parsing tasks of the previous chapter with the UI presentation of this one. We're presenting real-world data in our app. The last major step is to reconnect ourselves with the audio player scene of several chapters back so that we can choose a podcast episode from this list and start playing it. In the next chapter, we'll learn how to navigate between these scenes.

CHAPTER 10

Navigating Through Scenes

Few iPhone apps have only a single scene. Usually, you want to do different things in an app, and the scene changes based on what you're doing. For example, the Mail app takes you from a list of messages to the contents of one you've selected, or the App Store shows you a list of search results and lets you choose one to inspect further and possibly buy.

The key here is the idea of *navigating* between scenes. We tap on table rows or buttons to drill down into deeper levels of detail, moving from one scene to another. In most cases, we can also navigate back to where we started.

In this chapter, we'll learn how navigation works on iOS, how we can go from one scene to another and back again, and the different modes iOS offers for presenting our scenes.

Navigation Controllers

Let's take stock of where we are with our app. We have two scenes—the episodes list and the media player—that currently have no relationship to one another. The only reason either works is that we reset the "Is initial view controller" setting in the AppDelegate. But what we want, of course, is for selecting an episode in the table to bring up the player for that episode. We need to *navigate* from one scene to the other.

The most common tool for achieving this on iOS is the UINavigationController, a view controller that manages a stack of other view controllers. Typically, it starts with a "root" view controller, and then when we want to show another view controller, we put the new one on the top stack. When we want to go back, we remove (or "pop") the top view controller.

All the while, the navigation controller just knows to show the top view controller. Optionally, it has its own minimal UI: a *navigation bar* at the top of the screen with a back button, a title, and a right-hand button that may or may not be present. As an iOS user, you've surely seen this navigation bar many, many times before.

Adding a Navigation Controller

So our task now is to bring a navigation controller into our app. It will start with the episode list as its root view controller, and when we tap a row, we'll want to navigate to the player scene.

Go to Main.storyboard and zoom out enough to clearly see both scenes. We are going to add a navigation controller to the storyboard and connect it to the episode list scene as its root view controller. In the Object Library (^⌥⌘3), find the navigation controller icon, which looks like the blue left-pointing "back" arrow in a yellow ball. Start dragging this into the storyboard, and don't freak out that during the drag it shows *two* scenes. Drop it to the left of the episode list scene.

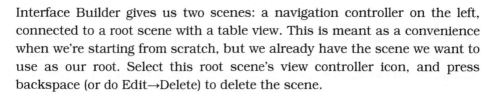

Interface Builder gives us two scenes: a navigation controller on the left, connected to a root scene with a table view. This is meant as a convenience when we're starting from scratch, but we already have the scene we want to use as our root. Select this root scene's view controller icon, and press backspace (or do Edit→Delete) to delete the scene.

Now we have a loose navigation controller scene without a root view controller. Select its yellow-ball icon and look at its connections (either Control-click to show the HUD, or visit the Connections Inspector, ⌥⌘6). Find the connection called "root view controller," and drag from its circle to the episode list scene to use our scene as the new root view controller for the navigation controller.

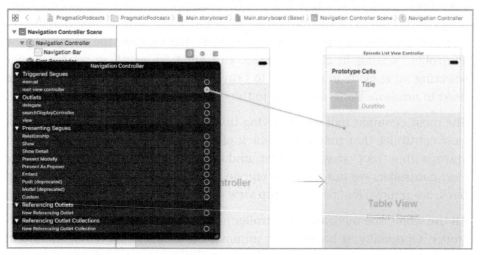

Making this connection actually makes several changes in our episode list scene. The table shifts down about 80 points, and a new Navigation Item icon appears in the Document Outline. Part of this is good change, and part is Xcode making a mistake.

Select the Navigation Item icon, and bring up Attributes Inspector (⌥⌘4). It only has three attributes: strings for a title, prompt, and back button. Enter Podcasts for the title. This causes the word "Podcasts" to appear at the top-center of the scene—the idea of the navigation item is that the navigation controller will use the title from this navigation item (if present) in the navigation bar. Each scene can have its own navigation item, so it's easy to change titles for different scenes in a navigation.

Now to fix Xcode's mistake. Select the episode list view controller (the yellow ball in its scene) and visit its Attributes Inspector. There's a check box here for Adjust Scroll View Insets. That's a setting that would be good if we wanted the table to go under the navigation bar, but if we wanted that we would have set the table's top constraint to its superview, and not to the Top Layout Guide, which accounts for space taken up by the navigation bar if it's there. So uncheck this check box. Now we should have a scene with a navigation bar showing the Podcasts title, and no extra space between the bar and the prototype table cell, as shown here.

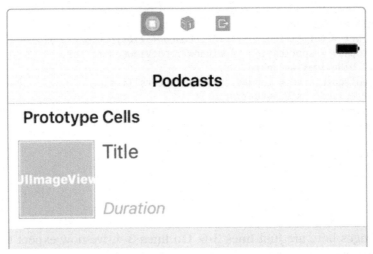

There's also an inconsistency in our storyboard. The episode scene is both the root view controller of the navigation controller scene, and it's the initial view controller, as indicated by the arrow pointing into it. We need to make the navigation controller be the initial VC. Select the navigation controller's icon, bring up its Attributes Inspector, and select "Is initial view controller."

The relationship between the three scenes should now look like the following figure:

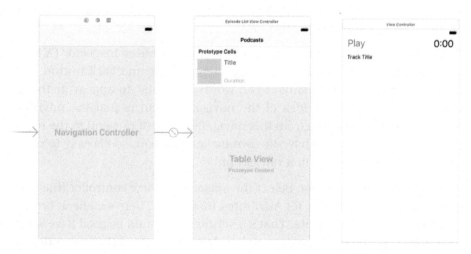

We can run the app now, but we get an empty table with the Podcasts title on the navigation bar. Where did our table contents go? They didn't get populated because our code in AppDelegate expects the first view controller to be the EpisodeListViewController, and it isn't anymore. Go to AppDelegate.swift and rewrite applicationDidBecomeActive() as follows:

navigation/PragmaticPodcasts-10-1/PragmaticPodcasts/AppDelegate.swift
```
Line 1  func applicationDidBecomeActive(_ application: UIApplication) {
   -      if let url = URL(string: "http://cocoaconf.libsyn.com/rss"),
   -        let topNav = application.keyWindow?.rootViewController
   -          as? UINavigationController,
   5        let episodeListVC = topNav.viewControllers.first
   -          as? EpisodeListViewController {
   -        let parser = PodcastFeedParser(contentsOf: url)
   -        parser.onParserFinished = { [weak episodeListVC] in
   -          if let feed = parser.currentFeed {
  10            episodeListVC?.feeds = [feed]
   -          }
   -        }
   -      }
   -    }
```

The changes here are just lines 3-6. On lines 3-4, we now expect the initial view controller to be a UINavigationController, which we'll store as the local variable topNav. A navigation controller's stack of view controllers is available as the array viewControllers, so lines 5-6 try to get the first member of this array as a EpisodeListViewController. With this change, our app starts working again, with the addition of the navigation bar at the top.

Awesome, our app is back! Now let's start navigating.

Segueing Between Scenes

At first glance, this looks like a lot of work to add what's little more than a title bar to our app, but we're now set up to start navigating between scenes. It gets pretty easy from here.

How easy? Like, *drawing one line* easy. In Main.storyboard, go to the episode list scene, select the table cell, and Control-drag from it to the player scene. At the end of the drag, a pop-up appears (shown here), listing a set of choices for Selection Segue, Accessory Action, and some deprecated choices. From the top section, choose Show. Once you release, this creates a new arrow between the episode list and player scenes.

More importantly, this gives us navigation to the player scene! Run the app again and tap on any of the table rows. The player scene slides in from the right, and the navigation bar updates to show a back button called Podcasts (the title of the previous view controller on the navigation stack) at upper-left, and clears out the title, since this scene doesn't have a navigation item. Click the back button to return to the episode list, and click another row to revisit the player. The player still plays the MP3 we hard-coded it to a few chapters back, but we can work on that next.

Updating the Player Scene for Navigation

In the storyboard, notice that the player scene now has a simulated navigation bar at its top. It may be overlapping some of the contents; if that's the case, as before, select the view controller, visit the Attributes Inspector, and turn off Adjust Scroll View Insets. Also,
we can give this scene a proper title by going to the Object Library at bottom right and dragging in a Navigation Item (the icon with the back button, but without the yellow ball). Drop it anywhere in the scene, and in the Attributes Inspector, give it the title Player.

While we're here, let's attend to one last piece of business: the player view controller class has just been called ViewController since we started the project. With other view controllers in play, it's now ambiguous. Bring up the file explorer in the left pane, slowly double-click ViewController.swift, and rename it to PlayerViewController.swift. Then edit its class declaration to its new name:

navigation/PragmaticPodcasts-10-1/PragmaticPodcasts/PlayerViewController.swift
```
class PlayerViewController: UIViewController {
```

Of course, now the storyboard has a scene that refers to a ViewController that no longer exists. Select the player scene's view controller icon (the yellow ball), go to its Identity Inspector (⌥⌘3), and change the class to PlayerViewController.

Customizing Segues

Now let's figure out how to make the player use the podcast episode that we clicked on. The secrets are in that line we drew between the two scenes. When we did that, the storyboard added an arrow with an icon between the episode list and player scenes.

This arrow represents a *segue*, an object for a transition between two storyboard scenes. The little icon in the circle shows the type of segue—this one is a "push" segue, where the incoming scene pushes the old one off the side. Along with knowing which scenes are connected and how, the segue allows us to interact with the transition in code.

Segues can have attributes of their own, and it is a good habit to assign each one an identifier, so that our code can figure out which segue is being performed. Click on the segue arrow, bring up the Attributes Inspector, and enter showPlayer for the identifier (any string will do; you just have to be consistent between storyboard and code).

In code, when a segue is about to be performed, the view controller currently on the screen gets two method callbacks prior to the transition actually taking place:

- shouldPerformSegue(withIdentifier:sender:) gives the current view controller an opportunity to permit or veto the named segue. If it returns false, the segue is not performed.

- prepare(for:sender:) is called right before the transition. The first parameter is a UIStoryboardSegue, an object that provides the identifier and both the source and destination view controllers. This gives the current view controller an opportunity to prepare the destination scene before it even appears.

The latter method is what we need to prepare the player scene. When prepare(for:sender:) is called, we can get the PodcastEpisode that was tapped on, and set up the player scene with its audio URL and title. Then, when the scene flies in, it'll be all ready for the user to tap Play.

That said, we don't want the episode list modifying the player scene's fields directly—they could change, after all. So let's go over to PlayerViewController.swift and give it a way of accepting an episode to display and play:

navigation/PragmaticPodcasts-10-1/PragmaticPodcasts/PlayerViewController.swift

```
Line 1   var episode : PodcastEpisode? {
   -       didSet {
   -         loadViewIfNeeded()
   -         titleLabel.text = episode?.title
   5         if let url = episode?.enclosureURL {
   -           set (url: url)
   -         }
   -         if let imageURL = episode?.iTunesImageURL {
   -           let session = URLSession(configuration: .default)
  10           let dataTask = session.dataTask(with: imageURL) { dataMb, _, _ in
   -             if let data = dataMb {
   -               DispatchQueue.main.async {
   -                 self.logoView.image = UIImage(data: data)
   -               }
  15           }
   -         }
   -         dataTask.resume()
   -       }
   -     }
  20   }
```

This gives us an episode property, with a *lot* going on in its didSet. Let's take it step by step:

- We start with line 3, handling an important problem with segues, one that isn't immediately obvious. A view in a storyboard isn't actually loaded until it needs to be onscreen...but that means the view *won't* be loaded when prepare(for:sender:) is about to segue to this scene, which in turn means that *none* of the IBOutlets (like titleLabel) will be available yet. Manually forcing the view to load if needed, with loadViewIfNeeded(), fixes this problem.

- On line 4, we set the contents of the titleLabel from the PodcastEpisode's title.

- Lines 5-7 unwrap the episode's URL and use it to call setURL(). This method was one of the first things we wrote, and sets up the AVPlayer to play the podcast audio.

- Finally, there's a big section from lines 8-18 that populates the big image view. If we can unwrap an imageURL, we create a URLSession (line 9) and give it a URLSessionDataTask (line 10). This works like the other image-loading data tasks that we've written before: its closure (lines 10-16) looks to see if we got any data (line 11), and if so, dispatches to the main queue (lines 12-14) to create a new UIImage and set it as the image of logoView. Finally, after declaring this whole dataTask, we start it on line 17.

Also, while we're in PlayerViewController.swift, we can now take out the code we had set up to play a hard-coded URL. Delete the entire viewDidLoad(), as well as the line titleLabel.text = url.lastPathComponent in set(url:).

Now the player is ready to receive a PodcastEpisode when it's on the receiving end of a segue. Switch over to EpisodeListViewController.swift and write a new prepare(for:sender:) method.

navigation/PragmaticPodcasts-10-1/PragmaticPodcasts/EpisodeListViewController.swift
```
Line 1  override func prepare(for segue: UIStoryboardSegue, sender: Any?) {
     2    if segue.identifier == "showPlayer",
     3      let playerVC = segue.destination as? PlayerViewController,
     4      let indexPath = table.indexPathForSelectedRow {
     5      let episode = feeds[indexPath.section].episodes[indexPath.row]
     6      playerVC.episode = episode
     7    }
     8  }
```

Lines 2 and 3 test the segue to see if the segue is the one we expect and that the destination can be cast to PlayerViewController. Line 4 uses the table's index-PathForSelectedRow to figure out which row was tapped and get its corresponding PodcastEpisode on line 5. If all of that works, we simply set the episode property of the PlayerViewController, triggering the didSet that we just wrote in that class.

And that's all we need. Run the app and give it a try: scroll down to any row and tap it. The player will slide in with its label set to the episode we tapped on, and when you tap Play, that episode will load and start playing.

Look at that—or more accurately, *listen* to that. We now have an honest-to-gosh working podcast player! It downloads and parses a feed, shows its episode, lets us pick one, shows some of its meta-data, and plays its audio. Maybe it's no Overcast or Pocket Casts yet, but we're only getting started with our iOS development career, right?

Modal Segues

Of course, once we have something that works, our first thought as developers often is how to make it better. One obvious limitation of our app thus far is that it only loads a single default podcast feed. Since we already built the table with the expectation that there can be many feeds (one per table section), let's add the ability to do that. Along the way, we're going to see a very different kind of navigation.

In the Project Navigator on the left, add a new file. Use the Cocoa Touch Class template, make it another subclass of UIViewController, and call it AddPodcastView-Controller. Go ahead and delete the stubbed-out methods like viewDidLoad()(), since we won't need them.

Adding to the Navigation Bar

In Main.storyboard, grab the view controller icon (the plain white box in a yellow ball) from the Object Library, and drag it into the storyboard. It will be conve-nient to drop it above the episode list scene, since that's the scene that will be showing it.

So how are we going to get to this scene? Right now the episode list scene is mostly full from the table view. But the navigation bar actually provides a standard place to add additional functionality. Scroll down to the episode list scene, and find the Bar Button Item in the Object Library (it looks like a box that just says "Item").

Drag the bar button item to the right side of the navigation bar in the episode list scene. A "well" to accept the drop will appear as you mouse over that part of the bar. Once we drop it, it just says "Item," but we can change that. Select it and bring up the Attributes Inspector. By default, the button has a custom title that can be edited here, but there are a number of "System Items" that use common wording or icons across apps and localize in other languages as needed. Use the System Item pop-up to change its type to Add, which will change the bar button to a plus sign (+).

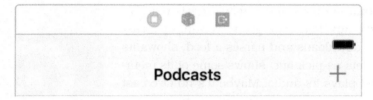

Going Modal

Like the table cells, we can Control-drag from this bar button item to another scene to create a segue to that scene. So do that; drag from the plus button in the navigation bar to the empty scene we just created. However, at the end of the drag, when the HUD pops up asking what kind of segue to create, choose Present Modally.

Go ahead and run the app again, and instead of choosing an episode, tap the add button. This segues to our new scene, but things are different: the new scene comes in from the bottom rather than the left. Also, it does not have a back button. In fact, we are stuck here and need to click Stop in Xcode to get out.

So what's the point? It's that a *modal* segue is different; a view controller presented modally must somehow dismiss itself, usually by providing a button like Done or Cancel. The reason we have modals is that sometimes we need to stop the current navigation and compel the user to take an action before continuing.

Building the Modal Scene

OK, let's get some contents in the new scene, particularly including a button that will let us get out. Select the new scene's view controller, and in the Identity Inspector (⌥⌘3), set its class to the AddPodcastViewController we recently created.

This can be a very simple scene, so we can use a nice trick to make our layout simpler. Add the following elements to the scene, top to bottom, with no regard for autolayout constraints.

1. A label with text "Add Podcast" in a large font

2. Another label with text "Enter the URL of the new feed" in a large font

3. A text field icon (the rounded rectangle icon that says "Text") and Placeholder text https://example.com/feed.rss

4. A button, titled "Done"

Here's where we save ourselves ten minutes of fiddling with auto layout. If we are OK with these items just appearing horizontally centered, with an equal vertical distance between each, then we can use a *stack view*, a superview that performs this sort of very simple layout. Select all four subviews with Shift-click, Command-click, or by drawing a box around them. Use the menu item Editor→Embed In...→Stack View, or the stack view layout button to the immediate left of the autolayout Pin pop-up button.

The previously cut-off labels immediately expand to their proper size, but the layout isn't quite right, because the stack view itself has no layout constraints. Select the stack view from the Document Outline on the left, bring up the Pin menu, and give it top, left, and right constraints of 0, then use the Update Frames button to fix up the layout.

Almost done. It just looks a little off because everything is left-aligned and spaced tightly. With the stack view still selected, visit the Attributes Inspector and set the Alignment to Center and Spacing to 10. This should clean up the layout nicely, and look like the following figure.

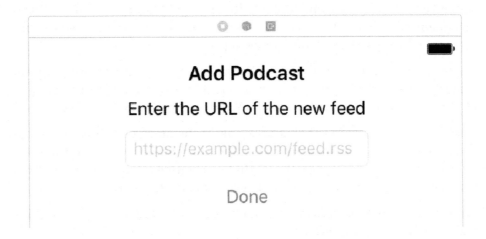

OK, now that we're laid out, let's deal with functionality. Clearly, we need an outlet to the text field, so that our code can retrieve whatever the user types into it. Bring up the Assistant Editor and Control-drag an outlet over to AddPodcastViewController.swift. Call the outlet urlField.

navigation/PragmaticPodcasts-10-2/PragmaticPodcasts/AddPodcastViewController.swift
```
@IBOutlet var urlField: UITextField!
```

Helping Your User Type

URLs aren't the easiest thing to type by hand, and we can give the user a little help in this regard. Select the text field and bring up the Attributes Inspector. A series of pop-up menus determines text entry and soft keyboard behaviors, like default capitalization and autocorrect. Select Keyboard Type, and select URL. This switches the default onscreen keyboard with one more appropriate for entering URLs: the common URL separators like colon and slash are accessible without hitting the symbol key.

Exit Segues

It's tempting at this point to think we will connect an action to the Done button, and it will be responsible for both reading the value from the text field and dismissing the modal somehow. Actually, there's a better and somewhat more interesting way to get out of modal presentations.

Hover over the third icon on the title bar atop this scene. A pop-over appears that says "Exit"; this represents a drop target for *exit segues*, which, instead of going to a specified scene, go back to a scene we've previously been in.

In fact, we're not limited to going back only to the previous scene. We can go back anywhere in our previous navigation. To make this work, we have to indicate *where* we want to go. We do that by creating an *unwind action*. This is a method in a previous scene that serves as our destination.

Since we want to go back to the EpisodeListViewController, switch over to that class and write the following method:

```
navigation/PragmaticPodcasts-10-2/PragmaticPodcasts/EpisodeListViewController.swift
@IBAction func unwindToEpisodeList(_ segue: UIStoryboardSegue) {
}
```

That's right; this method is completely empty, for now at least. All that matters is that it exists and adheres to a specific signature: it must have the @IBAction annotation, and it must take one argument of type UIStoryboardSegue.

Back in the storyboard, Control-drag from the Done button up to the Exit icon. When you release, a HUD menu appears listing all known unwind actions; unwindToEpisodeList() will be one of them, so choose that.

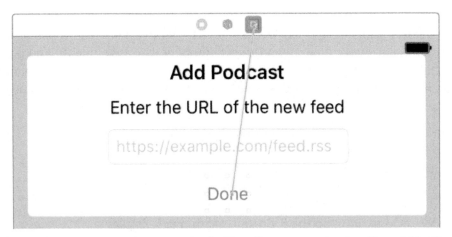

This new exit segue gets us unstuck. Run the app again, tap the add button, and once the modal slides in, tap Done. The modal scene slides back out the bottom where it came from, and we're back at the episode list.

Collecting Data on an Exit

This is great, but we do want our "add podcast" scene to, you know, actually add podcasts. So this is our final task: figuring out where and how to do it.

We have a couple of options. Since the exit segue is a genuine segue, prepare(for:sender:) is called on the AddPodcastViewController prior to performing the exit, so we have an opportunity to do some work there.

But then again, we just put a method in EpisodeListViewController as the unwind action, and this does more than give the exit segue somewhere to go; it actually gets executed as part of the unwind segue. Better yet, it passes in the UIStoryboardSegue object, so we can get a reference to the scene we're exiting, which will be the sourceViewController of the exit segue.

So rewrite unwindToEpisodeList() like this:

```
navigation/PragmaticPodcasts-10-2/PragmaticPodcasts/EpisodeListViewController.swift
Line 1  @IBAction func unwindToEpisodeList(_ segue: UIStoryboardSegue) {
   -      if let addPodcastVC = segue.source as? AddPodcastViewController,
   -        let urlText = addPodcastVC.urlField.text,
   -        let url = URL(string: urlText) {
   5        let parser = PodcastFeedParser(contentsOf: url)
   -        parser.onParserFinished = { [weak self] in
   -          if let feed = parser.currentFeed {
   -            self?.feeds.append(feed)
   -          }
  10        }
   -      }
   -    }
```

This starts with a big if let. We ask for the source view controller as an AddPodcastViewController (line 2), and the contents of its urlField (line 3), and a URL of that text (line 4). If *all* that works, then we create a new PodcastFeedParser and add any results to our feeds data model, exactly as we've done before (lines 5 through 10).

Run again, and click the add button. Type in the RSS URL of a favorite podcast. To speed this up, in the simulator, you can use Edit→Paste to paste the contents of your Mac's clipboard into the simulated iPhone's clipboard, and then long-press on the text field to bring up the iOS Paste menu. For this example, we can use the feed of our friends at the Core Intuition podcast (https://coreint.org), whose feed is http://www.coreint.org/podcast.xml. Remember to type the entire URL, including the http:// part, since we've done nothing to sanitize or clean up the input. Click Done and scroll down. You should find the episodes of the newly added podcast in their own section of the table, as shown in the figure.

Like our earlier feed from CocoaConf, the Core Intuition podcast doesn't have distinct images for each episode, so our code reuses the feed's main show logo for every episode. Even then, it's a good visual cue to help tell one podcast from another in our list, something users will appreciate.

So now, let's bask in the glow of our fully functional podcast client application.

What We've Learned

We've finally delivered all the goods in this chapter. By creating a UINavigation-Controller and creating a segue from the episode list cells to the player scene, we gave the user a way to select an episode and bring up the player for that episode. By using the prepare(for:sender) method, we were able to use the time just before performing the segue to pass data into the destination view controller, which let us set up the scene with its podcast URL to play and the metadata to show in its UI.

Then, to provide an "add more podcasts" feature, we looked at how to show scenes with modal segues, how they keep the user blocked until dismissed, and how exit segues give us a convenient way to go backwards through previously visited scenes.

Now that we have a functionally complete podcast app, our next challenge is to keep it working. In the next chapter, we'll look at the debugging features Xcode provides to find and fix problems in our app.

CHAPTER 11

Fixing the App When It Breaks

Congratulations! We have completed all the code for our app. Now we can get started on the real work we will be doing as a developer: debugging.

Bugs happen. Even the most awesome rock-star programmer writes bugs. In truth, developers spend only a fraction of their time writing code. A lot more time is taken up by debugging that code. So one of the single biggest favors we can do for ourselves is to become fast and efficient debuggers.

In this chapter you'll learn about several methods for debugging, starting with the most basic one, print(). We'll cover the various kinds of breakpoints, and then we'll take a nickel tour of LLDB, Xcode's default debugger. You will learn how to print to the console using a breakpoint and how to monitor a variable for changes. Finally, you'll find out how to make your app crash in the place that the problem exists and not several steps afterward.

By the end of this chapter, you'll have the skills for dispatching bugs fast so you can move on to bigger and better things.

Logging Messages

For novice developers, the first line of defense against bugs is to just write messages to the console to see what's going on. We've been doing this with the print() function way back in *for Loops*, on page 22, and have used it occasionally throughout the book, usually as a placeholder to make sure our app reached the new code we were writing.

The gist of print() is that it will print a message to the console that only we will see. (Foundation also has an NSLog() function that provides a timestamp and the process name of the app.) It might seem counterintuitive to create output that only we will see, but it is vitally important to have some means of verifying what is happening in our program.

Let's put ourselves in a situation where we might want to use print() to find our way out. For example, let's say we made a simple mistake when writing our episode parser and thought the title tag was actually called name instead.

That would be a simple mistake, but the results would be devastating, as we'll see. Open PodcastEpisodeParser.swift and change both instances of "title" to "name" (they're in parser(didStartElement:qualifiedName:attributes:) and parser(didEndElement:qualifiedName:)). Run the app, and notice that all the episodes are now missing their titles, as seen in the figure.

If we didn't know the root cause was the wrong element name, we'd have to think of reasons this might be happening. Since we have table rows and some of the episode metadata, there are a bunch of things we can rule out—fetching the URL and parsing the feed must be working to some degree. We might correctly guess that we're parsing the XML incorrectly, but we might also surmise that the label is hidden or transparent in the storyboard, that the label's IBOutlet is not connected, that tableView(cellForRowAt:) is failing to set its text, and so on.

We can mentally walk along the path our code takes from launch to the updated table, as shown in the following figure, in order to figure out where the problem might be, but we can't verify it without running some kind of test.

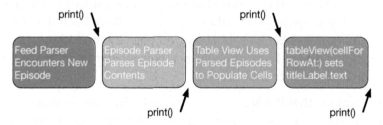

As you can see from the figure, there are at least four points in the operation where something could have gone wrong—maybe more, when we consider that some of these steps have multiple steps within them, or that the label could be wrong in the storyboard (it could be hidden, or the same color as the background, or misplaced, etc.)

By setting up feedback for every step in the process, we can now observe at what point in this chain things break down. By throwing down a bunch of print()s, we can at least focus our search—if we have a log statement atop parser(didStartElement:qualifiedName:attributes:) that logs the elementName, we'll realize that we never see name, and hopefully figure out that what we wanted was title.

Taking Control with Breakpoints

At this point, you might be looking at this and thinking, "There is something wrong with this. My Spidey sense detects Code Smell." Trust your Spidey sense. This solution is fraught with potential problems for your project.

Even if this approach has uncovered the bug, we've sprinkled nasty print statements all over our project. Ideally, we should never include a print command in code that we send to Apple. Although they may help for debugging, print statements do nothing for the end user, and are thus inefficient and slow our app for absolutely no reason. Additionally, any code we add to our project opens up the possibility of breaking something. What's the point of using something that might break our code in order to figure out how to fix it?

Wouldn't it be great if we could still print all our commands to the console without having to sift through all our code looking for those sneaky print statements?

Breakpointing Bad

The answer to our conundrum is to use *breakpoints*. You may have inadvertently already created a breakpoint when you clicked an error icon in the left gutter to try to see what it said. Now we are going to create breakpoints on purpose.

Breakpoints are a feature in the Xcode development environment that lets us freeze our app at a specific point and figure out what our code is doing. They are like a photograph of all the functions that are happening, what threads are running, and what all our variables are set to at a given moment in time. Understanding breakpoints is the key to many of the debugging techniques available to us in Xcode.

Breakpoints are part of the *Low-Level Debugger*. LLDB is the debugger for Xcode. Many of its functionalities have been built into the user interface, such as the ability to create and edit breakpoints, as we'll see shortly. It also has many other commands that are not included in the user interface and need to be entered via the Xcode console. By learning these, we can become efficient debuggers...plus, we can do things that look like magic and we can impress our friends and family.

We have already seen the easiest and most common way people create breakpoints in Xcode. Click in the gutter to the left of our code to create a breakpoint on any line. In PodcastEpisodeParser.swift, create a breakpoint

on the switch elementName that is the first executable line of parser(didStartElement:qualifiedName:attributes:).

Right now when we create a breakpoint, it is kind of limited. It will just signal the code to pause on this line. That's helpful enough, as it will let us know the app got that far, which is what we were tempted to use print()s for. Fortunately for us, breakpoints can do so much more than that.

Right-click (or Control-click) on the breakpoint to reveal the breakpoint menu, as seen in the figure. As you will see, one of our options is Edit Breakpoint. Let's go ahead and select that and see what we can do with it.

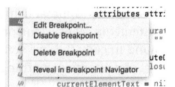

Take a look at the default options for editing breakpoints (as seen in the next figure). Notice that we have the following options:

- Add a condition for whether or not to stop on the breakpoint.
- Ignore the breakpoint a variable number of times.
- Add an action to perform when the breakpoint is hit.
- Determine if we want the program to pause or keep running after the program hits the breakpoint.

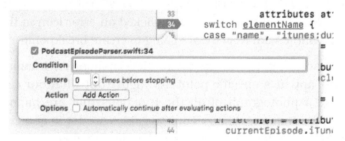

The ability to ignore a breakpoint is particularly useful if we are dealing with a large collection of items. If we were analyzing a collection of ten million keys and values but we only wanted to know what the forty-second value was, we could tell the compiler to ignore the first forty-one values and analyze the one we want to make sure it is "Life, the Universe, and Everything."

Breakpoint Logging

Rather than burdening our code with lots of print() statements, breakpoints offer something easier to remove when we have finished debugging our code. Click the Action popup button. Notice that one of our options is Log Message, as seen in the following figure.

Log Message lets you do exactly that: log a message to Xcode's debug console. Since we are attaching this behavior to a breakpoint, it is easier to go back later and filter out all of our debugging tools. We can surround expressions with the at (@) character to evaluate them as strings, so logging didStartElement: @elementName@ does the same thing as print("didStartElement: \(elementName)").

Better yet, instead of a lot of messy code, this approach leaves us with nice, neat breakpoints, like those in the following diagram. In fact, it gets better: breakpoints are saved only in the local user's Xcode configuration. So, if we send this project to our colleagues, there will be nothing for them to clean up. And when we want to clean up our own breakpoints, it's easier to find them with the Breakpoint Navigator (⌘7) and delete them than to search the code for every print() statement.

The Debugging User Interface

So far, what we've accomplished is pretty much what we got from using a bunch of print()s: we can tell how far our code got before something went wrong. But we still haven't narrowed down just where the problem is. Are we seriously going to have to put breakpoints all over it and edit each to add a unique log message?

At this level of debugging detail, we can do better. Go ahead and run the app. The usual parsing routine will call parser(didStartElement:qualifiedName:attributes:) and hit our breakpoint. When this happens, the Mac automatically switches the foreground application from the iOS Simulator to Xcode. The editor shows the app's source code, and the line we are stopped in is highlighted in green. By default, stopping on a breakpoint also causes two debugging-related panes (shown in the following figure) to appear automatically.

- Debug Navigator (⌘6): Shows the app's usage of CPU time, memory, and other resources. When the app is stopped on a breakpoint, it also shows the state of active threads.

- Debug Area (⇧⌘Y): As first mentioned in *The Xcode Window*, on page 54, this space below the source view can show output from print(). When stopped on a breakpoint, it also lets us look at variables and their values. In this figure, the Debug Navigator is on the left, and the Debug Area is on the right.

In the bottom right of the Debug Area are three important icons: a trashcan and two little boxes. The trashcan clears logged text from println() or breakpoints that log messages. The two boxes show or hide the two panes of the Debug Area: the left shows a variables view, and the right shows the log messages.

At the top of the Debug Area, there's a toolbar that includes a blue breakpoint icon, along with several  other tiny buttons. The breakpoint button turns all breakpoints on or off. The next button to the right is a Play/Pause button, which allows us to continue after hitting a breakpoint.

The next three buttons are the *step buttons*. The first, *Step Over*, allows the app to continue to the next statement in the current method and then stops

Debugging Grand Central Dispatch Issues

Back in *GCD Queues*, on page 123, we talked about the main queue and how we need to put any UI-related work on that queue, while ideally putting background tasks on other queues—ones that won't block UI refreshes. In the figure on page 192, notice that the Debug Navigator's list of threads and queues shows us the breakpoint is stopped in Thread 5, whose GCD queue is called "NSOperationQueue (serial)" (it's truncated in the figure, but while you're stopped on the breakpoint, enlarge the left pane to see for yourself).

Right above that, notice that the first thread we're *not* on is called com.apple.main-thread (serial). That's obviously the main thread, meaning that the code we're currently executing is not main, so it cannot touch UIKit methods or properties, unless it puts its work back on the main queue...and we've surely learned by now that the way to do that is via Dispatch.main.async().

again. Further right, the down and up arrow icons represent *Step In* and *Step Out*, respectively. Step In means that we will enter the statement on this line of code and stop on its first line. Usually, this is only useful if the statement is in code we've written, as the debugger can't show us the source for Apple's framework code (or third parties'). Step Out does the opposite: it lets the app continue until the current method returns, and stops on the first line in the calling method after returning.

Stepping Through Breakpoints

We are going to use the step buttons to solve our problem. Use the Step Over button to advance one line at a time after the breakpoint. A green arrow in the source will show us where we are after each step.

With our app stopped on the switch elementName instruction, we can look ahead to our various cases: the first one handles name and itunes:duration and sets currentEpisodeText to an empty string, so that later calls to parser(foundCharacters:) can fill in the string. The others, for grabbing attributes like enclosure and itunes:image, don't concern us right now.

So, click the Step Over button, which will execute the logic of the switch. It will stop execution on the first case statement. This is the one we expect it to enter eventually, but click Step Over again and it moves on to the next case. Click Step Over a few more times and it will eventually enter the default case.

Huh, guess that wasn't the element we wanted. We can click Continue to let the app go back to running until it hits the breakpoint again, this time with a different elementName.

We can keep doing it this way, but after a few trips, we should start to wonder if we'll ever go into the right case. There's a pretty good way we can find out: just drag the breakpoint arrow down to the currentElementText = "" line inside that case. Now that we've moved the breakpoint, click Continue. The app will start running again, and finally stop on our breakpoint.

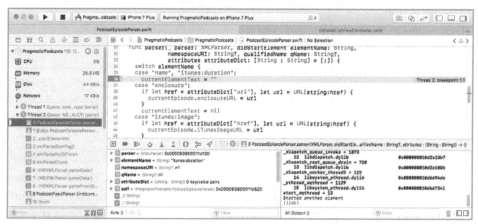

Progress! Or is it? Look down at the variables view on the left side of the debugging pane. It shows all the variables in scope, and elementName is itunes:duration. This is a case we don't care about; we're waiting for name (and, as a reminder, this is the bug: we deliberately changed that from the correct element name, title). Hit Continue, and we keep hitting itunes:duration, never name. So frustrating!

Let's say it occurs to us at this point that maybe it's not hitting name, because there is no element called name. How can we investigate this hypothesis further? Over on the far left, the Debug Navigator shows the stack trace—the chain of method and function calls that led us to this point. Line 0, at the top, is the method we're currently inside: parser(didStartElement:qualifiedName:attributes:). The next few lines are internal to iOS's frameworks, mostly the XML parser. We can click on those lines, but it will just show us the assembly language for those parts of the code (which is kind of cool, but doesn't help us now).

But further down the list of calls, we can find the Podcast-FeedParser.init(parser:) call that kicked off this parsing. This is in our own code base, so clicking it takes us to that source file. Better yet, the variables view updates to show what variables are in scope at that point, like the dataMb, responseMb, and errorMb that we receive in the URLSession downloadTask closure.

Best of all, we have data, the unwrapped NSData object. We can use the debugger to look at this and figure out why it doesn't have any name tags. Select data and right-click or Control-click it. A menu pops up with several options. Try "Print Description of 'data'."

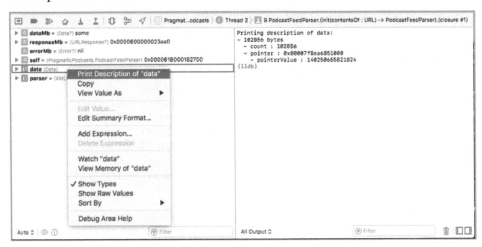

Over in the console, we'll see the results:

```
Printing description of data:
· 102856 bytes
   - count : 102856
  · pointer : 0x00007f8ea6851000
     - pointerValue : 140250655821824
(lldb)
```

For some data types, printing the object like this would give us a useful description, but with Data, all we get is a byte counter and a memory pointer, which isn't enough. For this one, we need to get our hands *really dirty*.

Click over in the console area, where it says (lldb). Did we mention this isn't just a log viewer, but in fact an interactive console? Because it is. There are a bunch of commands we can enter directly. For example, type po data and press Enter to "print out" the description of data. This gives us the same result as the menu item did.

The cool thing is, we aren't limited to just the objects as-is. We can actually write simple Swift expressions *in the debug console itself*. Remember back in *Coding the New Class*, on page 131, when we turned the podcast Data into a String so we could log it? We can do the same thing right here. Enter the following command:

```
po String(data: data, encoding: .utf8)
```

That's the same make-a-String-from-a-Data syntax we used when logging it with print(), except now we're interacting directly with the debugger. Press Enter and, *bam!*, the contents of the podcast XML fill the console:

```
· Optional<String>
- some : "<?xml version=\"1.0\" encoding=\"UTF-8\"?>\n<rss
version=\"2.0\" xmlns:atom=\"http://www.w3.org/2005/Atom\"
xmlns:cc=\"http://web.resource.org/cc/\"
xmlns:itunes=\"http://www.itunes.com/dtds/podcast-1.0.dtd\"
xmlns:media=\"http://search.yahoo.com/mrss/\"
xmlns:rdf=\"http://www.w3.org/1999/02/22-rdf-syntax-ns#\">\n\t<
channel>\n\t\t<atom:link href=\"http://cocoaconf.libsyn.com/rss\"
rel=\"self\" type=\"application/rss+xml\"/>\n\t\t<title>CocoaConf
Podcast</title>\n\t\t<pubDate>Wed, 16 Nov 2016 18:17:41
+0000</pubDate>\n\t\t<lastBuildDate>Wed, 16 Nov 2016 18:19:07
+0000</lastBuildDate>\n\t\t<generator>Libsyn WebEngine
2.0</generator>\n\t\t<link>http://cocoaconf.com/podcast</link>\n\t\t
<language>en-us</language>\n\t\t<copyright>
```

It's not nicely formatted, and has \n and \t escape sequences for newlines and tabs respectively, but we could totally copy-and-paste this into a text editor to clean it up and make sense of it. And at that point, we could look at the episode tags and realize that they use the element title and not name. All thanks to the fact that we can actually write single lines of Swift syntax in the debugger itself. That's pretty handy.

Of course, now that we've realized the error of our ways, go back to PodcastEpisode-Parser.swift and change name back to title in the two places where we deliberately made it wrong. Also, with our bug fixed, we can delete the breakpoint, either by right- or Control-clicking it in the source editor, or by selecting it in the Break-point Navigator and pressing the Delete key.

Setting Up Your Debugging Environment

When we're in serious debugging mode, it can sometimes help to make sure our debugging tools are ready to deploy immediately. With that in mind, we are going to set up a special debugging tab with an immersive debugging environment. In programming, being organized is vitally important. It will help our efficiency to have a dedicated space where all of our debugging tools are laid out consistently.

Think of your debugging tab like you would your kitchen. When you go to your kitchen to cook, you can get a recipe started right away because you know where all your tools are. If you didn't know where to find your measuring cups and the food processor, it would take a lot longer to get something started.

The Quick Look and Print Description Buttons

When we select a variable in the variables view, two inconspicuous buttons at the bottom of that pane provide some very handy features. On the right, the button with an "i" in a circle is "Print Description," which does the same thing as the "Print Description Of" menu item or the po debugger command.

The icon that looks like a little eye is "Quick Look," and provides a visual pop-over when the selected type allows it. For most types, this will just show the type and possibly a short description. But for visual types like UIViews or UIImages, it actually shows a visual representation of the object, and even provides a button to open the visual snapshot in Preview. This can be a *huge* help for debugging visual issues.

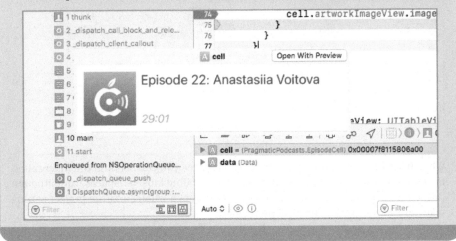

Some developers like to have a dedicated debugging tab. You can create a new tab by pressing ⌘T, just as you would in a web browser, but there is a better way to create a dedicated debugging tab.

Choose Xcode > Preferences or press ⌘, to access the Preferences window. The third tab from the left is Behaviors. This panel controls all of the behaviors an app will have at each and every stage of its life, along with controlling behaviors present in both automated testing and using OpenGL. Since these skills are a little beyond the scope of a beginner book, we won't be going over them, but we just wanted you to know they are there for when you want to take your next steps.

We want to make sure that we can see all of our testing tools while we are running and debugging our application. Find the Running section of the list. Instead of just waiting to hit a breakpoint, we want to see the debugger when the app starts, when it pauses, and when it generates output.

Joe asks:
How Do You Get Line Numbers in the Editor?

Maybe you've noticed that our screenshots of the breakpoint gutter on the left side of the code editor show line numbers, and you've wondered why your Xcode isn't showing line numbers. We are big fans of showing line numbers. It's a nice reminder that once one of our files hits 1,000 lines, it's clearly time to refactor that code. Also, it makes the breakpoint gutter a little wider.

To turn on line numbers, go to Xcode's preferences and select the Text Editing section. The first check box under the Editing tab is "Line numbers," and that's where you can turn them on.

While here, there are a number of other preferences you can set, and the Indentation tab lets you stake out your position in the never-ending tabs-vs.-spaces war (although this is also available as a setting on your project as a whole, and the project setting takes precedence over your local preference).

Another useful Xcode preference group is the "Fonts and Colors" group, which features various themes for styling your editor's color scheme and font sizes.

Click Start and look at the options available to us. You will see an option that says "Show tab named *empty text box* in *drop-down menu*." Click the check box to ensure that it is selected. In the text box, name it something appropriate, like Debugging. Lastly, go into the drop-down menu and select Active Window.

The last thing we need to do before moving on to other parts of the run cycle is to make sure our debugger is showing. If we look at the option two below the Show Tab option, we will see one that says "Show debugger with *drop-down menu*." Again, click the check box to ensure this option is selected and choose Variables & Console View from the options.

Next, let's move on in the left column to the behaviors we want when we pause our program. We want to show the debugger with Variables & Console View, but now we also want to select the option above that one, which selects a navigator window to show, and we want the Debug Navigator.

Lastly, in Generates Output make sure that you have it set to show the debugger with Variables & Console View. With all that done, make sure your options look the way they do in the following figure.

There! Now we have a handy debugging environment that will always be there for us when we need it. Since this is your debugging environment, make sure you go through and look at all the options you think you might want or need. There is nothing that says everyone must have the same options, so feel free to customize this to suit you.

What We've Learned

In this chapter, we explored some self-defense techniques against bugs. A bug we wrote in five seconds might take five hours to track down and correct. Being able to effectively use the tools provided to us to track down our issues faster means we free up more of our time for doing the fun coding stuff we want to be doing.

Next, we tackle our final challenge. We have our awesome bug-free app. Now we need to do the most important thing of all: publish the app on the App Store so that we can rake in the dough, or at least the accolades of our colleagues!

CHAPTER 12

Publishing and Maintaining the App

Look how far we've come! We started from nothing, learned our way around in playgrounds, and then started on our podcast app. By learning new things and adding new features, we've been able to build a genuinely useful app. So far, though, we're the only ones who've seen it.

In this chapter, we're going to get our app out of the Xcode build-and-run cycle and into the world where people can actually see and use it. We'll start by packaging the app for submission to the App Store and letting testers try it out before we release it to the world. We'll finish up by talking about what's next, both for our app and for our journey through iOS development.

One note before we get going: the material in this chapter is mostly about working with Apple's developer websites. Because that's something that we can't reproduce in a downloadable code example, and because Apple can change it at any time, we're taking a slightly different approach. We'll walk through the steps of submitting apps for testing or publishing in general terms, but we won't expect you to necessarily run through the process of actually publishing your copy of PragmaticPodcasts to the public.

Getting with the Program

To publish an app on the App Store, we need to have a paid account with Apple's developer program. The free level of membership lets us run apps on our own device, but to use the publishing resources of the App Store, we need to pay up. When you are ready to take this step, sign up at https://developer.apple.com/programs/.

You can join the program as either an individual or an organization. Joining as an individual means your own name is shown on App Store listings, which means the authors' apps literally show up as being by "Chris Adamson" or

"Janie Clayton." To join as an organization like a company or nonprofit, there are many more requirements, such as being legally incorporated and having a D-U-N-S Number that Apple can use to verify your organization's legal status. You can't just make up a cool doing-business-as (DBA) name and expect Apple to roll with it.

As of December 2016, membership costs US$99 per year and covers development for all Apple platforms: iOS (including iPhone, iPad, Apple Watch, and Apple TV), macOS, and Safari extensions. Along with the ability to publish apps through the App Store, membership benefits include TestFlight testing services (which we'll cover shortly) and access to pre-release versions of iOS, macOS, tvOS, watchOS, and Xcode. Members also get two *technical support incidents* per year, which provide answers from Apple support engineers to problems in your code. These are great for really tough problems that aren't easily fixed by searching Stack Overflow or Apple's own developer forums.[1]

Once you've joined the program, there are two sites you'll use to handle your development and publishing needs.

Member Center

Your account page [2] on the Apple Developer site is where you manage assets specific to your development process. The front page has links to helper sites like the Apple Bug Reporter[3] and the forums, but the essential resource here is "Certificates, Identifiers, & Profiles." These are the electronic assets that identify and authenticate both you and your apps.

Certificates authenticate your identity to Apple and Apple's identity to you. When you first used "Fix Problem" to run the app on your device, Apple set up these certificates in the OS X keychain on your Mac. Anytime we run on the device or submit to Apple, these certificates need to be found, which is important to remember when upgrading to a new computer. Fortunately, Xcode's preferences allow us to import and export developer accounts in a format that includes this data.

Profiles are used for two distinct purposes. A *development profile* allows an app to be run on one or more specific devices. Combined with a matching certificate, it tells the iPhone, "It's OK for this developer to install this app on this device." On the other hand, a *distribution profile* asserts your identity to

---

1. https://forums.developer.apple.com
2. https://developer.apple.com/account
3. https://bugreport.apple.com

Apple itself; it's used in the distribution process to prove to Apple that "we know this person, and it's OK for them to submit apps for review."

Finally, *identifiers* are just unique strings to identify a given application in the store, or to work with some advanced iOS features like iCloud and Wallet that need globally unique identifiers.

iTunes Connect

If the Member Center is the heart of development for the App Store, iTunes Connect[4] is all about distribution.

As a new member, your first task in iTunes Connect will likely be agreeing to multiple legal agreements for Apple to distribute your apps for you, and setting up banking information (so you can get paid!). Later, you can come back here to check out sales reports on published apps and see how the app is being rated and reviewed on the App Store.

The most important section of iTunes Connect is My Apps, where we assemble everything we need to get our app on the store: artwork, pricing data, descriptions and other metadata, and so on.

In fact, we haven't done any of those things yet, so let's go back to Xcode and get our app ready for the store.

Preparing the App for Submission

Currently, our app lacks the polish that we'd expect to see on the App Store. There's more to address than we can really do in a book of this size—entire books are devoted to iOS app design, after all—but at an absolute minimum, we really need a proper app icon. Since we haven't created one, what we see in our Simulator home screens is the iOS generic icon.

App Icons

By default, our app has no icon, and it has the name we gave it when we created the project. It looks like the figure—not pretty.

Let's get to work on that. We'll start with the name being cut off. Click the project icon at the top of the Project Navigator, select the Pragmatic Podcasts target, and click the Info tab. We can set some of the app's metadata here, including the Bundle Name, which defaults to the internal PRODUCT_NAME variable. Instead, just change the bundle name to something short like

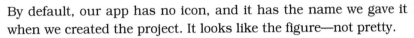

"PragCasts" or "Prag Podcasts" (which just barely fit without truncation when we tried it).

Now about that generic icon. The first step here is to bring in a real designer. "Why?" you might ask. Why slow things down by bringing in someone else?

Deadlines are a fact of life. We have all been forced by one deadline or another to do something we didn't want to do. But when that happens, skip features; don't skip design. The biggest mistake developers make is not having a designer in the loop from the beginning. The design of your app is the way that users will perceive it. After spending countless hours thinking about the internal workings of your app, you don't want to leave the users' interaction to chance. Just as classes need to be designed, user experiences need to be designed.

Interfaces designed by programmers tend to look like programming languages: specific and detailed but tedious. Users don't want tedious; they want it to *just work.* If you expose the switch to toggle the 20% feature, that leaves 80% to wonder at the complexity of the app.

Programmers fight for control; designers fight for the user. Make sure your app has someone fighting for the users. Don't ship an app that has not been designed from start to finish. If the idea is worth your time and energy, then it's worth getting a designer involved.

So, eating our own dog food, we had our designer friend Jaleh Afshar [5] design a proper icon for Pragmatic Podcasts.

One advantage of bringing in a designer who is specifically experienced with iOS design is that you now have someone to deal with the dizzying number of app icon sizes that are now required for App Store submission. In previous editions of this book, we've tried to list all of these. But now—between iPhones at single, double, and triple resolution, different app icons for iPhone and iPad, additional icons for the Settings app, Spotlight, CarPlay, Apple Watch notifications, and more—it is far too much for us to cover. Take a look at Icon and Image Sizes in the iOS Human Interface Guidelines if you're interested. But we're very much of the opinion that it can and should be your designer's problem.

Jaleh delivered our icons in the form of an Assets.xcassets file, as seen in the figure on page 205. We first saw this file back in *Image Assets*, on page 69, when we used it for a default app icon image (which, we can now reveal, was another of Jaleh's creations). Since we already have a Assets.xcassets file in our

---

5.   http://jalehafshar.com

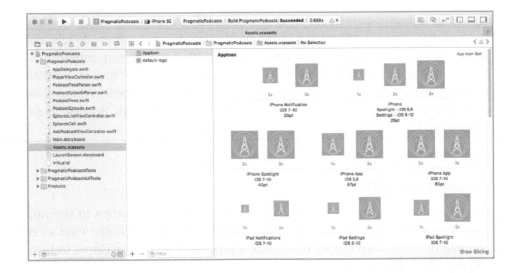

project, we took the app icons Jaleh mailed us and added them to our project's existing assets file.

With a proper name and icon, our app looks a lot more polished on the home screen, ready for our users to open it.

Launch Images

Another bit of visual polish we can attend to is what users see the instant the app is launched. When they tap the app icon, iOS presents a *launch image* until the app is fully initialized and showing its first view.

Prior to iOS 8, the launch image was a static .png file. Initially, Apple's guidance was that the launch image should look exactly like the app's first screen so that the user wouldn't notice the time it took to create and populate the first view. In practice, though, many apps use the static image as a "splash screen," displaying a logo for the app or perhaps its developer or publisher.

The problem with the PNG scheme is that designers had to create static launch images for every combination of screen size and portrait-vs.-landscape orientation, meaning they potentially needed a dozen or more different, yet related, launch screen designs. And that was *before* iPhones came in four different sets of screen resolutions and iPads in two.

Clearly, there needed to be an approach that wasn't tied to explicit screen dimensions. The LaunchScreen.storyboard offers a launch image that will work at any combination of size, resolution, and orientation. The trick is that this file is a genuine iOS view, in a genuine iOS storyboard, just like our app's Main.storyboard.

By default, LaunchScreen.storyboard is a completely empty view with a white background. But it's a view in a storyboard scene like any other—labels and image views can be added and then set up with Auto Layout constraints. Once fully laid out, the launch screen will adapt to screen size and orientation just like any other scene in the rest of the app. So all we need to do to have a fancy launch experience is to customize this view with colors, images, fonts, styling, and so on.

We'll leave that as an exercise...for your designer.

Setting the App ID

Our next step requires a little thinking ahead. We submit apps to the App Store via Xcode, but that won't actually work if Apple doesn't know what we're sending them. It turns out we need to do a little work on the developer website to prepare for our upload.

To upload an app to the store, we'll need a distribution profile. For that, we usually need an *App ID*. We say "usually" because there are certain edge cases where this isn't necessary. The trade-off is that while certain features like iCloud require a unique identifier for each app that uses the feature, there are a few scenarios where multiple apps can share a "wildcard" identifier and work together. The latter case is rare and hard to do, so it's best to just always create App IDs for our apps.

With your browser, log in to your account (https://developer.apple.com/account) and visit the Certificates, Identifiers, & Profiles section. In the Identifiers section, choose App IDs, and press the + button to create a new App ID. We just need two entries here: a name (which cannot have spaces or special characters) for use on the developer site, and the app's bundle ID. We created the bundle ID way back in *Creating Our First Project*, on page 51, when we combined a reverse-DNS style unique string with the name of the app. You can check the bundle ID in Xcode by going to the .xcodeproj in the File Navigator and looking at the App target; it should be something like com.pragprog.yourhandle.PragmaticPodcasts.

So, in the form, enter a memorable string for the App ID (we used PRAGMAT-ICPODCASTSIOS10), and under Explicit App ID enter the bundle identifier. We don't need any of the listed App Services for Pragmatic Podcasts, but keep in mind this is how you would signal to Apple that your app uses features like Apple Pay or Push Notifications.

Once you create the App ID, a "Registration complete" page says, "This App ID is now registered to your account and can be used in your provisioning profiles."

App IDs Are Forever

You might notice that the App IDs in the screenshots and bundle identifiers all have a gratuitous ios10 in them. This is just to make the app for this edition of the book unique from previous or future editions. You do not need to fix your App ID to a specific version of iOS, and, indeed, should not do so.

App IDs are globally unique, so once we create one, we can't use it again. That's why we have to tack on an IOS10 to disambiguate it from last year's or next year's example project.

Two takeaways here: App IDs are universal, and they're pretty much forever.

Creating a Distribution Profile

Next, we use the App ID to create a Distribution Profile. This is what Xcode's uploader will send to Apple to prove that we're a legitimate member of the developer program, authorized to upload apps for testing, review, and sale.

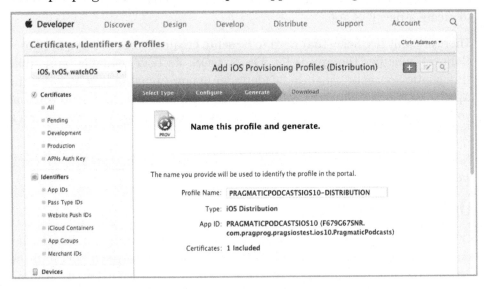

Still in the Certificates, Identifiers, & Profiles section, under Provisioning Profiles choose Distribution. Click + to create a new distribution profile. This lets us choose which kind of profile we want: whether we're sending an app to the iOS or tvOS App Store, or whether we're doing *ad hoc distribution*, which lets us send the app to a limited number of registered devices, usually for testing. We just want the regular iOS App Store, so choose that and click Continue.

Next, we choose which of our App IDs we're creating the profile for (the one we created in the previous section, of course), and on the following screen, which of our signing certificates will be used to prove our identity as registered iOS developers (there should only be one certificate, so choose that). After these screens, the profile file is created and can be downloaded to your computer. Click the button to download it, and then drag the downloaded .mobileprovision file onto the Xcode app icon to install it into Xcode.

By doing these steps, we've prepared Xcode to send our app to Apple. Now we need to tell the App Store what we're sending it.

Creating an App Store Entry

For App Store distribution, we also need to prepare at least a minimal entry in iTunes Connect to tell them what we're going to upload. Log in to iTunes Connect and visit the My Apps section. The main page here is a list of all apps ever uploaded from your account. It will initially be empty. Click the + button to create a new iOS app.

There are only five fields that need to be set to create a basic iOS app in iTunes Connect: whether the app is for iOS or tvOS, its user-readable name (like "Pragmatic Podcasts"), its bundle identifier (a pop-up menu that includes the App ID we just made), and a *SKU*. The SKU is an identifier unique to you and your organization. It's not visible on the App Store; it's just a way to track this app vs. any others you put on the store.

Now that we have prepared a distribution profile and an App Store record, we're finally ready to upload our app!

Uploading the App

Our first step to upload the app is to do a *release build*. So far, Xcode has been giving us *debug builds*, telling the compiler to insert symbols into the executable code that makes it easier to debug. That's what lets us stop on breakpoints and figure out what's going on. But at this point, our code should be fully debugged, so we can eliminate the cost and size of these debugging aids, and instead tell Xcode to build the fastest-running file it can. In practice, a release build will often run 10% or more faster than an equivalent debug build.

Archiving

It's possible to use the scheme selector to create a release build for the device—and this is a good practice for a final round of pre-submission testing—but let's cut to the chase. Select a connected iOS device or the Generic iOS Device from the scheme selector, then choose Product > Archive. The Archive command does two things for us: performs a release build, and packages it in a format that's suited for distribution.

When the Archive operation completes, a new Organizer window opens. It has two tabs: Archives and Crashes, with the Archives tab showing a list of apps on the left, and for each of them, every build of that app that's ever been created on this machine.

Each archive is listed by its build and version number. These are set in the build target's General info pane and have different uses. The version number is meant for the users and expresses the recency of the app and its features. The build is for internal use and tracks different revisions of a given version. In other words, a given version may have many builds. We need to update the build every time we want to make a new archive, and update the version when we want to do a new release to users.

With an archive selected, click the Validate button on the right. This does an up-front validation of the code and our signing credentials prior to uploading to Apple. It reports which signing identity will be used to identify the binary to Apple, and which distribution profile is associated with the submission (which it gets by matching the App ID to the app's bundle identifier).

Uploading

Now we're ready to upload our app to the App Store. For this to work, we need to have at least a minimal record entered into iTunes Connect that matches our app's bundle identifier, something we did back in *Creating an App Store Entry*, on page 208.

Click the Upload to App Store button to begin the transfer. It will take a while to get started, but eventually you'll see the progress bar as the upload begins.

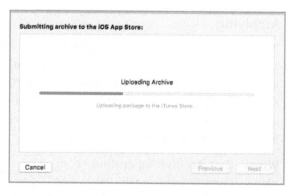

Eventually, the upload finishes and, after it's processed by Apple's backend, we'll get an email saying it's ready for testing or submission to the App Store. This means we're not on the App Store yet, but we've made a big step forward by getting the app off of our own machine. That's critical, because there's one big thing we should do before we release: *make sure our app actually works.*

Testing with TestFlight

Of course, we've been testing our app all along; we had a whole chapter about testing our code early on. But developers never see their apps the same way users do; we come in with biases and assumptions, and with insider knowledge of how the app works. A typical user has none of these things.

We need some typical users!

Lucky for us, uploading our app gets us a lot closer to typical users. Previously, we could only run the app on a device directly connected via USB cable to our Mac running Xcode. But now, from iTunes Connect, we can send the app to testers all around the world and have them try it out.

To do that, we're going to use a testing platform called *TestFlight.* This service allows us to send our app to testers of our choosing, lets them install it prior to its release on the App Store, and lets them send us their feedback. All they need is their own iOS devices.

Testing with Internal Testers

Let's try it out. On the iTunes Connect page, go to My Apps and visit the Pragmatic Podcasts app. Among the tabs at the top of the page is TestFlight, so let's go there.

On the left side of the page, there are three menu items at the top—Test Information, Internal Testing, and External Testing—followed by a list of platforms under the heading TestFlight Builds.

By default, we start on Test Information. Here we can enter a feedback email and (optionally) URLs for marketing and a privacy policy.

Let's move on to Internal Testing. These are builds that go to trusted members of your own development team. We can have up to twenty-five internal testers, and there must be at least one. In the Internal Testers area, click the + to add yourself as a tester. More testers can be added later via iTunes Connect.

To send a build to yourself or other team members, click Select Version to Test and choose the version/build you just uploaded. This will also ask if the app uses cryptography, since that is subject to U.S. export controls. Ours does not, so click No, but take note of the Export Compliance information that appears—we will need to go back and add a key to our app's Info.plist to declare that we don't use crypto.

Then click Start Testing.

Beginning a test cycle sends out invitation emails to all members of your team. The invitation includes two important links: a download link to your app, and a link to the TestFlight iOS app. Once you receive the email, open the email on your device, and download TestFlight from the App Store. When you run it, you'll also have to install a special profile; this is like the provisioning profiles that let Xcode put apps on your device, but in this case it lets the TestFlight app install the app to be tested.

Once the TestFlight app is set up, return to the email and click the Start Testing link. This will take you to a web page with a code you can redeem in the TestFlight app. When you redeem the code, you'll see the test instructions and description from the TestFlight page, and an Install button to download the app. Once installed, you can run the app from TestFlight via the Open button or just from home screen.

Run the app as usual, and look for any bugs you missed. Back on the Mac, the internal testing page will show that you've installed and run the app.

This is all well and good, but our own developers and colleagues aren't always going to be the most rigorous critics. For that, we need to go outside our organization.

Testing with External Testers

The opposite of internal testers is, of course, external testers. These are people who aren't your fellow team members in iTunes Connect. You might never know them by anything more than an email and their feedback on your app.

External testing works like internal testing in a lot of ways: you choose a version and build to test, and an email is sent to all the testers, allowing them to install the app via the TestFlight app and try it out. There are two big differences:

- You can have up to 2,000 external testers of your choosing. These can include your mom, your college roommate, your lover, your worst enemy (hey, they'll probably give honest feedback)...all they have to have is an iOS device and an email address.

- Apps sent out for external testing must pass a brief review by Apple before they're made available.

Let's try it out. Get one or more friends to agree to help test the app and collect their emails. Click External Testing from the left-side menu; this brings up a page showing which version/build combination we're testing and who our testers are. For our screenshots, Janie isn't on Chris's team in iTunes Connect, so she's the external tester. Click the + next to External Testers to add testers by name and email.

In the iOS section of the form, click the Add Build to Test link to choose any build we've uploaded (after a brief processing delay immediately following the upload). When we pick one, we go to a screen in which we describe what testers should focus on, a description of the app itself. Also, you must provide an email where testers can contact you, and a

marketing URL. A second screen asks for information that Apple's reviewers will need: your name, phone, and email, and whether a login is required to use the app (and, if so, a username and password they can use). Finally, there's an Additional Info field where you can communicate any other information that Apple's reviewers might need when looking at the app.

Approval can take as little as thirty minutes or as long as a few days if you submit on a weekend or holiday. At any rate, once approved, your external testers all receive an email linking them to the TestFlight app and our app to test, just as we saw with the internal testing.

Fixing Problems

And now we wait. Our testers will be notified by email that a new build is available, and by installing the TestFlight app, they can install our app. If they find bugs, they can return to the TestFlight app and click the Send Feedback button.

And chances are they will find bugs. It's just a matter of time, so we wait and...oh look, there's an email from Janie, with an attachment that gives us the specs of the device she was testing on. Let's see what her feedback says.

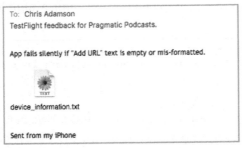

Ah, she raises a good point. It's hard to accurately enter URLs on iOS, and currently the app gives no feedback when the URL is junk or the download fails. We should at least show an alert or something in that case.

So let's fix this and send out a new build. We need two things: a way to catch errors in our parser, and a way to show an error.

The first is easier: switch to PodcastFeedParser.swift. In this file, we already have an onParserFinished closure property to handle success cases, so let's add a new property for errors:

publishing/PragmaticPodcasts-12-1/PragmaticPodcasts/PodcastFeedParser.swift
```
var onParserErrored : ((Error) -> Void)?
```

Notice that this onParserErrored closure will pass an Error as a parameter, unlike onParserFinished, which passes no arguments.

Next, we'll call this closure in the two places that can error: when loading data from the URL, and when parsing any data we received. In our init(contentsOf:), we creaste a URLSessionDataTask that can be passed the optionals dataMb, responseMb, and errorMb; although, the only one we've used so far is dataMb. So, after the curly brace that closes the if let data = dataMb condition, let's call our closure if there's an error:

publishing/PragmaticPodcasts-12-1/PragmaticPodcasts/PodcastFeedParser.swift
```
else if let error = errorMb {
  self.onParserErrored?(error)
}
```

As you can see, all this conditional needs to do is call the optional closure, passing in the error. It'll be up to the caller to decide what actually happens in the closure.

Our other possible error case is when we get some data, but it's garbage and the XMLParser produces an error. This calls back to the XMLParserDelegate with the parser(parseErrorOccurred:), a delegate method we haven't needed until now. After the existing parserDidEndDocument() implementation, add a simple error handler:

publishing/PragmaticPodcasts-12-1/PragmaticPodcasts/PodcastFeedParser.swift
```
func parser(_ parser: XMLParser, parseErrorOccurred parseError: Error) {
  onParserErrored?(parseError)
}
```

This allows the parser to tell us about an error, but what do we actually do about it? That decision belongs not in the parser, but in the UI. Specifically, we need to put it in the EpisodeListViewController, where unwindToEpisodeList() sets up a PodcastFeedParser after the add-podcast view controller dismisses. After the close brace that completes the parser.onParserFinished = { [weak self] in declaration, add the following code to add an error-handling closure.

publishing/PragmaticPodcasts-12-1/PragmaticPodcasts/EpisodeListViewController.swift
```
parser.onParserErrored = { [weak self] error in
  let alertVC = UIAlertController(title: "Error",
                                  message: "Couldn't load podcast",
                                  preferredStyle: .alert )
  let okAction = UIAlertAction(title: "OK", style: .cancel)
  alertVC.addAction(okAction)
  self?.present(alertVC, animated: true)
}
```

This creates a new kind of view controller, a UIAlertController, which gives us the modal error dialog we see throughout iOS. Its initializer takes a title, a message string, and a style, for which UIAlertControllerStyle.alert shows the typical middle-of-the-screen modal error dialog. The alert controller also lets us specify multiple buttons to be shown with the alert, each as a UIAlertAction. Each action takes a title for the button, a style, and a closure to be run when that button is tapped. We add the actions to the alert controller, and then our view controller shows the alert controller with presentViewController().

With this bug fixed—plus any others that come in—we need to kick off a new round of testing. Go to the target's properties and increment the build number, since we will want to track this build separately. Then, as before, we archive, upload to Apple, go to TestFlight in iTunes Connect, mark this new build as the one to test, and click Start Testing to send the new and better build to our testers. Testers will get an email telling them about the new build, and the TestFlight app will let them install it over the old one and continue testing.

Publishing and Beyond

After some give-and-take with our testers, we'll eventually reach a point where we're ready to release our app publicly. To do this, we need to provide the materials that will appear on the App Store page. This metadata is prepared in iTunes Connect, under the App Store tab.

There is a *lot* of material that needs to be provided for an App Store submission. The App Information section contains the basics of the app that we already provided, like its name, bundle identifier, and SKU. We can also assign one or two categories here, set a rating, and provide a custom license agreement (if we don't, a standard Apple license is used).

In Pricing and Availability, we set a price for the app. Prices are arranged in "tiers" that are similar across different regions and currencies. Tiers are shown in your local currency; once you select a non-free price, click Other Currencies to see how the app will be priced around the world.

Preparing for Submission

Most of the metadata that users see on the App Store is in the section titled Prepare for Submission. Filling out this section takes a while, and in companies or organizations, may be the responsibility of a project manager or release manager rather than individual developers.

Screenshots

Depending on whether the app is built for iPhone, iPad, or both, we have to provide screenshots showing the app running on those devices. For an iPhone app, we need to provide at least one screenshot for a 5.5-inch (iPhone 6 Plus, 6s Plus and 7 Plus). The screenshot for this size is scaled for use on other models, but you can also load screenshots specifically for 4.7-inch (iPhones 6, 6s, and 7), 4-inch (iPhones 5, 5s, and SE), and 3.5-inch (iPhone 4s, not supported by iOS 10 and thus only needed if you have set the app's deployment target back to iOS 9). The same approach is used for the iPad: we provide screenshots for the larger 12.9-inch iPad Pro, which is scaled to the 9.7-inch models unless we choose to upload screenshots specifically for that size.

There are two easy ways to get screenshots. From the Simulator, we can choose File > Save Screen Shot (⌘S) at any time to save a screenshot to the desktop. So by just switching devices in the Xcode scheme selector, we can collect screenshots at the needed sizes. If we want to get a screenshot from a device instead of the Simulator, we can use the Organizer window, which has a Save Screenshot button that grabs the device's current screen and saves it to the desktop. There are also third-party products and open-source projects that can mass-produce screenshots in multiple screen sizes and different language selections.

Descriptive Metadata

The Description is where we get to make the case for our app to shoppers on the App Store. The challenge is that although we can enter up to 4,000 characters of text, only the first line or two is visible by default, and only intrepid readers will click the More button that shows the rest. So it's critical to make our case with a catchy first line, like a witty slogan that captures the essence of the app, or a quote from a rave review.

We can also provide keywords that will assist with searching, along with support and marketing URLs. Because of the way the App Store works, this is our users' only way to contact us, so developing a page that greets users, helps them out, and gives them a way to provide feedback is a good defense

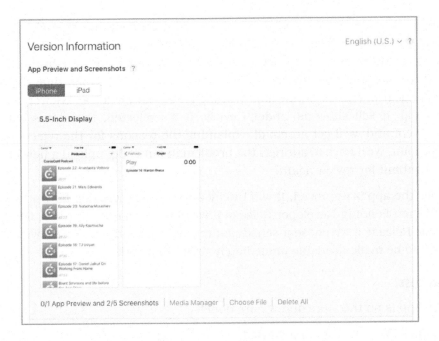

against one-star reviews, which unfortunately are the easiest and most common way for users to communicate with developers.

For presentation in the App Store UI and web page, Apple also requires a 1024×1024 app icon (which hopefully our designer has provided us with!), a publicly visible version number, and content information for assigning an age rating based on the possible inclusion of elements like profanity, violence, and simulated gambling.

App Review and Release

A section called App Review Information allows us to provide information in advance to smooth over any confusion with the app review process that could lead to a rejection. There's a Notes section for free-form information to send to the reviewers, and contact information for Apple to call or email us if they have questions.

If our app provided access to a service we hosted online, we would want to include a username and password in the Demo Account section.

The last section is called Version Release, and it determines how the app will be released to the public if and when it is approved. We have three options: automatically release it to the App Store immediately once it's approved; hold on for us to manually release it via iTunes Connect; or schedule it for release on a given date and time.

When all our metadata and screenshots are uploaded and entered, we can send it to Apple by clicking the Submit For Review button. At this point, the app goes into a queue for review by Apple. Review times dropped dramatically in 2016 and are now typically only a day or so, during which time the app will appear in iTunes Connect as Waiting for Review. Once a reviewer gets to the app, it will show as Under Review. If it's rejected, the status will be Rejected, and we'll get an email explaining the reasons for the rejection. At this point, we'll have to address the problem in our code, upload a new build, and submit for review again.

Once the app is approved, it will briefly appear as Processing for App Store, and then Pending Developer Release if we chose a manual release, Pending Apple Release if we chose a scheduled release, or Ready for Sale if we chose for it to be made available immediately upon approval.

Success!

Our app is on the store and we are done!

Kidding! We're just getting started.

Once version 1.0 is out the door, inevitably our attention will turn to version 1.1. We'll include features that didn't make the cut for 1.0, and incorporate feedback from users and reviewers. By visiting the Activity tab in iTunes Connect, we can see ratings and reviews from the App Store. There's also an App Analytics section that shows us sales data.

It's also possible that our app has bugs bad enough to crash the app. Hopefully not, but maybe we force-unwrapped an optional somewhere that we shouldn't have. When users allow their diagnostic data to be sent back to Apple, that actually shows up on our end in the Organizer. For any of the builds we've archived, the Crashes tab shows us where the app crashed. However, this only works if we keep the archive for that build on this machine. The internally stored archive allows the crash report to be *symbolicated*, meaning that the crash report's data about memory addresses where crashes occurred can be compared against the archive to figure out what line of code caused the crash. Without the archive, crash logs are almost impossible to make heads or tails of.

From here on out, we enter a cyclic process of developing the app further (using our unit tests to make sure we don't break anything that used to work), sending it to testers for external testing, and releasing updates to users via iTunes Connect. This is development, iOS App Store style.

What We've Learned

This chapter completes our journey with Pragmatic Podcasts. We've built a UI across several scenes, connected them to our code, and implemented the logic and behavior of our app with Swift. We've written unit tests, debugged the app, sent it to external testers, and published it on the App Store. These are the essentials of iOS app development.

But there's a lot more we can do on iOS than can be shown in a single app example. In our final chapter, we'll take a look at everything else in the iOS SDK, so you can start thinking about what you might want to do for your *next* app.

CHAPTER 13

Taking the Next Step

In the course of creating our app, we've mastered the essentials of iOS app development. We learned the Swift language, built a UI with storyboard scenes, connected them to code, and then used the essential frameworks like Foundation and UIKit to bring the app to life. We've learned enough to make and ship a real app.

Of course, it's obvious that there's much more potential in the iOS SDK than we've dug into with our simple podcast app. Looking through the App Store, we can see apps with features like mapping, purchasing, media, health tracking, and more.

So what do you want to do with your next app, and how can you do it? In this chapter, we're going to take a high-level overview of the rest of the iOS SDK, and show where to go for the features you need.

Everything mentioned in this chapter is available as part of the iOS SDK itself, and does not require separate downloads, installs, memberships, etc. Documentation for these features can be found in the Xcode documentation viewer (menu command Window → Documentation and API Reference, or ⌘⇧0).

User Interface

When creating scenes in storyboards, there are a number of user-interface components that we didn't need for Pragmatic Podcasts. These include things like text fields and text areas, sliders, progress indicators, and so on. UIKit also offers a *collection view* that is sort of like a two-dimensional table view— a grid view of cells that your app supplies with a delegate/data source scheme much like UITableView's. For embedding web content, the WKWebView (in the WebKit framework) provides the same rendering engine as the Safari web browser uses, as a convenient subview that can be added to your view like any other.

If none of the provided views does what we need, it's possible to create entirely custom views. To do so, we would subclass UIView and then override the drawRect() method, using the *Core Graphics* (introduced below). If the user needs to interact with this view, we can attach *gesture recognizers* to the view to detect taps, long-presses, swipes, and drags, and have these gestures call our code.

Along with different views, there are also some specialty view controllers beyond the base UIViewController and the UINavigationController we used in our app. The UITabBarController manages a bottom-of-screen tab bar, where each tab is connected to a separate view controller. The UISplitViewController provides the side-by-side master-detail arrangement of view controllers often seen in iPad apps. Both of these are examples of a view controller having *child view controllers*, where one view controller loads one or more child view controllers and their views when loading from the storyboard. This approach can be set up manually with the *container view* in the Object Library, and is useful for having two separate controllers on the iPhone, but combining them in one scene for the iPad.

Data Management

Like many (perhaps most) apps, Pragmatic Podcasts is heavily dependent on the network for its functionality. It fetches lists of podcasts, presents them in a UI, and lets us choose one to play. At the moment, we're really not managing any of the user's own data. But we certainly could. Let's say we wanted to remember all the podcast feeds our user adds with the plus button. We'd need to save those feed URLs somewhere. And with just that feature, we'd be in the data management business.

Persistence APIs

This gets us into the realm of data persistence: how to save the user's data from one session of the app to the next. This might not be as obvious a concern as it is on a computer, since iOS doesn't put the filesystem front and center. But make no mistake: there is a filesystem, and apps can use it.

In iOS, apps cannot access the filesystem outside of their own reserved space on the system. The app has a directory that contains folders for documents, caches, temporary data, and other specific purposes. The directories meant for long-term use, like documents, are backed up when the iOS device syncs with iTunes.

To access the filesystem directly, we can ask the FileManager class for the URL of the app's directory, then create paths to access folders and files with FileManager.

It's possible to read from and write to files with a low-level Stream API, or by using the read/write methods of the older NSData class that Swift's Data replaced, but usually neither of these is the right approach. If we want to work with documents, the best way to do it is with the UIDocument class. This is a higher-level abstraction, with which we just write a pair of methods to save our document object to a Data or instantiate an object from a Data. The framework takes care of the actual I/O, so we never have to write to streams byte-by-byte like with a lower-level approach. As a bonus, UIDocument also allows us to store our documents in iCloud, where they can be synced with the user's other devices.

Alternatives to Files

As a simpler solution for very small amounts of persistable data, we can ignore the filesystem altogether and use UserDefaults. This class is just a key-value store, meant for things like app preferences. The defaults are stored for us by the filesystem and are available on future runs of the app. They can also be exposed by the main iOS Settings app.

For secure data, like a user's passwords or other personally identifying information, iOS offers *Keychain Services*. The keychain is a cryptographically secured data store that our apps can use for storing user data long-term (if backed up to iTunes, it will even survive the device being wiped), without us having to implement the crypto features ourselves. Unfortunately, the API was written in C and is hard to use from Swift, but there are a number of open-source Swift "wrappers" to make using it easier.

Databases

Sometimes we want more than flat files or key-value stores: lots of apps need full-on databases, so they can store a lot of data in a structured form and access it quickly. iOS ships with *SQLite*, a simple relational database that supports most SQL (Structured Query Language) expressions. SQLite has a C-based API that can be called from Swift, albeit with some difficulty.

Core Data offers a higher-level approach to data persistence, giving you the power of SQLite without having to write and execute the SQL statements yourself. Instead, with Core Data you create entities and their relationships with a graphical editor in Xcode, then let Core Data take care of the rest. Pragmatic Programmers has a whole book on this topic: *Core Data in Swift: Data Storage and Management for iOS and OS X [Zar16]*.

User Data Services

Finally, there are a number of special-purpose frameworks that allow third-party apps like ours to interact with the user's content and data stored on the device and typically managed by Apple's built-in applications.

For example, the *Music Player* framework allows any app to access the Music app's library of songs, audiobooks, and podcasts. Apps can play these items independently, or set the items that the Music app itself is playing.

The user's photos are available by way of the *Photos* framework. This API lets apps query the photo database, get low-res thumbnail images immediately, and pass in closures to receive large full-resolution photos, a sometimes time-intensive task when dealing with 12 megapixel photos taken by the iPhone 7.

If the user has built up a database of names, addresses, and phone numbers, these are available through the *Contacts* framework, which has a rich data model for handling things like contacts with multiple phone numbers and email accounts for different purposes. For working with entries like boarding passes and concert tickets in the Wallet application, apps can use the *PassKit* framework.

Another thing many users store in the Settings app is their account information for social networks like Facebook and Twitter. Using the *Social* framework, third-party apps can ask to use these credentials, post to those networks with a built-in view controller, and make authenticated API calls to download posts or perform other service-specific actions.

Interacting with Other Apps

Apps can extend their functionality beyond their own virtual "sandbox." The way iOS implements this is in the form of *app extensions*. The idea is to provide "extension points" for specific sorts of functionality that an app could offer to other apps.

In iOS 10, there are more than a dozen defined app extension types. You can get a sense of what's available by going to your project's settings, and under the list of targets, click the plus (+) button to create a new target. The app extension templates will be shown along with all the other types of targets (like unit tests and UI tests) we might add to the project.

Some of the most commonly used app extension types are:

- *Share*: Share content from the application to destinations like the photo library, a printer, or social networks.

- *iMessage*: Put app-specific content into an iMessage.

- *Today*: Show timely content in the Notification Center.

- *Custom Keyboard*: Replace the iOS soft keyboard with a different UI for entering text.

- *Document Provider*: Provide files to other apps, often from online document services like Dropbox or OneDrive.

- *Photo Editing*: Implement a custom technique or UI for editing photos within the Photos app.

App Extensions are also how apps for Apple Watch are created. As you develop your iOS app, we can create a WatchKit app as an extension, and this relationship allows us to exchange data between the two. To learn more about developing for the watch, check out *Developing for Apple Watch, Second Edition* [Kel16].

Media, Graphics, and Gaming

iOS devices shine when it comes to games, sound, and video, and there are a rich set of frameworks for working with static and time-based media.

Graphics

For 2D graphics, the essential tool is *Core Graphics*, sometimes also called *Quartz*. Core Graphics is a drawing library that lets us draw resolution-independent lines, shapes, patterns, and text to an arbitrary "context." It doesn't matter if the context is a UIView we're drawing at runtime, or a PDF file stored on the filesystem—either way, the drawing commands are the same. This technology is what gives us user interfaces that look sharp at any size or resolution, from old non-Retina iPhones to the 3x display of the iPhone 7 Plus.

Quartz also gives us *Core Animation*, which allows apps to animate gradual changes like sliding their contents around, adjusting sizes, or fading in and out, rather than having UI elements just disappear or resize instantly. Many Core Animation features are built into UIKit components—we get smooth table scrolling for free—but in some cases, it's useful to use Core Animation directly, particularly when creating our own custom components.

While Quartz works with the drawing and presentation of graphics, *Core Image* works with the *content* of images. Core Image offers hundreds of filters that operate on images, mostly for effects like color correction, image sharpening, cropping, scaling, distortion, blurring, and so on. These filters can be chained together, one after another, to produce interesting composite effects, like a "chroma key" that takes out all pixels of a certain color and replaces them with another image. Core Image is also the technology of choice for writing the Photo Editing type of app extension mentioned earlier.

Media

Media is one feature of the iOS SDK that we've used already: we imported AV Foundation to play our podcasts, with the convenient AVPlayer. AV Foundation goes far deeper than this, of course, and has one of the highest class counts of the iOS frameworks. With AV Foundation, you can capture media from the camera or microphones, edit together parts of different sources to create new audio-video presentations, and export these to files.

AV Foundation also offers some audio-only classes for capture and playback, as well as an "engine" API for mixing sources together and performing effects on the audio they process. For video, these kinds of mixing and effects techniques actually incorporate Core Animation and Core Image: you can use Core Animation to provide motion elements like scrolling text, and Core Image to perform visual filtering on video frames.

Games

It's not often that a day goes by where at least one of the authors doesn't put in some serious time playing a game on their iPhone or iPad. After all, iOS is one of the world's most popular game platforms.

For 2D games, iOS offers *SpriteKit*, which lets us create flat "sprite" graphics, such as angry or flappy birds, and animate them over a background. This topic is so popular, it has its own Pragmatic title: *Build iOS Games with Sprite Kit (out of print) [PS14]*.

For 3D games, there are a couple of options. The cross-platform 3D standard *OpenGL* is available on iOS, although it's a C API that isn't really practical to call from Swift. Apple also offers *Metal*, a similar 3D API that is meant only for use on the graphics processing units (GPUs) on iOS devices, and which can be faster by being purpose-built for these chips rather than hardware-agnostic. Both are very demanding and require advanced development skills to write the "shader" code to determine how to render 3D objects on a 2D screen.

For the logic of a game, whether 2D or 3D, *GameplayKit* offers help in modeling a game's logic, providing things like path-finding, artificially intelligent opponent behavior, rule engines, randomization, and more.

Real-World Interaction

Some of the most important iOS apps are those that facilitate real-world interactions, with the user's environment and with the user him- or herself.

Location, Motion, and Mapping

It used to be that you'd be crazy to go driving around an unfamiliar city without a map. Now we don't think twice about visiting new places, since our iPhones can fetch maps or directions on demand (but please hand the iPhone to a passenger while you're actually behind the wheel).

The *Core Location* framework is used for dealing with locations on the surface of the Earth. You can use it to fetch the latitude and longitude of the device's current location, fetched from GPS (if equipped) or the known locations of available Wi-Fi networks. Core Location also offers *geocoding*, mapping locations to city/state/country information and vice versa. Apps that work with Apple's *iBeacons* for interacting with short-range points of interest, like departments of a store, do so using Core Location's CLBeacon type.

While Core Location tells you where you are, *MapKit* can tell you where you are going. With MapKit, an app can perform location-based searches for points of interest, or request driving or walking directions between two locations. MapKit also provides an MKMapView for showing maps as UIViews in your app.

On a much smaller scale, *Core Motion* uses the gyroscopes and compass in the device to sense motion and orientation. You can use this framework to find out when and how the phone is being moved around, which compass direction it's facing, and even get pedometer data as the user walks around with the device.

HealthKit

In the last few years, and especially since the debut of Apple Watch, iOS has shown a keen interest in health-tracking data. To the third-party developer, this is available through the *HealthKit* framework. This framework allows apps to access data like step count, pulse, weight, and more, as entered manually by the user or as monitored by their Apple Watch, the M7 motion-sensor chip in the iPhone, or other compatible devices.

Health data is uniquely sensitive and must be handled with more care than, say, a user's favorite podcasts or their lock screen picture. HealthKit apps require developers to provide an explicit privacy policy for how the health data will be used, and forbid a wide range of behaviors that fall outside of what can be addressed in code; for example, you cannot serve advertising based on the user's health data. Full details are available in HealthKit's docs.

Interacting with Other Devices

Finally, iOS devices can interact with many other kinds of devices, increasing the usefulness of both. *HomeKit* is Apple's protocol for Internet-of-things products, such as smart appliances, security systems, and so on. The HomeKit framework in iOS lets you discover the devices in a home and the services they provide, and communicate with them.

For general-purpose wireless connectivity, including the vast number of third-party devices that use Bluetooth LE ("Low Energy"), iOS offers *Core Bluetooth*. This low-level framework allows your app to discover nearby LE devices and send requests to them.

The Low-Level Frameworks

Most of the frameworks described thus far work with fairly high-level abstractions: locations, sprites, workouts, movies, and so on. These frameworks are implemented atop lower-level frameworks and libraries that sometimes offer additional features, but are generally more primitive and harder to code for.

For example, AV Foundation is built atop *Core Audio*, *Core Video*, and *Core Media*, all C-based APIs for working with buffers of audio or frames of video. There are things you can do at this level that are not exposed at the AV Foundation level, but it is usually more difficult: you are responsible for handling more things (like memory management and type safety), there are more ways the code can crash, and there is usually less documentation and sample code.

Furthermore, most of these lower-level APIs are meant to be called from C-language code. In almost all cases, it's technically *possible* to call them from Swift, but it is not particularly pleasant. Many of the C APIs cannot provide the kind of type safety that Swift enforces, so instead of having a function that takes a meaningful type like an AVPlayerItem for a podcast file or a movie, they'll take an UnsafeMutablePointer. That's all Swift can do to represent a C pointer that otherwise has no concept of type, and it's not kidding about the "unsafe" part; the number-one cause of crashing C apps is screwing up pointers, and bringing them into your Swift code doesn't make them any safer.

In Xcode's documentation viewer, most of these frameworks are listed under the System section, and our advice for the beginning programmer is to just *stay away*. For the intermediate and advanced developer, our experience has been that calling non-Swift APIs from Swift is more trouble than it's worth—the resulting code is not only hard to follow for Swift developers, it's less readable than its C equivalent. Instead, just write these parts in C or C++. An Xcode project can combine source files of different types, so if you have a lot of Metal or Core Audio code, just write all of that idiomatically in C/C++, and then expose a small number of Swift methods or functions to call into your C code from your Swift app.

What We've Learned

In this chapter, we've taken a look at much of the functionality offered by the iOS SDK, beyond the things we were able to make use of in Pragmatic Podcasts. By learning about how the frameworks are organized and what goes where, we have a sense of what to expect when we start to bring in these features in the next app we write. Fortunately, many design patterns repeat themselves throughout Apple's frameworks, so the idea of creating a closure for handling an asynchronous event is something we'll use again, whether that's an action to perform at the end of an animation, when your tweet gets posted, or when a video stops playing.

The next step, naturally, is up to you. What will you create? A utility? A game? Something that uses the device's location in an interesting way? Or maybe something to help users take care of their health. There are endless possibilities.

We can't wait to see what you come up with.

Bibliography

[Kel16]   Jeff Kelley. *Developing for Apple Watch, Second Edition*. The Pragmatic Bookshelf, Raleigh, NC, 2016.

[Mou16]   Christina Moulton. *iOS Apps with REST APIs*. The Pragmatic Bookshelf, Raleigh, NC, 2016.

[PS14]   Jonathan Penn and Josh Smith. *Build iOS Games with Sprite Kit (out of print)*. The Pragmatic Bookshelf, Raleigh, NC, 2014.

[Sad17]   Erica Sadun. *Swift Style*. The Pragmatic Bookshelf, Raleigh, NC, 2017.

[Zar16]   Marcus Zarra. *Core Data in Swift*. The Pragmatic Bookshelf, Raleigh, NC, 2016.

Index

Core Data

For databases on iOS, you need Core Data. Find out how to leverage it best from your choice of Objective-C or Swift versions.

Core Data in Objective-C, Third Edition

Core Data is Apple's data storage framework: it's powerful, built-in, and can integrate with iCloud. Discover all of Core Data's powerful capabilities, learn fundamental principles including thread and memory management, and add Core Data to both your iOS and OS X projects. All examples in this edition are written in Objective-C and are based on OS X El Capitan and iOS 9.

Marcus S. Zarra

(238 pages) ISBN: 9781680501230. $38

https://pragprog.com/book/mzcd3

Core Data in Swift

Core Data is intricate, powerful, and necessary. Discover the powerful capabilities integrated into Core Data, and how to use Core Data in your iOS and OS X projects. All examples are current for macOS Sierra, iOS 10, and the latest release of Core Data. All the code is written in Swift 3, including numerous examples of how best to integrate Core Data with Apple's newest programming language.

Marcus Zarra

(212 pages) ISBN: 9781680501704. $38

https://pragprog.com/book/mzswift

Embrace Swift Style and Gain Skill

Swift is the new language of choice on iOS. See how to use it the right way. And then expand your coding skills with these unique challenges!

Swift Style

Discover the do's and don'ts involved in crafting readable Swift code as you explore common Swift coding challenges and the best practices that address them. From spacing, bracing, and semicolons to proper API style, discover the whys behind each recommendation, and add to or establish your own house style guidelines. This practical, powerful, and opinionated guide offers the best practices you need to know to work successfully in this equally opinionated programming language.

Erica Sadun
(210 pages) ISBN: 9781680502350. $24.95
https://pragprog.com/book/esswift

Exercises for Programmers

When you write software, you need to be at the top of your game. Great programmers practice to keep their skills sharp. Get sharp and stay sharp with more than fifty practice exercises rooted in real-world scenarios. If you're a new programmer, these challenges will help you learn what you need to break into the field, and if you're a seasoned pro, you can use these exercises to learn that hot new language for your next gig.

Brian P. Hogan
(118 pages) ISBN: 9781680501223. $24
https://pragprog.com/book/bhwb

Secure JavaScript and Web Testing

Secure your Node applications and see how to really test on the web.

Secure Your Node.js Web Application

Cyber-criminals have your web applications in their crosshairs. They search for and exploit common security mistakes in your web application to steal user data. Learn how you can secure your Node.js applications, database and web server to avoid these security holes. Discover the primary attack vectors against web applications, and implement security best practices and effective countermeasures. Coding securely will make you a stronger web developer and analyst, and you'll protect your users.

Karl Düüna
(230 pages) ISBN: 9781680500851. $36
https://pragprog.com/book/kdnodesec

The Way of the Web Tester

This book is for everyone who needs to test the web. As a tester, you'll automate your tests. As a developer, you'll build more robust solutions. And as a team, you'll gain a vocabulary and a means to coordinate how to write and organize automated tests for the web. Follow the testing pyramid and level up your skills in user interface testing, integration testing, and unit testing. Your new skills will free you up to do other, more important things while letting the computer do the one thing it's really good at: quickly running thousands of repetitive tasks.

Jonathan Rasmusson
(254 pages) ISBN: 9781680501834. $29
https://pragprog.com/book/jrtest

Start Great Teams, Keep Teams Great

See how to get great teams started, and keep them great by doing retrospectives the right way.

Liftoff, Second Edition

Ready, set, liftoff! Align your team to one purpose: successful delivery. Learn new insights and techniques for starting projects and teams the right way, with expanded concepts for planning, organizing, and conducting liftoff meetings. Real-life stories illustrate how others have effectively started (or restarted) their teams and projects. Master coaches Diana Larsen and Ainsley Nies have successfully "lifted off" numerous agile projects worldwide. Are you ready for success?

Diana Larsen and Ainsley Nies
(170 pages) ISBN: 9781680501636. $24
https://pragprog.com/book/liftoff

Agile Retrospectives

See how to mine the experience of your software development team continually throughout the life of the project. The tools and recipes in this book will help you uncover and solve hidden (and not-so-hidden) problems with your technology, your methodology, and those difficult "people issues" on your team.

Esther Derby and Diana Larsen, Foreword by Ken Schwaber
(176 pages) ISBN: 9780977616640. $29.95
https://pragprog.com/book/dlret

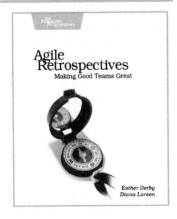

Pragmatic Programming

We'll show you how to be more pragmatic and effective, for new code and old.

Your Code as a Crime Scene

Jack the Ripper and legacy codebases have more in common than you'd think. Inspired by forensic psychology methods, this book teaches you strategies to predict the future of your codebase, assess refactoring direction, and understand how your team influences the design. With its unique blend of forensic psychology and code analysis, this book arms you with the strategies you need, no matter what programming language you use.

Adam Tornhill
(218 pages) ISBN: 9781680500387. $36
https://pragprog.com/book/atcrime

The Nature of Software Development

You need to get value from your software project. You need it "free, now, and perfect." We can't get you there, but we can help you get to "cheaper, sooner, and better." This book leads you from the desire for value down to the specific activities that help good Agile projects deliver better software sooner, and at a lower cost. Using simple sketches and a few words, the author invites you to follow his path of learning and understanding from a half century of software development and from his engagement with Agile methods from their very beginning.

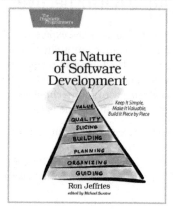

Ron Jeffries
(178 pages) ISBN: 9781941222379. $24
https://pragprog.com/book/rjnsd

Past and Present

To see where we're going, remember how we got here, and learn how to take a healthier approach to programming.

Fire in the Valley

In the 1970s, while their contemporaries were protesting the computer as a tool of dehumanization and oppression, a motley collection of college dropouts, hippies, and electronics fanatics were engaged in something much more subversive. Obsessed with the idea of getting computer power into their own hands, they launched from their garages a hobbyist movement that grew into an industry, and ultimately a social and technological revolution. What they did was invent the personal computer: not just a new device, but a watershed in the relationship between man and machine. This is their story.

Michael Swaine and Paul Freiberger
(424 pages) ISBN: 9781937785765. $34
https://pragprog.com/book/fsfire

The Healthy Programmer

To keep doing what you love, you need to maintain your own systems, not just the ones you write code for. Regular exercise and proper nutrition help you learn, remember, concentrate, and be creative—skills critical to doing your job well. Learn how to change your work habits, master exercises that make working at a computer more comfortable, and develop a plan to keep fit, healthy, and sharp for years to come.

This book is intended only as an informative guide for those wishing to know more about health issues. In no way is this book intended to replace, countermand, or conflict with the advice given to you by your own healthcare provider including Physician, Nurse Practitioner, Physician Assistant, Registered Dietician, and other licensed professionals.

Joe Kutner
(254 pages) ISBN: 9781937785314. $36
https://pragprog.com/book/jkthp

The Pragmatic Bookshelf

The Pragmatic Bookshelf features books written by developers for developers. The titles continue the well-known Pragmatic Programmer style and continue to garner awards and rave reviews. As development gets more and more difficult, the Pragmatic Programmers will be there with more titles and products to help you stay on top of your game.

Visit Us Online

This Book's Home Page
https://pragprog.com/book/adios4
Source code from this book, errata, and other resources. Come give us feedback, too!

Register for Updates
https://pragprog.com/updates
Be notified when updates and new books become available.

Join the Community
https://pragprog.com/community
Read our weblogs, join our online discussions, participate in our mailing list, interact with our wiki, and benefit from the experience of other Pragmatic Programmers.

New and Noteworthy
https://pragprog.com/news
Check out the latest pragmatic developments, new titles and other offerings.

Save on the eBook

Save on the eBook versions of this title. Owning the paper version of this book entitles you to purchase the electronic versions at a terrific discount.

PDFs are great for carrying around on your laptop—they are hyperlinked, have color, and are fully searchable. Most titles are also available for the iPhone and iPod touch, Amazon Kindle, and other popular e-book readers.

Buy now at *https://pragprog.com/coupon*

Contact Us

Online Orders:	*https://pragprog.com/catalog*
Customer Service:	*support@pragprog.com*
International Rights:	*translations@pragprog.com*
Academic Use:	*academic@pragprog.com*
Write for Us:	*http://write-for-us.pragprog.com*
Or Call:	+1 800-699-7764

CPSIA information can be obtained
at www.ICGtesting.com
Printed in the USA
BVOW07s2348230317

479349BV00002B/2/P